FIRE MONKS

FIRE MONKS

Zen Mind Meets Wildfire at the Gates of Tassajara

Colleen Morton Busch

The Penguin Press
New York
2011

THE PENGUIN PRESS
Published by the Penguin Group
Penguin Group (USA) Inc., 375 Hudson Street, New York, New York 10014, U.S.A. • Penguin Group (Canada), 90 Eglinton Avenue East, Suite 700, Toronto, Ontario, Canada M4P 2Y3 (a division of Pearson Penguin Canada Inc.) • Penguin Books Ltd, 80 Strand, London WC2R 0RL, England • Penguin Ireland, 25 St. Stephen's Green, Dublin 2, Ireland (a division of Penguin Books Ltd) • Penguin Books Australia Ltd, 250 Camberwell Road, Camberwell, Victoria 3124, Australia (a division of Pearson Australia Group Pty Ltd) • Penguin Books India Pvt Ltd, 11 Community Centre, Panchsheel Park, New Delhi – 110 017, India • Penguin Group (NZ), 67 Apollo Drive, Rosedale, Auckland 0632, New Zealand (a division of Pearson New Zealand Ltd) • Penguin Books (South Africa) (Pty) Ltd, 24 Sturdee Avenue, Rosebank, Johannesburg 2196, South Africa

Penguin Books Ltd, Registered Offices: 80 Strand, London WC2R 0RL, England

First published in 2011 by The Penguin Press, a member of Penguin Group (USA) Inc.

Grateful acknowledgment is made for permission to reprint the following copyrighted works:
Excerpt from "Genjo Koan" by Eihei Dōgen, translated by Kazuaki Tanahashi and Robert Aitken. Used by permission of the San Francisco Zen Center; Selection by Norman Fischer. Used by permission of Norman Fischer; Excerpt from *Deep Survival: Who Lives, Who Dies, and Why* by Laurence Gonzales. Copyright © 2003 by Laurence Gonzales. Used by permission of W. W. Norton & Company, Inc.; Excerpt from *You Have to Say Something* by Dainin Katagiri. © 1998 by Dainin Katagiri. Reprinted by permission of Shambhala Publications, Inc., Boston, Mass.; Excerpt from *Young Men and Fire* by Norman Maclean. By permission of University of Chicago Press; Excerpt from "How Plants Use Fire (And Are Used by It)" by Stephen Pyne from the companion Web site to the film *Fire Wars, NOVA* (WGBH). By permission of the author and WGBH; Excerpt from "Control Burn" from *Turtle Island* by Gary Snyder. Copyright © 1974 by Gary Snyder. Reprinted by permission of New Directions Publishing Corp.; Excerpt from *The Practice of the Wild* by Gary Snyder. Copyright © 1990 by Gary Snyder. Reprinted by permission of Counterpoint; Selection by Steve Stücky. Used by permission of Steve Stücky; Excerpt from *Zen Mind, Beginner's Mind* by Shunryu Suzuki. Protected under terms of the International Copyright Union. Reprinted by permission of Shambhala Publications, Inc., Boston, Mass.; Excerpt from *The Devil's Highway* by Luis Alberto Urrea. Published by Little, Brown and Company.

Photograph credits:
Page 1: top © Shundo David Haye, bottom © Johan Ostlund; Page 2: top © Shundo David Haye, bottom © Daniel J. Quinn; Page 3: top © Shundo David Haye, bottom Copyright © 2008 The Monterey County Herald. All rights reserved. Reprinted with Permission; Page 4: top © Shundo David Haye, bottom © David Zimmerman; Page 5: top © Ivan J. Iberle, bottom © Mako Voelkel; Page 6: top © Mako Voelkel, bottom © Tom Meyer; Page 7: top © Simon Moyes, bottom © Colleen Morton Busch; Page 8: top © Mako Voelkel, bottom © Daniel J. Quinn

LIBRARY OF CONGRESS CATALOGING IN PUBLICATION DATA
Busch, Colleen Morton.
Fire monks : Zen mind meets wildfire at the gates of Tassajara / Colleen Morton Busch.
p. cm.
Includes bibliographical references.
ISBN 978-1-59420-291-9
1. Fire fighters—California. 2. Wildfires—Prevention and control—California. 3. Zen Buddhism—Social aspects. 4. Zen Buddhists—California—Biography. 5. Tassajara Zen Mountain Center. I. Title.
HD8039.F52C35 2011
363.3709794'76—dc22 2011010226

Printed in the United States of America
1 3 5 7 9 10 8 6 4 2

Designed by Susan Walsh

Maps by Meighan Cavanaugh

For John,

gatekeeper, gate crasher, holder of the keys

Fire is more than an ecological process or an environmental problem. It is a relationship.

—STEPHEN J. PYNE, *fire historian*

CONTENTS

CAST OF CHARACTERS

Tassajara Monks

STEVE STÜCKY—San Francisco Zen Center abbot

Dharma name: *Daitsu Myōgen*, Greatly Pervading, Subtle Eye

DAVID ZIMMERMAN—director

Kansan Tetsuhō, Perfection Mountain, Complete Surrender

MAKO VOELKEL—head cook

Unzan Doshin, Cloud Mountain, Path of the Heart

GRAHAM ROSS—plant manager

Unzan Etsudo, Cloud Mountain, Joyful Way

COLIN GIPSON—head of shop

Shikan Zenka, Determined to See, Completely Burned

SHUNDO DAVID HAYE—former resident, fire scout

Shundo Gennin, Way of the Fleet Steed, Manifesting Virtue

DEVIN PATEL—student fire marshal

Kakusei Yushin, Jewel Stillness, Fearless Heart

LESLIE JAMES—senior practice leader, Jamesburg resident

Sho Sai So Kan, Settle/Finish, Encourage, Original Mirror

JANE HIRSHFIELD—former resident, poet

So Kai Un Go, Source Servant, Cloud Abode

Firefighters

STUART CARLSON—CAL FIRE station captain, Soquel Station, Santa Cruz County

JACK FROGGATT—Kern County Fire Department battalion chief Basin Complex fire branch director

GEORGE HAINES—CAL FIRE unit chief, San Benito–Monterey Unit

N
Wind
Tassajara Creek Drainage
CONFLUENCE
Firefighters evacuate
when fire reaches here
APPROX. 1 MILE
© 2011 Meighan Cavanaugh

To Jamesburg

rch Creek Drainage

Ashes Corner (4,400 ft.)
Monks turn around here

Lime Point

Tassajara Road

Hawk Mountain

Hogback

Flag Rock

Tassajara Zen Mountain Center (1,600 ft.)

Tony Trail
Lookout

Tassajara Environs with Fire Perimeter as of July 9

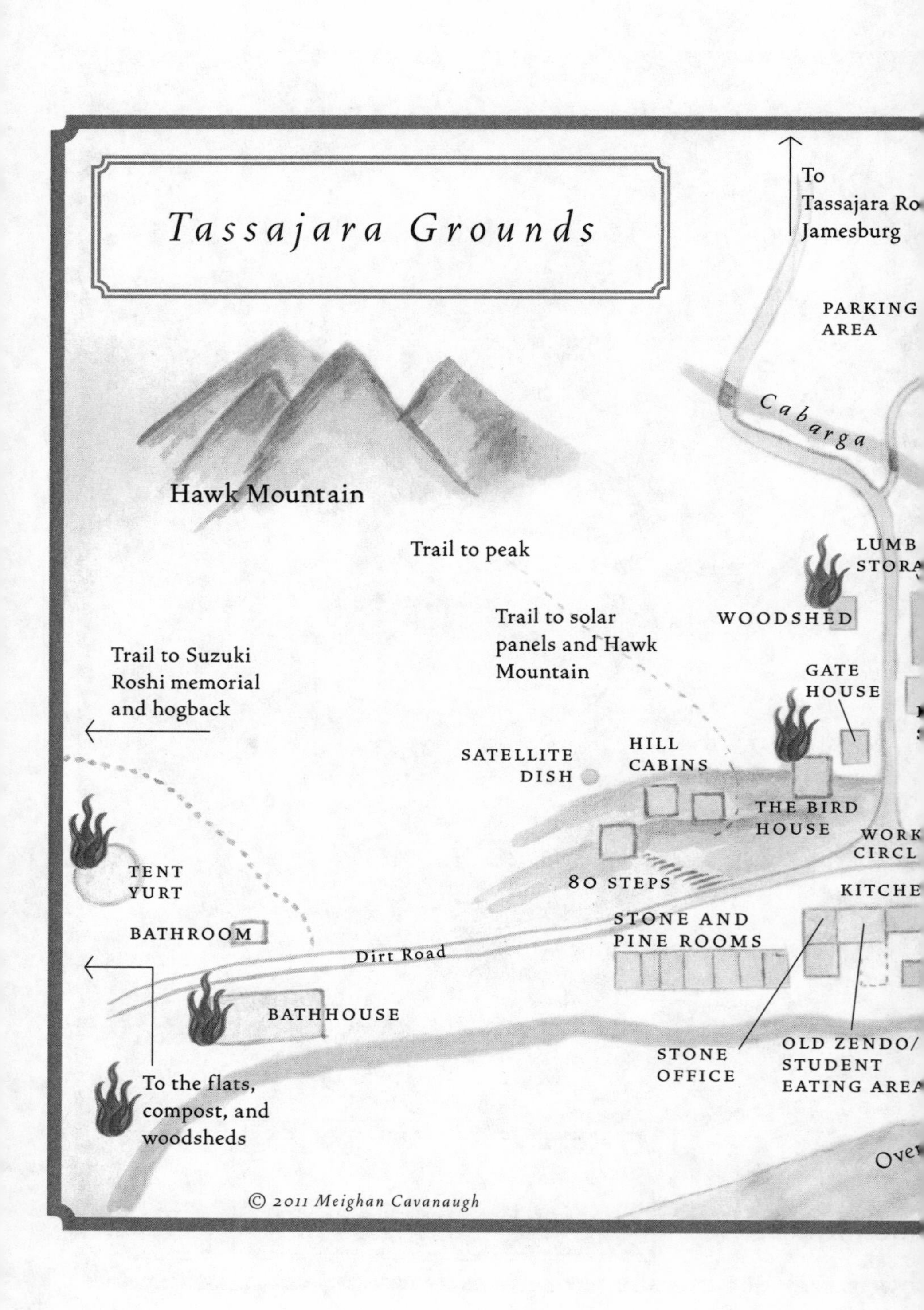

Tassajara Grounds
To
Tassajara Ro
Jamesburg
PARKING
AREA
Cabarga
Hawk Mountain
Trail to peak
LUMB
STORA
WOODSHED
Trail to solar
panels and Hawk
Mountain
Trail to Suzuki
Roshi memorial
and hogback
GATE
HOUSE
SATELLITE
DISH
HILL
CABINS
THE BIRD
HOUSE
WORK
CIRCL
TENT
YURT
80 STEPS
KITCHE
STONE AND
PINE ROOMS
BATHROOM
Dirt Road
BATHHOUSE
STONE
OFFICE
OLD ZENDO/
STUDENT
EATING AREA
To the flats,
compost, and
woodsheds
© 2011 Meighan Cavanaugh

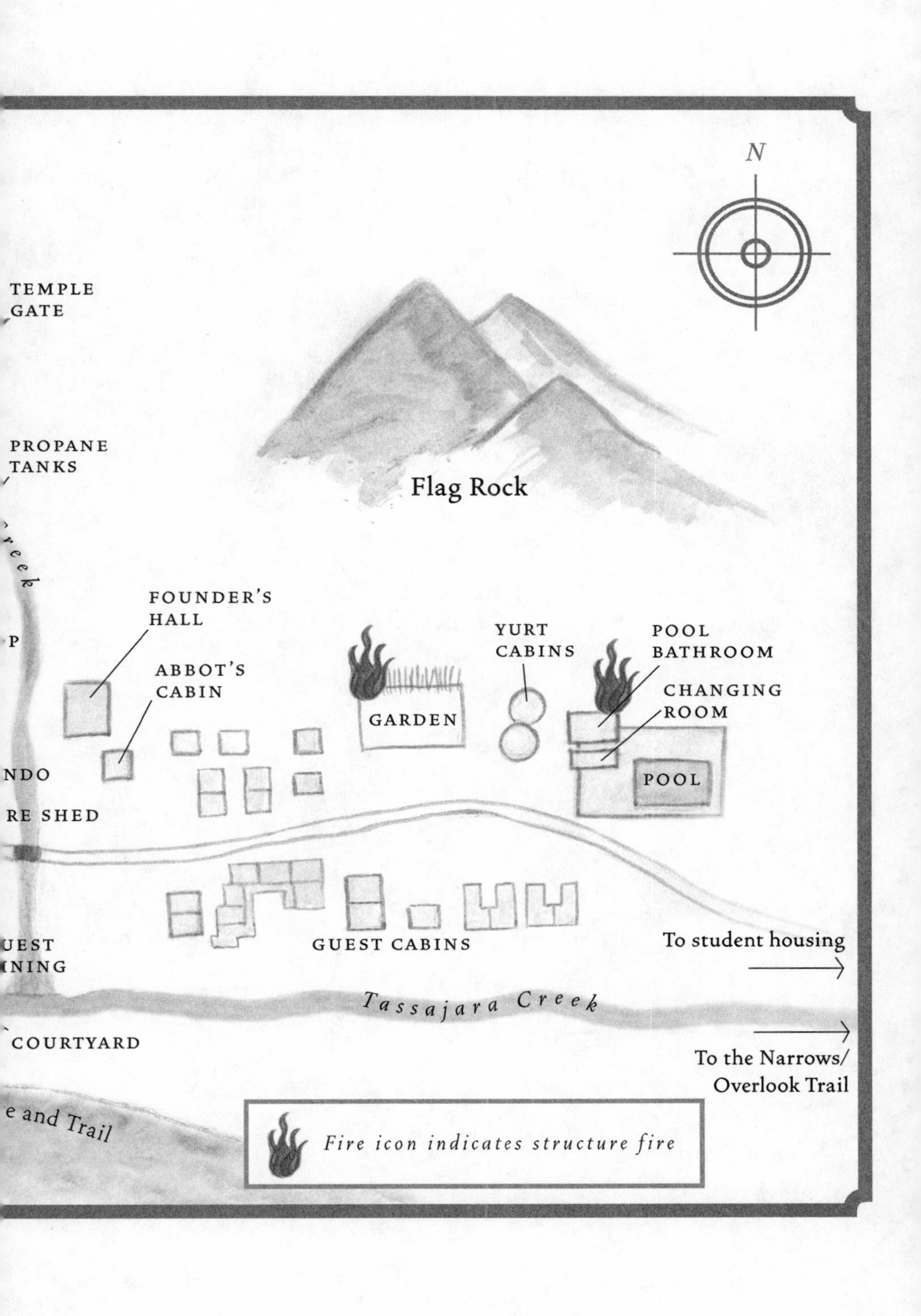
N
TEMPLE GATE
PROPANE TANKS
Flag Rock
FOUNDER'S HALL
ABBOT'S CABIN
GARDEN
YURT CABINS
POOL BATHROOM
CHANGING ROOM
POOL
GUEST CABINS
COURTYARD
To student housing
Tassajara Creek
To the Narrows/ Overlook Trail
Fire icon indicates structure fire

PROLOGUE

On June 21, 2008, lightning strikes from one end of drought-dry California to the other ignited more than two thousand wildfires in what became known as the "lightning siege." The fires stretched from the Trinity Alps in the north to Santa Barbara in the south. One of the blazes turned toward Tassajara Zen Mountain Center, in the Ventana Wilderness near Big Sur. For weeks the resident monks prepared for the fire's arrival, committed to staying to defend the monastery despite repeated orders to leave.

If you lived on the West Coast, you knew about the fires. If you lived in California, you smelled the smoke. The situation at Tassajara was featured in the national news. Connections to the monastery, famous for its hot springs, food, and peaceful environs, extend around the world. Even those who'd never been to Tassajara or heard of it before were intrigued by the seemingly paradoxical image of a *fire monk*. Suddenly, people who ordinarily spent a good deal of time sitting cross-legged in front of a wall faced a situation that required decisive action. What did that look like? And how could sitting still and doing nothing prepare you to act, and to act fast?

As a Zen student and regular visitor to Tassajara over the past ten years, I followed the fire closely. On the day it swept through the monastery, I was camping in Oregon, outside the band of smoke drifting north from California. As soon as I read Tassajara director David Zimmerman's account of the fire's arrival, I wanted to tell this story—from as close in as possible, but also with a wide lens. What was it like to meet a wildfire with minimal training in firefighting but years of Zen practice to guide you? I believed others might benefit from knowing, the fire being a perfect metaphor for anything that comes uninvited and threatens to hurt us or the people and places we love.

The word *Zen* is often used as a catchall synonym for paradox, simultaneously evoking the simple and the unfathomable. In *Fire Monks,* I wanted to portray Zen in all of its true complexity and relevance, as a continuous practice, a way of life that cultivates a particular kind of fearlessness whether or not there's a wildfire at the gate.

To write the book, I relied on official reports and logs, news coverage, written accounts and public talks, the *Sitting with Fire* blog created during the lead-up to the fire's arrival, and my own interviews—more than one hundred taped hours—with residents of Tassajara. I used first names in the pages that follow to distinguish the story's main characters; for practical reasons, many people I spoke with are named not in the body of the story but in the endnotes.

Over a period of two years after the fire, I made many trips to Tassajara, some during the summer guest season, others during the closed fall and winter training periods. Tassajara during a practice period and Tassajara during guest season are two sides of the same coin. Practice is always happening there—even in the summer months when there are guests who may have come simply for the hot springs and lavish vegetarian food—but it can look quite different depending on the season.

In a formal training period, practice looks like this: a wake-up bell at three fifty a.m., six periods of meditation, from forty minutes to an hour in length, interspersed with periods of work and study and occasional lectures. Simple meals are eaten in the *zendo* (meditation hall) at one's seat, in three bowls, nested and wrapped in cloths when not in use. There is about an hour and a half in the late afternoon for exercise and bathing. The day ends around nine p.m. after the last period of *zazen,* or meditation. On designated workdays and personal days, the schedule is slightly more forgiving.

In the summer guest season, a student runs up and down the paths at Tassajara swinging the wake-up bell and calling the resident community to meditation a full hour and a half later, at five fifteen a.m. The summer community consists of both long-term, year-round residents and summer "work practice" students often new to Zen. Though the zazen schedule is much lighter, the community works for most of each day to take care of Tassajara and its guests, mostly in silence. Whether it's tending to the altars, serving meals, or washing dishes, this work is considered an essential part of practice—not separate from the practice of meditation.

My first trip to Tassajara for *Fire Monks* took place during the winter practice period in November 2008, four months after the fire. David greeted me at the gate. When I commented on the smoky smell still in the air and the paths littered with leaves, he said, "That's Tassajara in the fall." I'd been there only during the summer, for "guest practice"—meditating and working with the community in the morning, relaxing as a guest in the afternoon.

During the book's writing, I witnessed Tassajara's recovery. Wildflowers bloomed on barren hillsides. Grasses sprouted, ferns unfurled, bright green shoots broke through the soil at the bases of charred tree trunks. The road became an obstacle course of potholes, runoff, rockfalls, and downed trees, until the county rehabilitated and graded it. New buildings gradually replaced burned ones. A community tested by a crisis continued to practice together and to examine their experience for whatever truths it might hold. Memories faded and then reappeared when I asked questions or when smoke hovered over the valley from a new wildfire in the distance.

At Tassajara, fire burned around some things and straight through others, in a course that might seem haphazard but was determined mostly by wind, relative humidity, topography. Similarly, the fire burned uniquely in each person. There wasn't one fire, but many. There was a shared fire—the event Tassajara's residents and friends experienced as a community—and the fires individuals lived through in the valleys of their own hearts.

When wildfire first threatened Tassajara, the question arose: Even if every building burned down to its foundation, wouldn't Tassajara survive? It's not the buildings that make Tassajara what it is. So, what does? What is Tassajara? It's a question that can't be fully met with words.

One of the monks who fought the fire observed in an interview: "The Tassajara that was here before the fire is not here anymore." But a smile tugged at the corners of his lips even before the next question came: What *is* here?

He paused, then answered, "Tassajara."

One

LIGHTNING STRIKES

To know the spirit of the place is to realize that you are a part of a part and that the whole is made of parts, each of which is whole. You start with the part you are whole in.

—GARY SNYDER, *The Practice of the Wild*

Saturday, June 21, 2008, one p.m.

Fire season had started early, in May, when people typically start dusting off barbecues and dreaming of long summer days. The Indians fire was one of those early-season blazes, ignited when a heat wave followed the driest spring on record in California. Weather staff for the Indians fire first spotted the lightning strikes several hundred miles off the Pacific Coast on the evening of June 20. Usually storms swept into the Big Sur area from the southeast. They often came with rain. But this one appeared seemingly out of nowhere, and it looked as though it might run all the way up to the northern edge of the state. By the morning of June 21, commanders had stripped resources from the Indians fire to assign to the lightning-ignited fires before those fires even started.

. . .

At one p.m. on June 21, David Zimmerman finished his gazpacho—a cooling summer tomato soup, crisp with cucumbers—and set aside his bowl. He picked up the phone and dialed the number for the Indians fire public information line. The drum had already sounded for work circle. He would be late, if he made it at all, but he wanted to get the latest official update on the wildfire burning through the wilderness five miles south (as the crow flies) of Tassajara.

Tassajara sits deep in the Ventana Wilderness, inside the boundary of the Los Padres National Forest, in rugged country designed to burn. At times, the satellite phone connection could sound as if you were placing a call to a Himalayan peak just to reach Salinas forty-six miles north. Today the connection with forest headquarters in Goleta was surprisingly clear. One of the fire info techs staffing the line answered—a friendly female voice David recognized. She reported that the fire had burned 51,125 acres as of six a.m. that morning, southeast of Tassajara. Northeasterly winds were blowing it away from the monastery.

The Indians fire had started with a runaway campfire on June 8. It was now June 21, the summer solstice. As Tassajara director, David had called the info line several times a day for nearly two weeks to check the status of the fire. He didn't have a personal phone, so he used the phone on the back porch or in the stone office. He'd put signs up around Tassajara for the guests, explaining the smoke. He'd noted that the fire was moving away from Tassajara, that staff were monitoring the situation closely and were in contact with fire officials, and that they had plans in place should evacuation become necessary.

He wasn't particularly worried. Other than the smoke, it was summer business as usual. The guest season had been open since early May. A dozen retreats for summer guests had come and gone. The various crews staffed by students—kitchen, dining room, bag lunch, cabin, garden, shop, dish shack—had worked out any kinks and settled into the schedule. Part of David's job was to coordinate the constant in-and-out flow of summer students and consult with crew heads to ensure that things ran smoothly. It could be tedious at times. Following the movements of the fire was new and engaging, like traveling abroad and learning to speak the local language.

David thanked the woman for the update. He cradled the receiver and stood up. Just then, the sky exploded. One loud whip-crack to the earth and then, a moment later, another. A brief downpour thrummed the roof, slapping sycamore leaves and splashing on the surface of the creek.

He'd seen the heavy gray clouds gathering overhead on his way to lunch. He'd thought they might get a little rain—rare in the summer, but not unheard of, and welcome, considering the lingering drought. But lightning? Thunder?

David could feel the expansion of heated air, smell the clouds giving up their condensation. He loved thunderstorms. Summer afternoon squalls tossed long shadows across Pennsylvania's green fields when he was a boy. But this storm stopped as suddenly as it started. The clouds closed up, and two strands of thought came together in David's mind: The drought-dry earth. And now lightning, like a match to the wilderness.

In David's life, there had been many match-strike moments like this, when everything changed, suddenly and drastically. Six months after his call on June 21 to the Indians fire information line, he sat in the library at San Francisco Zen Center, where he'd first learned to practice. Looking like someone more suited to wandering the halls of a library or museum than to holding a fire hose, David let his tea cool as he described how he came to be at Tassajara. Dark, well-defined eyebrows framed his round face. He answered my questions about his background with a determined precision to his speech yet an open focus to his gaze, suggesting that his past is no longer where he lives.

When he was five years old, his mother left the family. Unequipped to raise his kids alone, David's father was ordered by Child Protective Services to put David and his older brother in a children's home. For most of his childhood in Lancaster County, Pennsylvania, David bounced between the children's home, foster families, and stints living with his father, Paul, who struggled with alcohol abuse and the demands of holding down several jobs.

While living with their father, the boys were often left alone to meals of potato-chip sandwiches or TV dinners. They liked to pretend they were superheroes. David's brother, who later joined the U.S. Navy, would act out the destruction of whole towns, burning Matchbox cars, stomping on Lego buildings, and killing toy soldiers. David would transform himself into Wonder Woman—the feminine embodiment of goodness, strength, beauty, and compassion, in his eyes—with a white sheet, a towel for hair, his grandmother's tiara and clip-on earrings, and an imaginary golden lasso. When his father's truck pulled into the driveway, David ripped off his costume and threw himself in front of the television.

As for memories of his mother, David counted them on a few fingers. His recollections include a tender vision of her hanging laundry on the line in the backyard, her dress swaying in a breeze, and the sharp pain of witnessing an argument in which his father drew a knife from a kitchen drawer and raised it at his mother—the night before she left.

The Millersville Mennonite Children's Home, where he lived intermittently after his mother left, between the ages of six and nine, provided a stable and nurturing environment. The women who ran the home were chaste yet warm, strict but maternal. When he landed at San Francisco Zen Center in 1991 at age twenty-eight, the building on Page Street reminded him of the children's home, from the brick façade to the smell of old wood to its history as a residence for Jewish women. Early morning prayers, communal meals at long tables, a great, embracing silence—much seemed familiar. He wanted to learn to meditate. He'd been laid off from his job at the San Francisco AIDS Foundation and had student loans to repay. His father, not yet fifty, was dying of colon cancer.

At forty-six years old in the summer of 2008—the age his father was when diagnosed—David didn't want to die without waking up, without having tasted his life completely. That desire had led him to Tassajara and then to take priest's vows. But on June 21, listening to the lightning, he felt a deep unease. If the fire came Tassajara's way, what would they do? As director, he'd have to do more than talk to the friendly people staffing the fire information line and courier updates to the work circle. He knew something would be required of him, even if he couldn't anticipate exactly what it was. And would he be able to meet it?

Shortly after the thunderstorm, Colin Gipson drove Tassajara's green Isuzu Trooper up to Lime Point, a limestone outcropping on Tassajara Road partway between the monastery and Chews Ridge, beyond which the dirt road continues for another seven miles before turning to pavement.

In July 2008, Colin was head of shop at Tassajara, responsible for overseeing and often executing physical plant maintenance and repairs. The first time he came to Tassajara, in the spring of 2002, he was with a couple of friends from the Austin Zen Center. Driving in, he asked, "Where *is* this place?" One of his traveling companions pointed into the depths of a canyon at the end of a fraying ribbon of road. There's no hiding here, Colin thought.

Six years later, the forty-four-year-old former U.S. Marine with a youthful face and gray hairs sprouting from underneath the rim of his baseball cap could probably make the drive up the road with his eyes closed, after so many trips to town for supplies. The Isuzu was certainly more comfortable than his motorcycle, a Kawasaki KLR650 he took on long road trips between practice periods.

Tassajara Road was in pretty good shape on June 21—much better than it would be by the end of the summer, after baking in sun and shouldering the traffic of the guest season, or than it was in the winter, when rain and snow washed chunks of it away. Chinese laborers built the road in the late 1880s. Now Monterey County crews maintain it, grading it every spring after the rains end. Bay laurel, madrone, live oaks, scrub oaks, manzanita, sycamore, and western maple lined the road's edge—their leaves coated with road dust.

By June, the wildflowers that paint the limestone cliffs in April and May had dried up. Only the hardiest Indian paintbrush, yellow monkey flower, and yucca remained.

Colin pulled the truck off to the side of the road at Lime Point. He wore shorts, a T-shirt, a baseball cap, and a water bottle slung around his torso—his usual attire when he wasn't in priest robes. But there was something of the uniform about Colin even when he wasn't in robes. He kept a cool layer between himself and the world—the habit of someone raised to be "a pleaser" in a family with a legacy of troublemaking.

At Tassajara, something is always in need of repair. Some buildings date back to before the turn of the last century. The plumbing is full of patches and prayers. Colin was confident in his job as head of shop, something he couldn't say about other positions he'd held at Tassajara, in the dining room and kitchen. Practice positions, as job assignments are called there, are assigned not to take advantage of talents, but to teach the flexibility to develop ones you didn't know you had. Experience is not as important as willingness.

But Colin had driven to Lime Point that day—and quite a few days before that, since the Indians fire had started earlier in June—because of his experience. As a teenager in rural Texas, he'd worked as a volunteer firefighter, putting out brushfires.

This wasn't brush country, the grassy knolls of central Texas where he'd lived on his grandparents' ranch, west of Austin. This was the Ventana Wilderness—where the knife-edged peaks and valleys of the coastal Santa Lucia Mountains cut a jagged relief against the sky. The Santa Lucias are young as mountains go—only two million years old—and with mountains, youth corresponds to verticality. In the Ventana, elevation can change abruptly, from six hundred feet to nearly six thousand at Junipero Serra Peak. The one similarity to Texas was the heat. It was blazing hot up on the ridge, in the open sun. A weather station in nearby Carmel Valley recorded an afternoon high on June 21 of 103 degrees Fahrenheit.

From Lime Point, Colin could see in three directions: northwest toward Miller Canyon, west toward the ocean, and south-southeast toward Junipero

Serra Peak, where the Indians fire had been burning for two weeks. Hazy smoke draped the ridges near Fort Hunter Liggett, a U.S. Army training center. Fire management personnel were based there in what is known as an "incident command post" in the incident command system (ICS), a multiagency emergency response framework implemented in disasters, from wildfires to hurricanes to terrorist attacks, which grew out of a devastating fire season in California in the 1970s.

The smoke didn't look much different to Colin from when they'd started watching the Indians fire. Lucky us, he thought, we got through all of that lightning without any new fire. But then he noticed an oddly shaped cloud, more vertical than horizontal. He got back in the truck and drove another two miles up to the ridge approximately three thousand feet above Tassajara, where he had an even more panoramic view. Though he didn't know their names yet, he spotted the plumes of two lightning-sparked fires to the west—the Gallery fire, south of Big Sur, and the Bear Basin fire, north of Tassajara. "That was the moment I knew it was going to come in," Colin told me later. "The thing that had protected us with the Indians fire was that the wind was blowing it away. This was going to blow right to us."

As Colin walked back to the Isuzu, a couple drove by in a Toyota Corolla—probably day guests coming down the road for a soak in the hot springs. Too much brake, he thought, as the Corolla lurched downhill, taillights blinking. Better to put it in a low gear and coast. Following a safe distance behind, he mulled over how to break the news that the fire was coming their way.

Occasionally a backpacker wanders into Tassajara on foot, but most people arrive via the road. As Colin did the first time, they have plenty of time to wonder, Where *is* this place? Tassajara sits at the road's terminus, in a deep notch in the earth, rimmed by mountains. On the drive in, the world's glitter and self-importance gradually fall away. Humility comes naturally when you are standing at the base of so much vertical rock from within Tassajara, or looking down into the valley from a trail in the surrounding wilderness.

The first time I entered the coursing quiet of Tassajara, I felt as if I had landed somewhere I could truly rest—both out of my usual element and completely within the elements. There is no electricity in the guest cabins—light is obtained by kerosene lamp. There are no keys. The paths and internal road are earth and gravel. Residents silently greet one another in passing with a small standing bow called a *gassho*.

The basalt and granite walls of the stone rooms, some of the oldest cabins, were pulled from the streambed 150 years ago. The walls of the founder's hall were formed of clay from Tassajara Road. The roof beams in the kitchen were salvaged from a local stand of pine trees killed by beetles. The wood surfaces in the zendo were naturally finished with damp rags and monks' feet. Wood, dirt, stone, bare skin: These are the materials Tassajara is made of. Natural, sturdy, porous, impermanent.

The work circle, zendo, and courtyard between the guest dining room and kitchen constitute the central area of Tassajara. It's harder to say where Tassajara's heart is—to locate it in any one place. It isn't bound to structures but rather flows throughout the place like Tassajara Creek.

Despite that generous, endlessly renewing source of water, buildings have been lost to fire before at Tassajara. A grand turn-of-the-century sandstone hotel burned to the ground in 1949. The original zendo went up in flames in 1978. The current zendo was meant to be a temporary replacement but still stands today, on the site of the old hotel, across from the courtyard—an outdoor parlor of sorts for guests and residents.

At seven a.m. on Sunday, June 22, the courtyard at Tassajara was still quiet. Morning meditation had just ended. A student arranged the cloth napkins for guest breakfast, in alphabetical order by the name on the napkin ring. Another student, still wearing the black robe worn in the zendo, raked the gravel steps above the courtyard. A few early-rising guests wandered into the morning chill to fetch coffee. The smell of lemon-ginger scones pierced the smoke.

David had been up since before the wake-up bell. He'd just put signs on the dining room doors so that the guests would see them when they came to breakfast at nine o'clock. He'd decided to refer to the Gallery fire as the Big Sur fire in his announcement, since most guests would be familiar with Big Sur. The signs read:

There are currently two new fires in the Ventana Wilderness, both started by lightning strikes: one at Big Sur (10 miles west) and another at Bear Basin (8–10 miles north). The Big Sur fire is approximately 35 acres and is the primary cause of the smoke at Tassajara. The Bear Basin fire is approximately ten acres . . . The forest fire service crews and planes are giving these new fires their full attention. There is not an immediate concern for Tassajara, but we will keep you informed if the situation changes. We are prepared with evacuation plans should we be so notified by the Forest Service.

For Tassajara in the summer, Sunday was one of the busiest days of the week. Back when David's practice position was guest manager—*shika*, or "guest knower" in Japanese—he'd have had his hands full, sorting out issues with accommodations and arranging rides on the stage, a Suburban that at least once a day shuttles up to eight passengers between Jamesburg, Tassajara's outpost fourteen miles up the road, and Tassajara proper.

He'd liked being guest manager—taking care of people, making sure they were comfortable, and ensuring that their surroundings were aesthetically pleasing. As director, his responsibilities were more administrative. He missed the more creative aspects of his former role. He had to drive to meetings every two weeks at City Center, Zen Center's headquarters and temple in San Francisco, but he liked this part of the job. Despite having been born in rural Pennsylvania, David had urban sensibilities, with a particular fondness for theater and travel, though he could hardly afford much on his stipend of $560 a month.

Often, he returned to Tassajara late, after meetings in the city ended. The road was actually easier to deal with in the dark. The headlights illuminated the potholes, while the surrounding darkness blotted out any distractions. But when he drove the road in daylight, the beauty of the landscape always moved him. Especially when fog skimmed the ridges toward the coast, it looked like a Chinese painting. The scale of the Santa Lucias dwarfed the more modest mountains in Harrisburg, Pennsylvania, where his father, Paul, sometimes took him when he was young.

David and his father had had little contact with each other in the years before his father became ill. Shortly after David went away to college, he had told his father he was gay. His father saw homosexuality as an offense against God and had responded by disowning him. The two didn't speak for several years. AIDS was on the rise at the time and pegged as a homosexual disease. David suspected that his father, who'd remarried and had another child, feared that his son could have the virus and might infect his new family.

Once, after they'd reconciled, David visited his father and stepmother at their home in Colorado. Paul Zimmerman tried to apologize for his failings as a parent. "It was late. The TV was on," David told me. "My father came downstairs in his bathrobe. He wanted to talk. But I wasn't in a space where I could really engage him. I realized later what a loss that moment was." A few years later, his father slipped into a coma and died before David could make it to his bedside. David's stepmother had been vague about the seriousness of his father's condition, and David had thought he had more time.

David and the rest of the senior staff at Tassajara—a group of long-term residents holding vital temple positions, such as head cook and zendo manager—had a plan in place should they have to evacuate the guests, but David hoped that wouldn't be necessary. He knew how much it meant to the guests to come to Tassajara. Some saved up for it all year. He didn't want to disappoint anyone.

He noticed a familiar nagging feeling that no matter what he did, it wouldn't be enough. Practice had helped to shine a light on that old bit of suffering. It had loosened its grip. But it didn't make it go away.

There is a sign outside the house at Jamesburg, where the paved road turns to dirt. Snaky black script on pressed wood announces: *Tassajara Hot Springs, Zen Mountain Center, by Reservation Only.*

When Jane Hirshfield showed up at Jamesburg in her red Dodge van with yellow tie-dyed curtains in the summer of 1974, she was told she could not enter Tassajara without first going to San Francisco Zen Center. But she was twenty-one years old and not easily discouraged. Wearing a strand of bone-colored prayer beads around her neck, a Nepali *mala* given to her when she lived at Tassajara, the now fifty-seven-year-old poet refused to leave. "I unwittingly sat my first *tangaryo*."

Tangaryo is the Japanese Zen tradition in which a student demonstrates commitment and a desire to enter training by sitting at the monastery gate, for days if necessary. In Tassajara's adaptation of this tradition, for the first five days of the two yearly monastic practice periods, new students at Tassajara sit in the zendo for one long period of uninterrupted zazen, leaving their cushions only for bathroom breaks and at night to sleep. This unstructured, unsupervised sitting can be excruciating. There are no breaks, except to use the bathroom, and the new students are essentially ignored, left to negotiate the hours as best they can. As long as they remain in the zendo, they are allowed to stay on and practice.

Jane talked her way into staying at Tassajara for a week that first time. A year later, she returned to Tassajara for three years of residency, during which the future prize-winning poet put down her pen and focused on studying the Dharma, the teachings of Buddhism. Since then, she's returned most summers to teach a workshop on poetry and practice.

Driving in to Tassajara the day after the lightning strikes, Jane stopped in Jamesburg to say hello to an old friend, Leslie James. When the Marble Cone wildfire threatened Tassajara in 1977, Jane and Leslie were part of the small crew that stayed to defend it. Leslie has lived in Jamesburg, helping to coordinate the monastery's comings and goings, since 1991.

About fifteen minutes after leaving Jamesburg, Jane reached Chews Ridge, where the view opens to the fertile plain of the Salinas Valley on one side of the road and the spiny peaks of the coast range fencing out the ocean on the other. From here, she saw the plumes, three distinct pillars of rising smoke—two to the right of the road and one to the left. She didn't know about the lightning strikes the day before, but she took photos to show the staff when she arrived.

The guests are going to be evacuated sometime tomorrow, Jane thought to herself, and the other residents—except for a select group—most likely a couple of days later. They would need her car to drive residents out.

A few thousand feet below Chews Ridge, Jane rounded the bend at the Horse Pasture trailhead. It was this 160-acre parcel east of the road that San Francisco Zen Center first considered for purchase in 1966, before buying Tassajara Hot Springs instead. Its grassy meadows provided pasture for grazing when stagecoaches were the only transport to Tassajara. The 1977 fire had scorched the area as well as most of the road. By now the trees seemed to have completely recovered, all evidence of the earlier conflagration long hidden inside new growth.

Jane recalled driving into Tassajara in the middle of a summer night at the start of the 1977 fire. She and two others were returning from Fresno, where they had bought peaches to dry on the rooftops for winter. Tassajara's resident fire crew chief—Jane's partner at the time, Ted Marshall—slept beside her in the truck's front passenger seat. Marshall woke up, noted the orange glow in the sky, said, "Beautiful dawn," and fell back asleep. But Jane looked at the sky and thought, That's not where dawn should be. By morning, the air was thick with smoke.

Jane remembered the gritty work of digging fireline, a protective barrier of bare earth, until she was utterly exhausted. She remembered the nauseating ride she and Leslie James took down Tassajara Road in the back of a truck, flying through a curtain of fire. And feeling happy, nonetheless, to be one of the few who would try to keep the monastery from burning.

The 1977 Marble Cone fire was one of the treasures of her life. "When I smell forest fires now, an affection rises in my heart," she told me with moist eyes on a warm November afternoon in 2009. "It's such an extraordinary experience to participate in something so real—and so enormous. In the early stages there is a lot of smoke and the light turns red. But when it's closer and the smoke's even deeper, the air turns a kind of blue green and everything gets extremely quiet. It's almost like being underwater. It's as if the whole world is holding its breath."

This time around, Jane wasn't a Tassajara resident. She would not be asked to stay. And even if she was, she knew she didn't have the physical strength to warrant saying yes.

Yes! That's what Suzuki Roshi said when he saw Tassajara for the first time in the spring of 1966. The question, coming from his future successor, Richard Baker, was: Do you like it? Should we buy it?

Shunryu Suzuki had come to America in 1959 to be the head priest at a Zen temple: Sokoji, in San Francisco's Japantown. But that original calling had led to something much bigger. Young Americans had started showing up at Sokoji eager to learn to meditate. By 1966, Suzuki Roshi (*roshi* means "venerable teacher" in Japanese) had established a loyal and dedicated, if somewhat unruly, following. "They were a striking mix of individualists and eccentrics who would never have ended up together, following that disciplined life, if not for Suzuki. Now they were getting up in the dark, practicing zazen in full or half lotus, chanting together in an ancient, unfamiliar language, wearing robes, eating in silence, working hard, and making every attempt to follow a life far more structured than the ones they'd rejected," wrote David Chadwick, an early Suzuki student, in *Crooked Cucumber*. Together, they were blazing a path for American Zen.

American Zen didn't look just like Japanese Zen. And an American Zen training monastery would not look exactly like the monasteries where Suzuki Roshi had trained in Japan. Many of the words and forms of Japanese Zen, along with aesthetic and cultural influences, would carry over, but traditional vows of celibacy would not. In fact, in modern times, Japanese Zen priests were allowed to marry, as Suzuki Roshi had. But at this American Zen monastery—the first—women and men would actually practice and live together, side by side, as equals. People would train at Tassajara for a period of time and then return to their lives "outside the gate," continuing to practice within the context of work, marriage, and family.

"Just like China!" Suzuki Roshi proclaimed, gazing at the Ventana's precipitous peaks and valleys. He danced in celebration in the middle of Tassajara Road.

By bringing Zen to America—specifically, Soto Zen, a sect of Japanese Zen marked by an emphasis on zazen and the view of practice as enlightenment itself—Suzuki Roshi would continue Zen's emigrant lineage. In the fifth century, Bodhidharma, an Indian sage, first introduced meditation practice in China; from there, Zen had spread to Japan, Vietnam, and Korea, taking on the flavor of the host cultures. America—and Tassajara—would now become what China had for the ancient Indian traveler, a new home for Zen Buddhism. A place of origination, adaptation, immersion.

Suzuki Roshi had been looking for several years for the right place to offer more monastic training than was possible in San Francisco. The opportunity to buy Tassajara came along, observed Chadwick, "at a time when there was enough maturity and open-mindedness in America to support, in this way, a teaching that challenged many commonly held assumptions about space, time, being, life and death."

After a frenzy of fund-raising and with the assistance of some high-profile supporters like Alan Watts, Gary Snyder, Allen Ginsberg, Joseph Campbell, and the Grateful Dead, San Francisco Zen Center purchased Tassajara for $300,000 in late 1966, naming it Zenshinji, or Zen Mind Temple.

Tassajara came with its own rich history. Native Americans had used the hot springs for healing long before the descendants of Europeans discovered them. The Esselen, a peaceful tribe that once inhabited the area now known as the Ventana Wilderness, had cared for the land by intentionally setting fire to underbrush to clear paths for travel and replenish the soil. One local Esselen family, the Nasons, still live up Tassajara Road, managing a ranch, working as wilderness guides, and occasionally appearing at Tassajara to give talks on the area's Native American heritage.

The first known structures at Tassajara were built in the 1800s by a local hunter. By the early 1900s it had become a popular resort. Robert Beck, who owned the resort before selling it to Zen Center—short for San Francisco Zen Center—said that in Tassajara's early days, they gave meals away and sold whiskey to make money. Immigrants from the Watsonville area near Santa Cruz came to Tassajara because the water reminded them of the springs back home in Yugoslavia. In those days, visitors didn't just soak in the springs, they drank the mineral-rich water, called "granite wine."

Robert and Anna Beck purchased Tassajara in 1960, a decade after the hotel had burned down. In 1966, they hired a young Zen student named Ed Brown to wash dishes. Brown learned to bake bread in Tassajara's kitchen. When one of the Becks' cooks quit, he started cooking for the hot springs guests. After Zen Center acquired Tassajara, he became *tenzo,* or head cook. Later, Brown wrote the *Tassajara Bread Book* and *Tassajara Cooking*—launching a bread-baking revolution and making the monastery a household name in vegetarian cooking. He still teaches cooking classes at Tassajara and around the world.

When the Becks wanted to sell Tassajara, they had many offers. The Monterey County Roughriders—who would ride on horseback up the Arroyo Seco and over the Horse Pasture Trail to Tassajara—put in a bid. So did the publisher of *Sunset* magazine and the vice president of Pacific Gas & Electric. On behalf of Zen Center, Allen Ginsberg asked Bob Dylan if he would buy Tassajara, but Dylan wanted to build a house there, and that squelched the deal.

The Becks' decision to sell Tassajara to Zen Center, for less money than they could have received from other interested parties, ultimately helped Buddhism flourish in America. For Robert Beck, who wasn't a Zen student himself—he was a teacher and antiques dealer—the deal had a destined quality. Before Beck died in 2007, he recalled the negotiations as feeling "foreordained, and it was just a question of filling in the details." Remembering Suzuki Roshi, he said, "He exemplified the best that humans could be. He was an exemplary character, with his failures, his flaws, his faults, he still went bravely ahead and said this is possible. It's possible to go beyond what we think we can do, and we don't have to be heroic, we can be simple and express our convictions."

Much has changed in the four and a half decades that Zen Center has owned Tassajara. But what's remarkable is how much remains the same. The practice that Suzuki Roshi nurtured has been largely preserved, handed down from one generation to the next. Tassajara remains a place for rigorous monastic training. Every year, around seventy serious practitioners of Zen leave behind whatever ties them to their lives as they know them and commit to three to six months of intense silence, study, and sitting.

But for four months of the year, Tassajara's gate is open to whoever wants to come—regardless of an interest or lack thereof in Zen practice. Some stumble upon Tassajara in their quest for natural hot springs. Some are drawn in by a workshop—in yoga, conscious relationships, ecology, cooking, poetry. Some in need of a respite have been sent there by sympathetic friends. Some have tattered copies of the *Tassajara Bread Book* on their kitchen shelves. Some are Zen students, working in exchange for the opportunity to practice residentially, part time or full time, for a few days or the entire summer. Quite a few wear priest robes.

Tassajara is known by name around the world by people who have never been there and whose personal connection to the place may be based on a beloved recipe for jalapeño cornbread or a lecture from Suzuki Roshi's *Zen Mind, Beginner's Mind*, now translated into Czech, Dutch, Finnish, French, German, Icelandic, Japanese, Portuguese, Russian, Spanish, and Vietnamese. While fires were burning around Tassajara in June, Zen Center vice president Susan O'Connell flew to Mongolia for an international Buddhist women's conference. She worried about being far away and out of touch, until she turned on the television in her hotel room and saw footage of Tassajara in a report on the California wildfires, on Al Jazeera.

All kinds of people call Tassajara home. Tassajara may belong to Zen Center, but that doesn't stop anyone who's ever been there from feeling that it belongs to them somehow. Or that they belong to it.

. . .

Every morning around nine a.m., shortly after the bell sounded for guest breakfast, head cook Mako Voelkel led her crew in a service. Eight or so students stood around the altar fashioned from a sycamore that fell during the first winter Zen Center owned Tassajara. A candle glowed faintly in the daylight. Incense twisted toward the roof beams. They chanted briskly, in a monotone, not emphasizing any one word over another, from thirteenth-century Soto Zen founder Eihei Dōgen's *Instructions for the Zen Cook*: "Of old it was said, 'When steaming rice, treat the pot as one's own head; when rinsing the rice, know that the water is one's own lifeblood.'"

Mako wasn't supposed to be born. She revealed this fact undramatically on a damp January day six months after the 2008 fire. It was the beginning of the winter practice period—the new students were still sitting in the zendo. I'd driven in to Tassajara to do a first round of interviews. We sat in one of the stone rooms, a fire glowing in the wood stove. Mako explained that having carried one child, her mother was told she couldn't get pregnant again. When Mako was conceived despite doctors' predictions, she was not expected to survive. At thirty-six years old, Mako radiated an undeniable robustness, a willful inner strength that had pushed her out of the womb and into the world.

She was born in Baltimore, to a Japanese mother and an American father of German descent. Her features—both delicate and bold—reflect those mixed roots. Her presence is powerful, extroverted yet self-contained. She holds herself upright but often stands with her hips askew, forefinger cupping her chin, in conversation. When she laughs, which is frequently, she throws back her head with a sharp "ha!" Her brown hair turns cinnamon in the summer, when she has hair—she shaved her head when she became a priest in 2004.

Before that, Mako studied philosophy as an undergraduate and pursued a graduate degree in neurobiology, figuring that if she wanted to understand the mind, she ought to understand the brain first. "But there wasn't enough big picture in it for me," she told me of the days spent peering through a microscope. In 1997, when she was twenty-five years old, she moved to San Francisco.

She'd learned transcendental meditation at fifteen and had heard of San Francisco Zen Center, but she was wary of organized religion. She'd read about abuses of power by spiritual teachers. She thought Zen Center seemed too big and institutional, maybe too patriarchal, and what she knew of Zen seemed like "mind tricks." But she decided to check it out for herself. She started to meditate at City Center. She volunteered in the library. "I'd go when it was closed," she told me, "which is funny, because I wanted to meet people." She was searching, she later realized, for *sangha,* or community, one of Buddhism's three treasures, along with the Buddha and the Dharma.

One evening, she gave what's called a way-seeking-mind talk, introducing herself to the community, talking about her life and her path to practice. Through that talk, she connected with a senior priest interested in Buddhist logic. And through that relationship, she was drawn into the sangha at City Center. Eventually, she became a resident.

But she wanted to complete some unfinished business—her philosophy master's degree, held up by a paper on philosopher Immanuel Kant. She'd started it many times but could never finish. In December 2001, she sat a seven-day meditation intensive called a *sesshin*. Sesshin means to "gather" or "receive" the mind. It also means sitting in meditation from long before dawn to well after dark on a cushion, facing the wall, with breaks for work and rest, but only enough to make so much sitting possible. A kind of sheer, objectless concentration and feelings of profound connection and contentment can arise, a sense that the self and all of its concerns have dropped away. But the mind can also be rambunctious, distracted, tired, angry, bored, anxious, obsessed. The Zen meditator's aim, whether in a regular forty-minute period of meditation or over the course of many days, is to accept whatever emotional or mental states arise and not hold on.

This particular sesshin that Mako sat occurs every December in Buddhist communities all over the world in honor of the Buddha's enlightenment. When the seven days ended, Mako whipped out her paper. She got her master's degree. Not long after that, she put it in a drawer. She wanted to study the mind, she'd realized, by simply studying *her* mind. By 2002, she'd sold her car, her computer, and her motorcycle to pay off student loans and move to Tassajara. A year later, she met her partner, Graham Ross, on the steps to the hill cabins.

In the text Mako chanted every morning with her kitchen crew, Dōgen calls the job of tenzo—or head cook—"an all-consuming pursuit of the way." This essential position is typically given to someone who has been in residence for a while and who has held other prominent positions. Mako had lived at Tassajara for five years when she became tenzo. She'd served as work leader previously. Before that, as a full-time fire marshal (ordinarily the position is only part-time), she'd revamped the fire and safety systems at Tassajara—organizing and updating manuals and crew instructions and refurbishing equipment.

The tenzo is responsible both for the feeling of practice in the kitchen, since those who are cooking inevitably spend less time in the zendo, and for feeding the monks. At Tassajara, he or she is also responsible for guest meals in the summer. Mako knew how many gallon-capacity containers of chopped mushrooms a case of mushrooms yielded, where to get quality ingredients at a reasonable price, and how to have them on hand when the cooks needed them. But a big part of her job was preserving harmony in tight quarters, within the kitchen sangha. Inevitably, there were collisions—of bodies, of personalities, of sugar and salt.

After the morning chant, Mako would ask if anyone had concerns to bring up. Then she sent the crew off to their various tasks—chopping onions, baking cookies, or washing floors—with some guiding words: Today, let's try to do just one thing at a time. Give whatever you're working with your undivided attention.

. . .

After dinner on Sunday evening, June 22, participants in the "Poetry and the Intimacy of All Things" retreat gathered in the tent yurt. They sat cross-legged on the floor on round meditation cushions called *zafus*. Some quietly continued conversations they'd started at dinner. Jane lit a candle, offered incense, and rang a small bell to gather the group's attention. Then they went around and introduced themselves.

The mood in the room was warm, cheerful, anticipatory. If anyone else had noted the plumes of smoke, they didn't say. Jane didn't share her suspicion that their retreat would be canceled. She opened the workshop as usual, explaining how the week would be structured, answering questions, closing with what she calls a "tiny *teisho*," or teaching talk.

Pens were uncapped, notebooks opened. A few people stretched out their legs. Buddhism is really very simple, she told them. Not complicated at all. She could distill it down to seven words:

Everything changes.

Everything is connected.

Pay attention.

On Monday, June 23, Governor Arnold Schwarzenegger declared a state of emergency in California, citing "extreme peril to the safety of persons and property" in Monterey and Trinity counties.

That morning, unaware of this development, the guests picked up their napkins outside the dining room and glanced at David's latest fire update before checking out the menu: Firefighter Hotcakes. The inspiration of a creative guest cook, the name elicited a few chuckles. When people doctored their pancakes with butter and maple syrup and ate their first forkful, they were surprised to find chocolate chips and chili flakes tucked inside. But a bigger surprise came later that morning, when Sergeant Wingo of the

Monterey County Sheriff's Office called to order the "mandatory evacuation" of Tassajara.

David spoke to Wingo on the phone in the stone office. "The guests will be taken out immediately," David said. "But we plan to have willing residents stay behind." He explained that they had a fire crew in place at Tassajara, good sources of water, and the experience of successfully defending the monastery in two previous large fires.

If the seventy residents currently at Tassajara, or any portion of them, chose to stay against the orders of the Monterey County sheriff, Wingo replied, he needed dental records and next-of-kin contacts for every individual remaining on the grounds.

Following the evacuation procedures the senior staff had established after the lightning strikes, David sent a crew to round up the guests. They knocked on cabin doors, left notices on beds, emptied out the bathhouse, and sent scouts to the Narrows, a popular swimming hole about a twenty-minute walk down Tassajara Creek. They reached the yurt where the poetry retreat was being held just as Jane had given the participants a writing prompt. Instead, they took their notebooks and pens back to their cabins and packed them into suitcases. By eleven thirty a.m., all forty-six guests were accounted for. It took another half hour for the communications crew, wearing yellow and red bandannas, to sort them into vehicles. By noon the guests were heading back up the road, along with twenty-three students who'd chosen to leave. The poets in Jane's workshop had spent less than twenty-four hours at Tassajara.

David found Jane. "Would you please stay for a while?" he asked.

"Absolutely."

That Jane had been through a fire at Tassajara was deeply reassuring to David. She had already shared her thoughts with him about what to expect from authorities and what preparations to make. Though Tassajara had an infrastructure in place to respond to fires, with student crews trained to operate the pumps and lay hoses, the current summer residents hadn't experienced a wildfire before. People would look to David, as director, for an answer to the question "What happens now?" He didn't want the answer to be, "I have no idea." He certainly didn't want to have to ask the sheriff.

He had a note in his pocket—a message from Jane's old friend Leslie, who was in San Francisco at an abbots' council meeting along with Zen Center's two co-abbots. David had asked Leslie to attend the meeting in his place. For more than twenty years, Leslie had divided her weeks between Jamesburg and Tassajara, where she'd held nearly every staff position, including director—some several times. A slight woman with long white hair and brown eyes, Leslie floated easily between the monastery and the secular world up the road, sometimes in robes, sometimes in blue jeans.

"Keep people who want to stay and are able-bodied and emotionally stable until at least six p.m. unless it becomes clear fire is close," her note read. "Abbots are willing to come but realize what we need is people with expertise. Go slow sending residents away."

"Zen Center" is actually three centers: City Center, on Page Street in the Lower Haight district of San Francisco; Green Gulch Farm, in a fog-hemmed coastal valley across the Golden Gate Bridge; and Tassajara. They inhabit three different ecosystems: urban, coastal, and wilderness. They have discrete cultures, schedules, and ways of relating to the forms and traditions of Zen practice. But like a tree whose trunk forks in three directions, they share the same roots. They are separate even as they are deeply interconnected.

All three centers depend on revenues from Tassajara's guest season—for nearly half of all operating expenses. If Tassajara burned, much would be lost that could not be measured in dollars. But shutting down Tassajara for any amount of time in the summer could deal a blow to Zen Center's material well-being. The abbots, meeting in San Francisco, knew this. David knew it, too.

Two

FIRES MERGE

Numbers never lie, after all: they simply tell different stories depending on the math of the tellers.

—LUIS ALBERTO URREA, *The Devil's Highway*

Monday, June 23, two days after the lightning strikes

Around noon on Monday, after the guests had left, David called an urgent meeting in the screened-in student eating area for the forty-seven remaining residents. "Saturday's lightning strikes started three new fires in the Ventana Wilderness, and they are growing rapidly. By order of the Monterey County Sheriff's Office, we've evacuated the guests. Actually, the sheriff requested that we evacuate Tassajara completely, but I explained that we need people here to prepare. It's not clear yet what kind of help we might receive. The state's resources are challenged right now, but hopefully they'll send several crews as they did in '99," he said, thinking of the Kirk Complex fire, which threatened but ultimately missed Tassajara.

"Our primary concern is everyone's safety," he continued. "We don't know how long we have before the fire will arrive—or even whether it will arrive. It could be three days. It could be three weeks. But we are in regular contact with the fire service and we will keep you informed. Since things could change quickly, please pack a bag so that you are ready to go with short notice."

He took a breath and tried to keep his tone informative, neutral. "The sergeant who ordered the mandatory evacuation has asked each of us to provide the names of our dentists and emergency contacts." He left out the sergeant's words—"so we can identify bodies."

Silence. Startled looks back and forth. A few muffled, nervous laughs. No one said anything, but questions hung in the air. You're telling me I'm safe, but you want the name of my dentist? Wasn't I just making strawberry pie?

"I know it sounds alarming," David continued, "but it's just a precautionary measure."

A sheriff's deputy had arrived to collect residents' identifying information as the guests were being taken out. David had explained that many of the students would need to make phone calls to get the requested information, sharing three phone lines. The deputy had declined an offer to join the community for lunch. He waited nearby while they held their meeting.

David paused to gather his thoughts. Was he forgetting something important? "No one will be asked to stay who does not wish to. We have a lot of work to do. We'll be identifying those priorities just as soon as we can. We are lucky to have Jane Hirshfield here with us, who defended Tassajara during the 1977 fire, and maybe she can guide us in our efforts."

Jane bowed. David asked her if she'd like to add anything. Around the room, there were not a lot of familiar faces. Many of the students were new to Tassajara—having arrived only in May. Many were young, she noted, in their twenties—energetic, fit, tattoos hidden under their clothes. A few were old Tassajara hands, people she'd seen year after year, priests and senior staff who'd held many practice positions. Everyone was in work clothes—shorts or jeans and T-shirts, or *samues,* two-piece informal outfits worn by monks during periods of temple work—mostly dark fabrics to hide the dirt.

She'd seen the same array of expressions around the circle of the poetry workshop the prior evening—a mix of apprehension and excitement. Writing a poem could be frightening if you thought you already needed to know how to do it. So it was with a wildfire. You just had to start somewhere and be willing to get dirty.

Jane didn't say anything about the evacuation she'd already correctly predicted or the one she still believed was on its way. She tried to underscore the message that hung on the wooden board outside the zendo called a *han,* struck each morning and evening to call the community to meditation: *Listen, everyone. Birth and death is given once. This moment now is gone. Awake each one awake. Don't waste this life*. The mallet had worn a deep groove into the faded word *now*.

They need not panic, she assured them, thinking of the effect of the sheriff's request. It would be days, maybe weeks, before the fire actually arrived. The important thing was just to do what they could in each moment to make Tassajara safe. Look around you, she encouraged the few dozen residents who remained, students and staff included. That broom you see leaning up against a building? Don't wait for someone else to move it. Make it your responsibility. A single spark can change everything.

Don't worry, she said again. "We are safe at Tassajara. They'll throw most of us out long before there's any chance of danger, and if they think there's any real danger to life, they'll make everyone leave." Specific tasks could be figured out later, as well as who might stay for the duration. But first, people needed to know that they were not in immediate danger.

David asked the residents to return to the student eating area after packing a bag and gathering their emergency contact numbers. The work leader would wait there to collect the information for the sheriff's deputy.

"Does anyone have questions?" he asked.

There were more than he had answers for. If it's a mandatory evacuation, then why are we allowed to stay? When will we know if fire crews are coming down here? What if I stay now but decide to leave later? Will the stage be running? Someone from the kitchen crew was worried about getting lunch out, even though the guests were gone. What about the schedule?

Each new student is given a copy of the monastic regulations when they arrive at Tassajara—rules that help the monks live together "in mutual respect, peace, and harmony." The first item listed is a "commitment to completely follow the zendo schedule." This means be on time for morning meditation. In fact, be early. Be in your seat five minutes before the final roll-down on the han signaling the start of the officiating priest's morning offering rounds. Be on time for work. Be on time. Be in time.

It may sound confining, but the schedule is not intended to restrict. It's meant to release. Without a schedule, you have to wonder what you should be doing from one moment to the next. Should you wake up now or roll over and go back to sleep? Preferences must be weighed, decisions constantly confronted. And since reality does not align itself with personal preferences, organizing yourself to support them is usually an invitation to suffering.

Zen has a solution to this problem: "The great way is not difficult, just avoid picking and choosing." Just follow the schedule. Take up the tasks of whatever position you've been assigned, without being tugged around by likes and dislikes, and stop when the bell rings. Cook. Clean. Serve meals. Turn compost. Trim candles. Scrub toilets. Sit meditation. One is not higher than the other. A Zen student undertakes work as a practice—this is in the rules, too—"by entering deeply and wholeheartedly into the work given us to do."

That afternoon at the work circle, David told the residents, "We have a lot of hard, physical labor ahead of us. We're going to need as much help as we can get. But it's important that you understand: If you choose to stay, you're choosing to defend Tassajara if the fire comes while you're here."

At that meeting, some residents decided to leave. One student who stayed noted how still and in-between Tassajara felt then. "It was as if the set for a play had suddenly been stripped from the stage," she told me. Her head ached and her lungs felt heavy. She knew that the smoke was only likely to worsen and that she should probably leave, too, but she wanted to stay. She went to the kitchen, where she'd spent many hours as a guest cook, and collected the recipe box and binders containing the lineage of Tassajara's kitchen to be taken to Jamesburg. That afternoon, the regular evening service at five forty-five in the zendo, often not fully attended, was packed. "Everyone was in there," she recalled. "Suddenly we all needed to show up to the one thing that was still known amid all that was so uncertain."

. . .

After supper there was yet another meeting, this time in the creekside guest dining room. The tables inside were set for the next meal, the napkin table outside sprinkled with a fine sifting of ash.

From her seat, Jane could see the bloodred orb of the sun, orange shadows on the hillsides. She listened as residents started to discuss the schedule. Should they alter the usual summer routine, a student asked, maintaining morning and evening meditation, doing fire preparations during the working hours, when people would normally be at their regular crew jobs? But there were problems with that approach, another resident pointed out. Every crew's schedule was slightly different. Some crews worked three days on, one day off. Some worked four days on, one off. Would they still have days off?

Jane had been keeping a quiet profile, making suggestions gently to David or other senior staff members and only when her opinion was requested. But listening to this discussion, she realized she had to speak up. This fire just might find Tassajara unprotected and empty by default, she feared, if they didn't stop talking and get to work.

She'd stopped by the office earlier and asked for a sheet of paper—a whole sheet, not one of the recycled quarters from a cut-up page, used for messages—to start a list of everything they needed to do. They needed to dig fireline, removing even roots from cleared bands of earth. They needed to get crews organized, trim overhanging branches, clear brush, and rake leaves. Anything that might be extra flammable had to be moved to where it could not catch a building on fire. You can't know what is the thing that will make a difference, she told them, you just do everything you can think to do.

"What about the zendo schedule?" a resident asked. "What about zazen?"

"This is a work sesshin," said Jane. "It's not *not* practice."

"Fire sesshin," someone added, and the mood in the room shifted. They decided they would work earlier in the mornings and later into the evenings, when it was cooler and less smoky. They would begin right then, at eight o'clock in the evening. Those who were able and wanted to would work. The zazen schedule would continue but would be optional.

With the day's last light, they hiked up to the hill cabins above the work circle to start clearing. The guest cook who'd gathered up the recipes cleared oak leaves from around cabins with a small brush. Of this experience, she wrote in her journal, "I couldn't tell if we were preparing Tassajara for its death or its rebirth." For the next thirty-six hours, the community worked together removing fuels, limbing trees, and digging fireline around the perimeter of Tassajara. They started at five thirty a.m. and continued until darkness fell, taking individual breaks as needed and meeting several times a day for work circle or a meal in the guest dining room. They worked mostly in silence, but occasionally someone started singing or told a story for respite from the heat, smoke, mosquito bites, poison oak, and blisters. At the end of the day, they washed away the sweat and grime and weariness at the baths and walked back to their cabins in darkness—the flammable kerosene lanterns had been removed from the paths.

The feeling of shared presence that normally abides in the zendo had drifted outdoors, to all of Tassajara. But even as they relished the camaraderie of their collective efforts and the rare privilege of having Tassajara to themselves in the summer, some also had their doubts: We're Zen students, not firefighters! One student's apartment building in San Francisco had burned down less than a year before. His neighbor had died. Had he offended some god of fire? Another lived in New Orleans when Katrina hit. First flood, now fire, threatened her home. Some voiced their concerns, either out in the open or privately, to roommates and friends: They took out all the guests. What are we still doing here?

Jane walked around, reassuring even as she encouraged an attitude of not delaying until later what could be done now. She moved at least fifteen brooms, propped against the outer walls of wooden buildings. Mostly she looked: *What else? What haven't I seen?* Everywhere she looked was something: a wicker chair, a box of firewood outside a cabin door, a pile of dead branches in the dry creekbed just below the shop and its store of lumber and fuel. When she discovered a knee-deep cache of dried, fallen leaves behind the courtyard cabins, she rallied most of the remaining residents to rake them. They used garden carts and trash cans to haul the leaves onto big tarps, then lifted the tarps into trucks and drove them out to the flats. "A leaf is light," Jane said later, "but moved in that quantity, it was heavy labor."

This is what sangha looks like: a chain of bodies clearing leaves or passing thirty-pound sacks of flour hand to hand from the town truck to the kitchen—built by Tassajara's first Zen students. But it's not just about manpower. Sangha is also a mirror. It's what Colin sensed when he arrived that first time at Tassajara and thought, There's no hiding here. It's the connection Mako craved, the nourishment David remembered from the children's home. What better way to learn your habits of mind than to place yourself among a group of other beings with their own habits of mind, deep in a canyon? Sometimes it's like pinball, personalities bouncing off one another, making a racket. Sometimes it's as sweet as a soft rain. Living in sangha, you learn to make harmony, to see harmony in difference, to accept change. At Tassajara in particular, the sangha is always in flux. People come and go.

On the afternoon of June 24, a day after the summer guests had gone and three days after the lightning strikes, the southern perimeter of the group of fires now known as the "Basin Complex"—the Gallery fire, the Basin fire, and a single lightning-struck tree—was six miles northwest of Tassajara. A team of field observers came to inspect the grounds. David and a few others showed them the standpipe system, a set of dedicated high-flow water pipes and outlets designed for firefighting. They showed them the pump that could draw water from the fifty-thousand-gallon swimming pool and the creek-side pump that fed the standpipe and irrigation systems. They pointed out the clearing they'd accomplished thus far. They toured the shed stocked with fire gear: boots, fire-resistant jumpsuits, leather gloves, goggles, and headlamps; McLeods and Pulaskis (combination tools used to dig fireline) and shovels; fire shelters—individual heat-reflective tents deployed as a last resort by firefighters trapped by flames or caught in a burnover; and a well-worn copy of *Essentials of Fire Fighting*, 4th edition. Everywhere they went in Tassajara, the creek-song followed them.

Jane joined the tour. She had cued the staff beforehand: "You have to speak their language. We have to let them see that you are prepared, and willing and capable of staying, or they will throw you out." She jumped into the conversation often, telling the scouts how residents had stood their ground in 1977 and succeeded. She felt that she could serve as living proof that however unlikely it looked, Zen practitioners could help, not hinder, in fighting the fire.

When the field observers left, David felt good about the encounter. No one had encouraged them to stay, but no one had demanded that they leave, either. It seemed they'd overcome the strikes against them—the main one being the narrow road through a deep canyon full of brush that dead-ends at Tassajara. If fire closed the road, the only way to access Tassajara, there would be no escape from the valley, no way to move people in or out in an emergency.

Before they'd left, the firefighters fingered the protective clothing in the fire shed, nodding approvingly, saying, "Oh, yeah. You've got the good stuff."

On the morning of June 25, the incident management team predicted that the fires in the Basin Complex would burn together in the next twelve-hour period and that the fire would spread northeast toward Tassajara Road in the next twenty-four to seventy-two hours.

Governor Schwarzenegger visited the incident command post that morning in Monterey for a briefing with the team, made up of members from local, state, and federal agencies staffing various positions, from safety officers to fire behavior analysts, and logistics and finance specialists. Schwarzenegger had already mobilized the California National Guard a few days earlier. "We haven't seen this kind of condition, this early in the year," he observed at a press conference. "There is no fire season anymore. The fire season is really all year round." More than seven thousand firefighters were working the fires, more than fifty helicopters and fixed-wing aircraft, more than five hundred engines. Schwarzenegger said the state's resources were "spread thin." He advised California residents to take health precautions—to stay inside with windows and doors closed and curtail outdoor activities, especially people with respiratory conditions. "Stay home and stay inside."

As the governor spoke in Monterey, those still at Tassajara—about forty-five residents—sat around tables in the guest dining room beside the creek, listening to a rundown of priority tasks for the day, nearly all of which would require spending time outside in the smoky air, breathing heavily from exertion. Many were feeling the effects of the smoke: dizziness, headaches, a scratchy throat, fatigue. Their muscles throbbed; their bug bites itched. Blisters broke on their hands and feet.

Just before nine a.m., in the middle of the meeting, David was called to the stone office to take a phone call. His voice trembled with emotion when he returned several minutes later and announced that a fire commander stationed at the observatory on Chews Ridge had ordered another evacuation. Fire had entered the Tassajara Creek watershed. "The Basin and Gallery fires are burning together and moving toward the road. Fire engines are staged and ready to leave for Tassajara. They need us out now to avoid a bottleneck on the road. Please go to your room, gather the bag you packed, and meet in the work circle in thirty minutes."

There was the slightest beat of stunned silence before the creek rushed in, filling the void with its coming and going.

Jane had already walked from one end of Tassajara to the other and up to the Suzuki Roshi memorial site, saying wordless good-byes. In the work circle, people were beginning to gather, embrace, load into vehicles. She said good-bye to David, who was warm but visibly distracted. She hugged Mako and her partner, Graham, Tassajara's thirty-five-year-old plant manager.

She felt a deep fondness for the couple, an intimacy beyond their actual familiarity. Mako strongly resembled a friend from Jane's time at Tassajara thirty years before, and the couple reminded her of her own partnership with Tassajara's fire marshal during the 1977 fire. All of this tugged at her heart along with the plumes of smoke rising from the ridge.

But she knew many were being asked to leave who would have stayed if they could, and she deliberately modeled, *We go now. That's what we do. We go.*

Eight was not enough. That was the number of residents David had been told could stay behind. Aware that three times that amount had stayed at Tassajara during previous fires, he had tried to negotiate for more. With more hands, they'd have a better chance of getting the remaining work done and making a stand against the fire if it came through Tassajara. Eight, the commander had said again.

A convoy of vehicles stretched from the work circle past the shop and pointed up the road. A carload of four senior students, former residents whose presence David had requested after the guest evacuation because of their particular skills and knowledge of Tassajara, arrived from San Francisco just as the departing vehicles filled up. Those four plus five others—residents David thought had useful skills and the physical capacity to engage a wildfire—made nine, one more than they'd been granted permission to keep. But the fire commander who'd called with the evacuation order hadn't been to Tassajara. David had never even heard his name before the morning's urgent call. As students loaded into cars, David decided to up the number. If they kept five more, they'd have fourteen, and fourteen could fit in two evacuation vehicles if it became necessary for everyone to leave.

David turned to Mako and Graham. "Who else should we keep?"

He hadn't made a list of candidates, maybe in defiance of this moment of inevitable, and inevitably unpleasant, picking and choosing. David knew well what it was like to lose your home, and here he was, in the position of deciding who could stay and who would go. That pained him, even if he intended to use his power responsibly, for the benefit of all. But he knew what mattered for Tassajara. Who was strong and physically capable? Who had a practical, useful skill, such as carpentry? Who knew the infrastructure? Who could handle the emotional stress and strain of being in the middle of a wildfire? Who would promote harmony in the group?

It was a spontaneous, somewhat random process. They started going to vehicles, knocking on windows, asking certain individuals to stay. These individuals tended to be young and male. In many cases, they weren't the most senior students or residents of Tassajara, but rather those who could dig ditches, fell trees, fix a malfunctioning pump—and maybe run from flames.

Sonja Gardenswartz had lived at Tassajara for ten years. A former head cook in her late fifties, Gardenswartz had answered the phone in the stone office that morning. When the commander said that everyone had to leave Tassajara right away, she'd told him he had to speak with the director. She'd already told David she wanted to stay and cook for the fire crews, and David had said yes. But at the last minute, he decided instead to keep a younger female resident who was strong-bodied, emotionally resilient, and skilled in both the kitchen and the shop.

"I'm sorry," David told Gardenswartz. "I changed my mind. You need to leave with the others."

He watched what looked like anger flash across Gardenswartz's face, her fair skin already flushed pink from rushing to the lower barn for the bag she'd stuffed with her belongings. To be told yes and then no would be painful for anyone. In Gardenswartz's case, David suspected, it might be worse that the denial came from him. As the current guest manager, Gardenswartz was also a member of the senior staff. But Gardenswartz had a history of feeling overlooked at Zen Center, while David had been fast-tracked to positions of responsibility.

"Are *you* leaving?" she asked.

The question, in David's mind, implied that an old rotator cuff injury that limited his physical contribution to work at Tassajara ought to count against his staying as well. But it wasn't really a question, and Gardenswartz didn't wait for an answer before walking away.

Later, she told me that several factors—closed communication and a lack of experience, coupled with the confusion and intensity of the moment—had perhaps obscured "a wider view of what might be needed in the circumstances, that maybe youth and physical strength were not the only qualifications to consider." Had she known at the time what she later learned—"a mandatory evacuation does not mean they will haul you out"—she might have made a different choice herself that morning and refused to leave.

Hard as it was to deny Gardenswartz—and to dismiss three other Tassajara senior staff members, also women—David was sure he'd made the right decision. He counted up those he had asked to stay—four women and ten men, a mix of senior staff and students who'd arrived at Tassajara for the first time only a few weeks before.

He'd pared them down from forty-plus to fourteen. Fourteen wasn't nearly enough, but it was better than eight.

Around ten a.m., after the evacuation convoy left, the remaining fourteen regrouped and recalibrated their preparation efforts. An hour later, one green U.S. Forest Service (USFS) fire engine with a crew of eight arrived. David, Graham, and Tassajara's resident fire marshal, Devin Patel, gave the crew a tour. The firefighters helped residents clear brush and dig fireline, but shortly before four p.m., the engine captain told David they wouldn't be staying the night. The crew left before dinner.

David felt duped. Based on the urgency of that morning's mandatory evacuation order, he had emptied out most of Tassajara, expecting that the firefighters would stay—and that there would be many engines, not one. The numbers in his head from the 1977 and 1999 fire logs—sixty firefighters, twenty engines lining the road—dwarfed this response.

That evening, David and Graham drove up to Chews Ridge and the Monterey Institute for Research in Astronomy (MIRA) observatory, built to take advantage of the clear atmosphere above the Santa Lucia Mountains and lack of ambient light in the Ventana. During the Basin Complex fire, MIRA served as a safety zone, lookout, meeting site, and operations base for firefighters, as it had in the 1999 Kirk Complex fire. Ivan Eberle, MIRA's caretaker, had invited David and Graham for a visit to get acquainted with the fire commanders who held briefings there and to view Google Earth maps of the fire's progression.

Eberle had stayed at MIRA throughout the 1999 fire. He was familiar with the lingo, tactics, and politics of firefighting. He had relationships with local firefighters. But for David and Graham, it was like being thrown into another world. When they first arrived, to David's surprise, they encountered the USFS engine captain who had pulled his crew out of Tassajara just a few hours earlier.

Inside Eberle's living quarters, a group of firefighters in varying uniforms—including several members of the USFS engine crew—gathered around the dinette table. Some wore USFS uniforms. Others were from CAL FIRE, California's state firefighting agency. As the firefighters ribbed one another like members of opposing sports teams, David and Graham glimpsed the complex and sometimes conflicted relationship between the agencies. "We learned that CAL FIRE was more proactive," David told me later. "The Forest Service was in charge, but it seemed like CAL FIRE wanted to be."

Firefighters came and went from the room. Eberle played a YouTube video of a "fire tornado"—a spinning pillar of black smoke churning through a stand of oak trees in a grassy meadow on the Indians fire, southeast of Tassajara. He told David and Graham that the fire whirl had run three miles, burned over an engine crew, and ripped a fifteen-inch limb off an oak tree. Could that happen at Tassajara? David wondered. He wouldn't want to be anywhere near that.

At one point, Eberle told me later, a "consultant" on the fire joined the conversation, someone he had not met before who reported directly to the incident commander. As Eberle listened to the talk around his table, he heard that the incident management team for the Basin Complex fire, concerned about the rugged terrain and lack of resources, did not plan to provide structure protection within the fire area. Eberle felt he'd received assurances of protection from a commander previously assigned to the area who had consulted him for his local knowledge and experience. But now he heard that crews were pulling out, that they wouldn't even wrap buildings before leaving them to the flames.

Graham heard something slightly different. His impression was not that the fire service was abandoning the area completely but that incident command staff was shifting personnel around, trying to cover two huge fires. "They were bringing the fires together under one command structure and separating east from west."

It's not unusual for Graham to have his own considered take. Sometimes he wears glasses, sometimes not, depending on whether he feels the need. His mind is disciplined yet curious; serious yet playful. He once continued to sit zazen all night long during a seven-day sesshin at Tassajara, inspired by old stories of monks who tested the marrow of their practice by sitting upright for years at a time. In conversation, Graham pauses as long as it takes for the words he seeks to arise. He can move from a look of intense concentration to a soft, high-pitched giggle and back all within one sentence.

As plant manager, Graham had intimate knowledge of Tassajara's hidden places, the systems below the surface and out of sight that keep the place running. Twice a day he checked the potable water supply, running tests for the county. He maintained the pumps that fed the irrigation system. He monitored the energy supply from solar panels installed high on the hill above the work circle and tracked power usage—in 2008, about half of the electricity used to light the kitchen, staff offices, student housing, and zendo came from the sun. Graham also ensured that Tassajara's phone lines were in working order. He came to the position with some background in carpentry, but he learned the job more by observation, in his words, by "seeing clearly what's happening and responding," by "attuning to plumbing as attuning to zazen." Ever since the fires had started, Graham had spent more time than usual thinking about water—running beneath the earth, down the creekbed, through the pipes at Tassajara—and about how to ensure that they would have a constant supply when they needed it.

When they returned from MIRA, Graham and David said good night below the birdhouse, a resident cabin perched on a cliff above the work circle. The darkness around them was alive with the rush of the creek and the rustlings of the Ventana's animal inhabitants—crickets, wood rats, rattlesnakes, raccoons, deer, the occasional cougar. Normally Graham would have to walk down to the flats at the far end of Tassajara to return to the cabin he shared with Mako. That night he walked only as far as stone three, one of Tassajara's most desirable guest rooms, along the creek. David had requested that the fourteen remaining residents move into the central area, where they would be easy to reach in an emergency.

Back at his cabin, David looked longingly at the stack of books on his night table. Normally summer afforded him time to read. He could work through several novels reading a bit each night before bed. Not now. All he wanted to do was sleep at day's end. It was exhausting integrating new information on the fire each day, making decisions that powerfully affected others, and then, on top of that, dealing with people's reactions.

He set his notebook on the table. It was full of names. The official fire command structure seemed to be in constant flux. The day's events and the meeting at MIRA had reinforced David's mounting confusion about who had authority on the fire and who could be trusted. From now on, he decided, he wouldn't take what anyone said as the unshakable truth or assume that the people in uniform were keeping Tassajara's best interests in mind. He would rely on his own authority, even if it made him uncomfortable to do so.

After about six months at the children's home, David was sent to live with a foster family. Once, while spanking him for something he no longer remembers, his foster mother felt faint and demanded that he bring her a glass of water. When he did, she spit it out and said, "This isn't cold enough!" He brought her another and she spit it out again: "Can't you do anything right? I'm in pain and you're not helping me!" Knowing that his actions could cause others to suffer caused an old anxious feeling to stir in David, only now he knew that trying to make it right would only make it worse. At any moment, despite good intentions, he might misstep. A novice in fire, he could only be willing to learn and to make his best effort.

Find out for yourself, Suzuki Roshi had told his students at Tassajara when they were trying to figure out what an American Zen monastery would look like—a messy, confusing, yet exciting process. The mind of a beginner is as open and receptive as a tilled field in spring. The mind of a beginner doesn't know. It assumes nothing; it tests everything. It asks of all it encounters: Is that so? In this business of wildfire, all of Tassajara's residents were novices, feeling their way in the dark.

Three

THE THREE-DAY-AWAY FIRE

To carry yourself forward and experience myriad things
is delusion.

That myriad things come forth and experience themselves
is awakening.

—EIHEI DŌGEN, *Genjo Koan*

Thursday, June 26, five days after the lightning strikes

Midday on June 26, Chris Slymon sat down at the computer in Jamesburg to post an update on *Sitting with Fire*, the blog he'd started the prior afternoon when a few dozen Tassajara evacuees had arrived in Jamesburg.

Stunned and ravenous, they had unloaded boxes of fruit, cheese, loaves of bread, and various spreads for lunch, having raided the walk-in refrigerator and dry goods storage at Tassajara before leaving. (There were plenty of extra supplies since the Tassajara kitchen had been prepared to feed close to fifty that night.) After lunch, Jane Hirshfield had hugged Leslie good-bye and slipped away before the start of a four-hour meeting in which the evacuees sorted out the complicated logistics of where each and every person would go—and the animals. The evacuation caravan had included the monastery dog and a couple of cats.

Residents accustomed to greeting one another with a bow embraced when the meeting ended, uncertain whether they'd meet again. Then they reshuffled themselves into cars, preparing to scatter in all directions. Some were relieved to leave the fire zone, while others felt profound disorientation and distress, a state of shock at the quick turn of events.

They had spent thirty-six extraordinary hours together, engaged in the task of preparing for the fire, yet individual responses to the sudden upheaval of the evacuation varied. While Zen holds that the construct of a "self" is actually empty, because like everything else it is always changing, people inevitably bring their own perspectives to the circumstances they encounter. As 1977 Tassajara fire marshal Ted Marshall told me: "You show up with your own life experience."

One summer resident's friends had thrown her a "monkette" party when she left behind a lucrative career in video production in Austin, Texas, to dive into practice at Tassajara. Heading out of the smoky valley only three weeks after she'd arrived there, she had no idea what she'd do next. "I'd just left my whole life," she told me.

The student whose San Francisco apartment had burned down returned to a temporary home at City Center, with six small boxes containing his entire worldly possessions and fresh memories of the sounds of his neighbor banging around in the hallway, attempting to escape the burning building. He felt helpless, useless, and resolved to get back in to Tassajara as soon as he could.

For Judith Randall, a member of the senior staff who hadn't been asked to stay, the time at Jamesburg was the hardest part. As the zendo manager, or *ino,* the fifty-nine-year-old priest had sat morning and evening zazen while most residents worked outside. Sometimes she was the only one in the meditation hall. She had carefully removed ritual objects, statues, scrolls, and portraits from the zendo, founder's hall, and abbot's cabin. Randall had coordinated the morning's evacuation at Tassajara, directing residents to their assigned cars, then she'd purposely driven the last car out with only one passenger so that she could pick up the stranded if there were any breakdowns on the road. It wasn't until she arrived at Jamesburg and was confronted with the question of where she wanted to go that the full weight of the evacuation had hit her. She couldn't think. Eventually she drove to San Francisco to be near her teacher, taking a van full of evacuees.

On Sitting with Fire, *there were pictures, links to official fire* reports, satellite images, Google Earth maps of fire activity—a wealth of information for anyone curious about what was happening at Tassajara. "The short story is that Tassajara is currently threatened by two wildfires," read Slymon's first post, published the afternoon of the resident evacuation. The Indians fire did not seem to be moving their way, but the Basin Complex fire continued to mount a direct threat, burning south and east toward Tassajara.

Which meant it was also burning toward Jamesburg. The day after the resident evacuation, Jamesburg was put under an "advisory" evacuation. This first of three alert levels warns residents to prepare for possible evacuation. The next, "voluntary," is a more forceful recommendation to leave. The final level is "mandatory." Residents are told to evacuate immediately—as Tassajara was on June 25. Though California residents cannot legally be forced to leave, even in a mandatory evacuation, the language conveys a sense of urgency and authority to strongly encourage them to do so.

The Basin Complex fire was under what is called "unified command" within the ICS, which meant that fire management decisions, while ultimately the responsibility of the incident commander, included input from the USFS, the Monterey County Sheriff's Office, and CAL FIRE, the state firefighting agency. From June 23 to 25, the twice-daily status summaries from the incident management team were consistent, predicting a threat to Tassajara in the next twelve-hour period and fire spread toward Tassajara Road thereafter. The Basin Complex fire's acreage continued to increase—20,600 acres had burned by the evening of June 25. Containment estimates hovered at a mere

3 percent. Incident Commander (IC) Mike Dietrich had his hands full in Big Sur, where sixteen homes had just been lost.

On June 26, IC Dietrich told a reporter for KAZU, an NPR affiliate in Monterey: "This country is straight up and down and brushy and very unsafe." Since it was likely that the Indians and the Basin Complex fires would also merge and become one fire, Dietrich explained, "that's a strategy that we're looking at." The "strategy" under consideration seemed to be: Do nothing and let the fire dictate its course. "There's no good place in the middle of the wilderness to fight the fires," IC Dietrich said. In 1977, the Marble Cone fire had spread through the Ventana despite significant efforts to contain it. This time, Dietrich and his cohorts on the incident management team planned to let the fire burn inside a big box drawn by the old 1977 "dozer lines"—wide firebreaks cut by bulldozers.

Thirty-one years after the Marble Cone fire, the incident commander on the Basin Complex fire invoked that fire as a strategic model for how to fight this one. Indeed, there were many similarities. Like the Basin Complex fire, the Marble Cone fire was lightning ignited. It was an aggregated fire—the result of several smaller fires that burned together. At 178,000 acres burned, it was the biggest fire the state of California had ever seen. Estimates of the combined acreage for the 2008 Basin Complex and Indians fires were approaching that record figure.

For Tassajara residents, too, the 1977 Marble Cone fire provided a gauge for what to expect. One of the first things David had done after the lightning strikes was to read the Marble Cone fire log. Tassajara had been ordered to evacuate in 1977 as well. After initially following those orders, residents had made covert trips into Tassajara at night. One group had even driven through a roadblock while some students distracted the officers posted there. A couple of days after being told by the USFS not to expect help, hotshots—the gritty elite of firefighting—had arrived at Tassajara.

Hotshots hike extreme terrain on foot, carrying thirty-five-pound packs, chainsaws, and other tools to do the backbreaking work of digging a trough of bare earth to catch flames and stop their spread through fine surface fuels like grasses, twigs, pine needles, and leaf litter. They also light backfires to consume fuels and create a safety zone—an area that has burned won't burn again.

At Tassajara, when the main fire was still off in the distance, the hotshots lit the hill behind the monastery, across the creek. They disappeared either up- or downstream to continue their work as a crew of residents extinguished spot fires from drifting embers inside Tassajara. Once that large area had burned, there was less chance of a firestorm in the canyon, and a group of residents returned to prepare for the main fire's arrival. Jane and Leslie rode in the last vehicle to return to Tassajara from Jamesburg before fire closed the road.

For two weeks in 1977, Zen students cut firelines and set sprinklers on the roofs of the central buildings. From time to time a fire crew arrived, took baths, ate some of that truckload of peaches, then hiked upstream. When the Marble Cone fire finally burst into the canyon over Flag Rock one August afternoon after several weeks of lingering nearby, a small fire crew was at Tassajara. The crew boss invited then abbot Richard Baker to do the honors of igniting a backburn on the slope across from the stone office. The monks who worked alongside firefighters to defend Tassajara became known as the Tassajara "cool shots."

Reading the Marble Cone log in 2008 gave David reason to believe that help was coming, eventually. The record also provided a glimpse of what to expect after a fire passed through—as well as what couldn't be expected but could happen anyway. At the end of August 1977, the skies above Tassajara were still smoky and spitting ash. That fall and winter, hundred-year rains streamed down the charred watershed and flooded Tassajara. The creek turned chocolate brown and swelled several feet. Some twenty-five hundred sandbags were placed around buildings, and a few hundred creekside trees were felled to prevent damming. Tassajara Road, which had been closed for days during the fire's passage, washed out in six places. Food and supplies had to be ferried across impassable areas on garden carts and wheelbarrows. The students worked through the winter and spring practice periods to protect

Tassajara from the post-fire floods. Then, on the final day of the spring 1978 practice period, the zendo—the original zendo, the one that was a bar before it was a meditation hall—burned to the ground.

The fire started in the middle of a ceremony in which the abbot answers a question about the teachings from each member of the sangha. Both questions and answers indicate understanding. Within a few minutes, fire engulfed the building where Suzuki Roshi had given his talks, seated in front of the old fireplace converted into an altar; where before that, whiskey had warmed the bellies of hunters; where even before that, an Esselen Indian might have made a meal of acorn mush over a campfire.

A monk visiting from Japan tried to dash back into the burning building to save the two-thousand-year-old stone Gandharan Buddha statue on the altar, probably smuggled on a donkey cart from inside the borders of present-day Pakistan or Afghanistan before Zen Center purchased it from an American art dealer. "First I stopped him," Jane told me. "Then I changed my mind. We walked back in together and half the ceiling was burning, so I pulled him out again." The next day, the two sat staring at the remains of the zendo. "I'm sorry I didn't let you go in at the beginning to get the Buddha," Jane said to the Japanese monk.

The monk looked at her, then pointed at the old altar. "Buddha," he said. He pointed at the ashes: "Buddha." Then he pointed at Jane. "Buddha," he said again.

Because of problems with the emergency water pump after the floods that followed the Marble Cone fire, the resident fire crew at Tassajara in the spring of 1978 wasn't able to get water on the zendo fire in time. They'd saved Tassajara from a wildfire only to lose its most significant building the following spring, probably because of a faulty pilot light on a propane gas refrigerator. No one was injured, yet nothing was left of the zendo but fragments of stone walls. Drums and bells melted in the flames. The Gandharan Buddha toppled from the altar. Some who were at Tassajara at the time, like resident fire crew head Ted Marshall, recalled that the Buddha shattered into pieces, none larger than a teacup. But Roger Broussal, the restorer who worked on the statue at the de Young Museum in San Francisco, told me it had split into several large chunks, and pieces of schist had stripped away "in layers or sheets, almost like shale."

After the new zendo was built, the Buddha was placed on the altar, on a pillow with red and gold accents, where he has sat for three decades. Two feet tall, with a chiseled, slender torso, he's a fit Buddha, not rotund or androgynous. His eyes are half-lidded, the left eye set slightly higher than the other by the original sculptor's hands. Aside from chips in his right ear and knee—some pieces were lost forever in the zendo's ashes—there is little evidence of the damage. His lips press together in a hint of a smile.

Within twenty-four hours of the resident evacuation on June 25, linked lengths of PVC pipe zigzagged across the dining room roof at Tassajara in a white, angular web. In 1977, David had learned, students used garden hoses, sprinklers, and blankets to keep the roofs wet. This time they constructed something more complex yet elegant. When they turned on the jury-rigged sprinkler system for the first time and it worked, drawing water through the standpipe system from the twenty-thousand-gallon spring-fed water tank up the road and showering it over the rooftops, plant manager Graham smiled and said, "Ah, Dharma Rain."

When CAL FIRE captain Stuart Carlson arrived that afternoon, he admired what Tassajara's residents had already accomplished—the rooftop sprinklers, the firelines, the cleared ground around the solar panels and cabins. He'd been headed to the Sierra Nevada mountains for a weeklong backpacking trip when he got a call asking him to come to Tassajara to advise the residents and help them prepare for the fire. "I'm on my way," he said. He brought his eighteen-year-old son with him.

Stuart had been coming to Tassajara for years to give first-aid training and assist in fire safety evaluations and drills. He first arrived as a Zen student in 1987—but his connection to meditative practices predated that. When he was growing up, Stuart was introduced to meditation by his godmother, a member of the Franciscan order, and later to Zen by a brief encounter in the San Bernardino National Forest in the 1970s with poet and natural world spokesman Gary Snyder, who once worked as a fire lookout. Snyder read his poem "Control Burn"—"Fire is the old story. / I would like, / with a sense of helpful order, / with respect for laws / of nature / to help my land / with a burn, a hot clean / burn"—and Stuart's ears pricked up.

Having grown up in rural Santa Cruz County, he'd been in the woods his whole life. His first and favorite family dog was a coyote his father had nursed back to health from a gunshot wound. He spent summers at Pico Blanco Boy Scout Camp near Big Sur, racking up merit badges. When Governor Jerry Brown created the California Conservation Corps (CCC) in 1976, Stuart was among the first group hired. He wanted to "heal" the forest. He worked at Pico Blanco on a CCC crew during the 1977 Marble Cone fire.

"My poor mom got a house full of Vikings," the fifty-three-year-old youngest of three boys told me when we talked at Tassajara in June 2009. He'd returned to Tassajara the summer after the fire to give his annual first-aid training. A drizzle had turned into a downpour and we'd sought shelter in the student eating area. The kitchen crew chopped vegetables nearby at two long tables.

"We were all surfers, wandering around with dirty bare feet on her white carpets," Stuart recalled with a sympathetic laugh. Both of his parents were activists, though his father's politics were considerably more radical than his mother's. His father was an animator at the Walt Disney Studios and a founding member of the Motion Picture Screen Cartoonists Guild during the House Un-American Activities Committee era. From his father, whom he described as "a hard-core labor man and true conservationist in the Teddy Roosevelt mode," Stuart inherited the desire to take care of others, even at risk to himself.

In 1984, a few years after signing up as a seasonal firefighter with the California Department of Forestry (CDF), now known as CAL FIRE, Stuart found out his girlfriend was pregnant. He applied for a permanent position for financial stability but, like many firefighters, got hooked by the "esprit de corps and feeling of family" as well as the sense of being useful to his community. He was promoted to captain in the early 1990s. As station captain at Soquel Station, near Santa Cruz, Stuart oversees a four-person engine crew. He's responsible for the upkeep of equipment, vehicles, and the station itself, budget management, and the training and supervision of firefighters.

"I'm hard on them at first," Stuart told me. "It's easier to be a jerk and then a nice guy later on." It's not so easy to imagine Stuart playing tough. He's gregarious, with a warm, tenderhearted demeanor. He has soft eyes, wavy hair, a flirtatious smile, and a quick, slightly nervous laugh. He studied traditional Japanese karate for years but is more surfer than black belt, agreeable and amiable by nature.

Under the surface, though, there's the pain Stuart has seen over a firefighting career that's spanned thirty years. The worst are the tragedies close to home, the people he knows—like the local teacher whose rayon nightgown brushed against a gas burner on her kitchen stove and burst into flame. "Even her hair burned off her head," recalled Stuart, who was first on the scene.

Stuart's had a few close calls himself during his career, but they weren't on his mind when he showed up at Tassajara with his son—and plans for his girlfriend to join him over the weekend. He wasn't going there in any official capacity. "The Forest owned the fire," he told me.

The Forest—the Los Padres National Forest and the USFS—"owned" the fire because it was on their land. Stuart works for CAL FIRE, and even though the agencies cooperate on fires in mutual aid agreements, Stuart readily admitted that the USFS and CAL FIRE don't always get along. In part, the friction is a result of a difference in mission, especially when it comes to structure protection. "The Forest Service is a land management agency, a resource management agency. We're a resource protection agency. We're a fire department. Structure protection is what we do."

That might mean dashing into a burning building, but it also means preparing structures so they aren't fire hazards in the first place. It means clearing brush so that when a fire moves through, the only fuels available to it aren't anywhere near buildings. Grunt work, most of it. But Stuart knew the work ethic of Zen students. They made his most gung ho firefighters look lazy. Given the prep work that residents had done already and the creek's constant water supply, they were in a good position to make a stand and defend Tassajara. It would take only an engine or two to back up the monks.

Fire season was off to a running start. Three major fires had raged in Stuart's home county of Santa Cruz already, and it was only June. Stuart sensed it was going to be a wild season. After a dinner of squash-and-mushroom casserole, roasted vegetables, and pear crisp that first night at Tassajara, he went to bed early, lulled to sleep by the creek.

On June 27, the day after Stuart's arrival, sixty-five firefighters descended into Tassajara to help cut firebreaks. Members of a CDF/CAL FIRE inmate crew from Fenner Canyon, the men worked for a dollar an hour and a day off their sentence for every day worked on a fire.

"Hey, Captain Carlson!" one of them cried out, recognizing Stuart from his days leading a California Youth Authority crew.

Some of the inmate firefighters couldn't scrub the look of bewilderment from their faces. Many had grown up in the inner city and had never seen a landscape anything like this. But it wasn't the first time a prison crew had found themselves at the monastery.

In 1999, when the Kirk Complex fire threatened Tassajara, both inmate and professional crews dispatched to assist the residents were prepared to spend weeks at Tassajara if the road closed. Some staffed the kitchen, helping to turn out meals that featured tofu, or "white Spam," in lieu of meat. Firefighters helped out with cabin repairs, soaked in the hot plunge at the bathhouse at day's end, and hung their laundry on the line. When zazen instruction was offered to the firefighters, rows of battered leather boots lined the zendo shoe racks.

Subdued by early rain, the 1999 fire never made it to Tassajara. Their last night at the monastery, firefighters moved from their tents into guest rooms. The next morning, as they prepared to pull out and clouds gathered overhead, a crew captain protested, "It wasn't supposed to rain!" Gaelyn Godwin, director of Tassajara at the time, wrote later about the bond that developed between firefighters and monks and caught the media's interest—a bond of mutual kindness, concern, and generosity.

Another firefighter left in 1999 with these parting words: "If you want to live here, you'd better learn to live with fire."

Diane Renshaw, an ecologist who began practicing at Tassajara in 1978 when the mountains were recovering from the Marble Cone burn, agrees. "Fire is one of the primary ecosystem processes that defines the character and beauty of the Santa Lucia Mountains," Renshaw told me. And you can't talk about fire in California, she added, without talking about chaparral, a plant community that is so widespread, it could well be the unofficial state ecosystem.

In the daily status reports issued by the incident management team, there is a designated space for noting fuels involved. For the Basin Complex, the first word was always "chaparral," followed by timber and "dead loading" from diseased tan oaks. Covering more than seven million acres in the state, *chaparral* is an umbrella term for a variety of drought-tolerant and fire-adapted plants that thrive in the warm, dry summers and mild, wet winters of Mediterranean climate zones. The chaparral found around Tassajara includes maroon-barked manzanita, chamise, ceanothus, and the distinctive spear-shaped blooming yucca, which exists in a profoundly cooperative relationship with a moth that lays its eggs exclusively on the yucca's white petals and, in turn, pollinates the plant.

What chaparral lacks in height—it grows dense and relatively low—it makes up for in depth. The roots of "old growth" chaparral can work their way through crevices in the bedrock to depths of twenty-five feet or more, where cool temperatures and moisture prevail. Different species of chaparral have different methods of post-fire regeneration. Some resprout, some reseed, some send shoots above the soil from underground bulbs. But all chaparral species are energy-efficient, using available resources wisely. After a fire, chaparral shrubs take advantage of increased available light and soil nutrients.

According to Renshaw, the scientific community has learned much about fire since Smokey the Bear started educating the public in 1944. How fire behaves and the role it plays differs from one ecosystem to another. Within one designated land area, such as the Los Padres National Forest, there are many different plant communities. Conifers such as Coulter and ponderosa pines grow primarily at the higher elevations. Thin-barked Santa Lucia firs favor fire-resistant rocky areas and wet canyons. The steep drainages around Tassajara, especially those that face south, are carpeted with chaparral, while the road is fringed with oaks. Down in the riparian corridor of the Tassajara valley, tall sycamores and alders shade the creek. Big-leaf maples thrive on the lower canyon slopes.

Such ecological diversity makes for a complex fire ecosystem—one that includes some species that do not tolerate fire, others that have developed regrowth strategies to cope with it, and some that depend on a wildfire's smoke and heat for their survival. In the plant realm: Whispering bells, golden eardrops, and the radiant orange fire poppy bloom only after fires. In the animal kingdom: "Fire beetles" (*Melanophila*) mate and lay their eggs in the hot wood of burned trees just after the flames have died down.

It's true that living in the Ventana means learning to live with fire. But learning to live with fire is tricky, because there isn't one kind of fire. There are crown fires, slow creeping fires, wind-driven fires, stand-replacement fires, smoldering fires. There are fires in chaparral, fires in pines, fires in oak savannas, fires in buildings made of wood, clay, and stone. There is fire in the center of each human heart. Knowing what kind of fire you live with, a Zen student knows, is an endless, constantly changing, moment-by-moment process.

Word of the situation at Tassajara had begun to spread, in part because of media attention. Days after the June 25 evacuation, a reporter from the *Los Angeles Times,* tipped off by an evacuated resident, had driven down the road with a photographer to interview residents. On June 28, a week after the lightning strikes, the published article noted the cooperative efforts of monks and professional crews in the 1977 and 1999 fires and indicated that the residents hoped for a rerun.

The fridge in the courtyard where guests store personal items was full of wine, but the fourteen residents left at Tassajara in late June 2008 went for the Clif Bars and Hansen's cherry soda instead. With the Fenner Canyon inmate crew digging fireline, the residents' work schedule had eased slightly. They'd begun to hold meetings around a block of tables pushed together in the dining room so they could consult fire maps and share ideas.

"The spirit is good and the group very solid," noted David Haye, who goes by his Dharma name Shundo, in his journal. A forty-four-year-old expat Brit who was previously the fire marshal and work leader at Tassajara, Shundo had left at the beginning of June to be head cook at City Center in San Francisco. He was one of the four who'd arrived at Tassajara to help with fire preparations just as the student evacuation caravan was pulling out on June 25. Among the small group now charged with protecting the monastery, he felt glad to be on the team, if also a bit guilty for the privilege.

It made sense for Shundo to be there. As a former fire marshal, he could show new resident fire marshal Devin Patel the ropes. A cyclist and runner, he knew every hiking trail within a ten-mile radius. And many of the others who'd remained at Tassajara were his peers. Shundo sat his first practice period in 2002 along with David and Mako. Having "come up through the ranks" and been on senior staff together, they shared a strong connection, Shundo told me more than a year after the fire, his English accent softened by years spent abroad.

Typically, every summer day at Tassajara brings new arrivals and departures. During the fire preparations, the number of residents at Tassajara hovered between fourteen and twenty-two. But sometimes the total number of people there, including firefighters and volunteers, fluctuated dramatically.

When the inmates arrived, David had recruited four students who'd stayed near Jamesburg to return to Tassajara to help with food preparations for the additional sixty-five people. Anyone David asked to return had to be physically capable and willing to stay for the fire's arrival.

By the morning of Saturday, June 28, the remaining senior staff members had identified a group of nine who would stay if yet another paring down became necessary. "As soon as we were down to fourteen," David told me later, "the question came up: How are we going to organize? Who is going to make decisions?" Normally, decisions that affect residents fall to the senior staff, temple officers who meet briefly every morning before work meeting. But half of the senior staff had been evacuated. Those who remained settled on a group of six residents, made up mostly of senior staff, to function as a decision-making team. This "core team" included David, Mako, Graham, Colin, fire marshal Devin, and Shundo.

Late in the morning on June 28, a CAL FIRE battalion chief appeared at Tassajara, saying that all "nonessential" people should pull out. With a fire map spread out on the hood of his truck, he pointed to the fire's creeping eastern perimeter, nearing the Church Creek divide north of Tassajara, and beyond it, the road. The prior evening, a visiting safety officer and Jon Wight, the captain of the Fenner Canyon inmate crew, had emphasized to residents the liability of Tassajara Road. Wight had said the road would be "extremely dangerous" as the fire approached. No one would be able to travel on it, either to enter the valley or to leave. Now, having personally observed how prepared residents were, Wight came to their defense. In the end, the chief didn't pressure residents further to reduce their numbers. For the time being, all fourteen would stay.

At this point, fire could come from any direction. And yet, observed Shundo, "it looked like the fire was building up and getting closer, and then it seemed to peter out. There was a definite dip." The firefighters clearly had intended to impress upon them that this was serious business. But the fire was still three days away—as it had been estimated to be for more than a week, earning it the name the Three-Day-Away fire among Tassajara residents.

. . .

On Sunday, June 29, David walked into the kitchen and told Mako that the Fenner Canyon inmate crew was packing up. They would be gone before lunch.

"What do you mean they're leaving?" Mako asked, arms crossed, big eyes opened wide. She and her skeleton kitchen crew had just made enough three-bean salad to feed nearly eighty-five people. "I thought they were supposed to stay for a few days. We've got so much food." The town truck that had brought in kitchen helpers had also ferried in extra supplies in anticipation of feeding the firefighters.

"I thought so, too," David said, shrugging.

The Fenner Canyon inmate crew had accomplished a lot in a couple of days—mostly digging trenches on the steep northern slopes for firebreaks—but inmates and monks had not had the kind of time they'd had during the 1999 fire to forge a bond. This time, the inmates slept in sleeping bags on the concrete deck at the pool. They didn't work together with residents so much as in parallel. One inmate told Mako he was a Buddhist, but there were no boots lined up on the zendo shoe rack as there had been in 1999. There was still so much work to do, and the zendo was mostly empty.

Still, crew captain Jon Wight recalled sadness and frustration when their orders came to pull out on June 29. It was the second time he'd been told to leave Tassajara. The first was only an hour after they'd arrived on June 27, but he'd argued with the commander and received permission to stay. He'd originally been told his crew was going down to Tassajara to ride out the fire. The residents had welcomed his crew with warmth and respect. "Driving away," Wight said later about leaving, "I won't say I cried, but I wanted to. I had such a good feeling about the type of people they were and the way they treated us. I felt like we were abandoning them."

Later that morning, firefighters and monks gathered in the courtyard, circling around a large upright boulder. A student who'd returned after the resident evacuation to help in the kitchen had made cookies for the inmates.

He distributed a brown paper bag of cookies to each of the men. "Just be careful when you bite down," he announced, unable to resist, "there's a tiny metal file in each cookie."

The inmates laughed, though their wardens weren't amused. After that, everyone took a group picture in the parking lot—orange suits clustered in the middle, flanked by uniformed crew leaders and wardens, and monks in work clothes. The monks thanked the firefighters for their hard work. Wight assured them that another crew would be on the way if the fire moved closer. Then the engines pulled out, and the residents were left alone.

Four

IN THE SHADOW OF ESPERANZA

It is hard to know what to do with all the detail that rises out of a fire. It rises out of a fire as thick as smoke and threatens to blot out everything—some of it is true but doesn't make any difference, some is just plain wrong, and some doesn't even exist, except in your mind, as you slowly discover long afterwards. Some of it, though, is true—and makes all the difference.

—NORMAN MACLEAN, *Young Men and Fire*

Sunday, June 29, eight days after the lightning strikes

At Jamesburg, the phone kept ringing. The far-flung sangha called for updates and with offers to drop everything and drive into the valley to help. Chris Slymon, *Sitting with Fire*'s creator, broadcast a thank-you, saying, "We are unable to accept any offers to help work at Tassajara as we cannot increase the number of people we have staying down there." The post's larger font drew attention to the unwritten message: *Do not come to Tassajara.* He suggested that those who wanted to help could open their homes to the displaced.

Some could not be so easily dissuaded. One Zen student who had lived at Tassajara in the 1980s decided to drive down Tassajara Road. Videocamera in hand, he shot footage destined for YouTube of smoke-churned skies above Tassajara and interviewed eighty-five-year-old local Esselen "Grandpa" Fred Nason, who just a few days earlier had ridden his horse in front of a fleet of bulldozers rehabilitating old firelines from the 1977 and 1999 fires, to safeguard Native American sites in their path.

But few ventured past the closure signs at the Los Padres National Forest boundary. For many, checking *Sitting with Fire* regularly was enough—or was the only option. Slymon passed along whatever he knew to readers hungry for information about what was happening down at Tassajara.

As the month of June drew to a close, he summarized the situation. The Indians fire was "almost-but-not-quite controlled," but the Basin Complex fire was burning out of control, extending its northern, southern, and eastern perimeters. "The current plan for controlling the fire to the north and east," reported Slymon, "involves the construction of a large box within which the fire is allowed to burn and within which they work only to protect structures such as Tassajara . . . There are many scenarios for protecting Tassajara that vary with the direction in which the fire approaches." The one constant was unpredictability. Fire behavior, and firefighting strategies, couldn't be set in stone because they depended so completely on weather.

"Well, life goes on (toilet paper and tissues)," he wrote, speaking of supplies still being driven in to Tassajara for the resident fire crew, "and life changes (electrolyte powder, oxygen and hoses, hoses, and yet more hoses)."

Talking about the weather may be a euphemism for conversation with a lack of substance, but nothing could be further from the truth when it comes to wildfires. Weather makes or breaks fires. Big fires create their own weather. When firefighters and civilians die in wildfires, weather plays a pivotal role.

Most recently, and most directly relevant to the Basin Complex fire's management, was the 2006 Esperanza fire in Southern California. Ignited by an arsonist and stoked by hot, dry, October Santa Ana winds, the wildfire killed five USFS firefighters defending an empty, half-built residence on a ridgeline west of Palm Springs.

As is usually the case in tragedies, several factors lined up to create the conditions for devastation. There was a temperature inversion in place that morning. When fire entered the canyon below the octagon-shaped house where the firefighters of Engine 57 had stationed themselves, superheated flames—1,200 degrees Fahrenheit—punched through the inversion layer. A twenty-four-thousand-foot plume acted as a chimney, drawing winds into the fire downwind of the house and blowing walls of flame up the canyon at speeds of 50–70 mph toward the house. Flames wrapped around the angled sides of the structure, leaving the crew nowhere to hide. The extreme heat and winds created an "area ignition"—all combustible material in the area caught fire simultaneously, without needing to come in contact with flames. The firefighters' Nomex, flame- and heat-resistant clothing that chars at 824 degrees Fahrenheit, disintegrated.

The captain of Engine 57 must have determined that the spot, perched on the rim of a steep canyon, was safe. So what went wrong?

The Esperanza fire made its fatal run up a steep drainage. The 1949 Mann Gulch fire in Montana and the 1994 South Canyon fire in Colorado had already provided grave examples of what could happen in that kind of terrain. In addition, crews on the Esperanza fire—there were several engines in the area—had trouble reaching one another on the radio because assigned frequencies were overwhelmed by radio traffic. They resorted to using unassigned frequencies, where those managing the fire couldn't hear them.

In the world of wildland firefighting, the firefighter who arrives first at a fire usually names it and assumes command of the incident, at least initially. Who is ultimately "responsible" for a fire depends on who owns or manages the land where the fire starts or spreads to. The Esperanza fire start, and the accident site, were in CAL FIRE's area of responsibility. A CAL FIRE engine arrived first, at just after one in the morning. As the fire burned into the San Bernardino National Forest, the CAL FIRE battalion chief functioning as incident commander requested U.S. Forest Service support. Five USFS engines, including the doomed Engine 57, were dispatched within a half hour.

According to an investigation conducted by the USFS and CAL FIRE, unified command for the fire was established (and radio broadcast) at three ten a.m. An independent federal inquiry three years later, however, found that unified command wasn't put in place until after the fatal burnover. Either way, here is the bitter irony of Esperanza: Five USFS firefighters, not mandated by their agency to provide structure protection, died defending an empty residence burning within the jurisdiction of CAL FIRE, whose mission clearly includes protecting property.

Esperanza means "hope" in Spanish, but this was no hope-giving event. Rather, it seeded doubt and an abundance of caution. Why did our men die? fire commanders had to ask. And there was no good answer. No good response but to refocus on firefighter safety going forward. Basin Complex IC Mike Dietrich spoke at the memorial service for the Engine 57 firefighters when he was still fire chief for the San Bernardino National Forest. In 2008, it's unlikely that Dietrich or any other firefighter had forgotten the stricken faces of family members at those firefighters' funerals.

The USFS firefighters who'd come to Tassajara since the start of the Basin Complex fire mentioned the Esperanza fire often. We can't put our men down here, they'd say. Not with one road in and out. Not to protect structures.

It got under CAL FIRE captain Stuart Carlson's skin. "They kept on saying we lost these firefighters on this fire in San Bernardino County. So what they were saying is we're not doing structure protection. Well, they've lost a lot more people doing wildland firefighting throughout their history, so why are they doing wildland firefighting?"

There were ways in which Tassajara evoked Esperanza. The steepness and remoteness of the terrain. The access issues. But there were also key differences. The burnover in Southern California had happened on a ridge—a dangerous place to be during a wildfire. Tassajara is situated in a riparian corridor. Fire would have to work hard to descend into the relatively moist Tassajara valley anywhere near as hot and fast as it had swept up the ridge on the Esperanza fire.

The federal inquiry into the Esperanza fatalities concluded that a lapse in situational awareness played a destructive role. Firefighters need to know what is going on around them, be able to perceive the potential for change, and be willing to modulate those perceptions based on what is actually happening on the ground. Zen monks, too, are trained to attend closely to the dynamics of their environment. They try to stay in contact with reality, to realize that things constantly change, and to respond to each moment's cues.

Call it situational awareness or call it beginner's mind. Mindfulness is the everyday practice of a monk. It can save the life of a firefighter.

As June gave way to July at Tassajara, the remaining residents kept preparing for the Basin Complex fire, not knowing if it would arrive or when. They tested the Mark 3 pump at the creek, had meetings, studied fire maps, drank mullein herb tea—good for the lungs. They dug a hole for the Gandharan Buddha statue in the bocce ball court, just in case. Shundo Haye took pictures of helicopters passing overhead and gorgeous orange sunsets, stone walls tinged red. On Tuesday, July 1, he wrote in his journal: "Not knowing is the habit. We become elemental—earth air fire and water."

On July 2, Shundo and another resident named Bryan Clark scrambled up past the solar panels to Hawk Mountain, stopping every so often to look back at Tassajara. It glistened below them, damp and green thanks to Dharma Rain. Shundo had become the core group's scout, patrolling trails around Tassajara on foot, often accompanied by Clark. Some days Shundo ran all the way up the Tony Trail behind Tassajara to monitor the smoke spooling from densely forested ridges in the Willow Creek valley, a drainage that intersects with Tassajara Creek a few miles downstream from the monastery.

The trail up Hawk Mountain was relentlessly steep. On the steepest pitches, they crawled more than walked. At the top, they caught their breath while taking in the view. An orange gray haze hung over the road to the north, obscuring the thick white band of limestone from which Lime Point takes its name. The sun poked through the haze, a tiny pinprick of light, though it was only four p.m. The fire had established itself upstream in the Tassajara Creek drainage, but twists and turns in the terrain prevented Shundo and Clark from seeing it, even from this high vantage point.

Shundo dug into his day pack for his Canon G9. He'd been taking photo after photo, trying to capture the endless transformations in the sky, the relationship of sky to earth and fire to cloud, and to get the pictures to Slymon to post on *Sitting with Fire*. A former BBC sound engineer, Shundo had a sense of how important it was for people outside the valley to see what it looked like at Tassajara. An amateur photographer, he wanted to record and share the spectacular, singular beauty of the fire.

"All the world is on fire," said the Buddha after his enlightenment. Addressing a thousand fire-worshipping ascetics in Gaya, India, in what's known as the Fire Sermon, the Buddha spoke of the fires of the senses that stoke greed, aversion, and delusion and lead to suffering. "Monks, the All is aflame. What All is aflame? The eye is aflame. Forms are aflame. Consciousness at the eye is aflame. Contact at the eye is aflame. And whatever there is that arises in dependence on contact at the eye—experienced as pleasure, pain, or neither-pleasure-nor-pain—that too is aflame." Here were the Buddha's words, nearly twenty-five hundred years old, unfolding in the Ventana.

Working through each of the gates of perception—the eyes, ears, nose, mouth, body, mind—and the fires at each gate, the Buddha taught that "disenchantment" is the path to liberation. He urged the monks not to stamp out the fires of the senses, but simply to see that they are there and to recognize them for what they are—sensations, perceptions, thoughts, not solid or fixed, but always burning, transforming.

The monks at Gaya were immediately enlightened. At least that's how the story goes. Awakening can happen in a moment with the right words, the right conditions. But it can't be held on to. Awakening too is on fire. It comes and goes.

Shundo's entrée into Zen practice had been a happy accident. While visiting San Francisco, he'd gone to a cyclists' club gathering and met a woman there who lived at City Center. She introduced him to practice. The two married and moved to Tassajara. She eventually wanted to leave, but Shundo didn't. It seemed more important, he told me later, to follow through on what he'd started at Tassajara. Unlike most of his peers on the core team, who'd been at the monastery for six or seven years straight, Shundo has come and gone several times. While a resident, he left Tassajara twice to tend to relationships—once with his ex-wife (the couple eventually divorced), once with another Zen student. While his peers were all becoming priests, he was told by his teacher to sort out his romantic life first. *All is aflame.* Shundo knew that truth intimately.

As Clark and Shundo started their descent down Hawk Mountain, a helicopter with a bucket swinging beneath it stirred the murky air overhead. It headed toward the Narrows, probably to get more water. David had announced at the morning meeting that the Basin Complex fire had burned more than 52,000 acres, mostly in wilderness. Almost two weeks after the lightning strikes, they had begun to wonder if they'd ever see actual flames. All they could do was wait and make good use of the fire's delayed arrival, continuing to dig, clear, rake, limb, scout, and drill.

The small group of residents remaining at Tassajara had found a rhythm, a coherence. Some even sat zazen in the zendo in the morning or evening, but attendance was still optional. They held a short service each morning after work meeting in the dining room, where they'd posted a copy of poet Gary Snyder's "Smokey the Bear Sutra" on a bulletin board—a 1969 early homage to deep ecology written in the form of a Buddhist scripture. A small poster of Japanese calligraphy propped on the altar read: *One mind is like water.*

The mood at work meetings was marked by the kind of grave and playful humor that flourishes among those who share close quarters in conditions of extreme fatigue and potential hazard, like a company of soldiers in a war zone or a fire crew. On July 2, one of San Francisco Zen Center's two abbots, Steve Stücky, was scheduled to come to Tassajara. The wooden board outside the zendo would be struck and incense offered upon his arrival. At Zen

Center, the abbacy is a position of both spiritual and organizational leadership. While many residents and some watching from afar felt that the abbot's arrival was long overdue, some wondered if his presence would throw off the congenial, consensual dynamic they'd established.

The prior morning, July 1, a CAL FIRE captain had arrived with new fire maps to brief them on the fire's presence less than three miles up the Tassajara Creek drainage. Forecasted northwest winds would nudge it closer. But the captain expressed confidence that residents could ride out the fire. This confidence was based in large part on Tassajara's natural defensibility—its abundant water and its location at the bottom of a canyon, as opposed to a ridge. And his confidence was shared by Stuart, who had taken to teasing the residents, "I'm just going to sit back with a cold Coors when the fire creeps in and let you all take care of it."

Now that the fire had reached the local watershed, they had decided to take turns doing four-hour night watch shifts. Shundo had signed up for the first shift that night to set an example that senior staff weren't exempt from the duty. When they returned from Hawk Mountain and Clark went to the kitchen to see if he was needed there, Shundo headed for the bathhouse, a slender building situated along the creek. He offered incense and made three bows in front of the altar, where a verse hangs: "With all beings, I wash body and mind / free from dust / pure and shining / within and without." After entering the men's side, he stripped off his sweaty clothes and went straight for the creek to cool off.

Nearly two millennia after the Buddha's Fire Sermon, in the Mountains and Rivers Sutra, thirteenth-century Zen teacher Eihei Dōgen wrote, "There is water in the world, but there is a world in water. It is not just in water. There is also a world of sentient beings in clouds. There is a world of sentient beings in the air. There is a world of sentient beings in fire.... You should thoroughly examine the meaning of this."

So what happens when the world of water and the world of fire meet? As Shundo lay in the cool creek and felt the current fork around him with steady, unrelenting force, it was pretty easy to imagine the world of water quenching the world of fire.

Shundo's father used to call him a "lazy layabout." How different his life was now from when he lived in London, working for the BBC and playing in a jazz band. Now his mum had to explain to acquaintances that her son was a Zen monk, waiting for a wildfire in the American wilderness.

He'd loved London, but he'd always known he wouldn't stay. By contrast, the first time he'd seen Tassajara, he'd sensed that he'd never want to leave. Shundo left the bathhouse, bowing once at the altar before slipping on his shoes. Time for dinner, and he was ready.

Inside Tassajara, the residents had little time to fret—preparations kept them busy. Dharma Rain now extended from one end of the valley to the other, covering most of the buildings. A regular twice-daily watering schedule kept the grounds moist and green. Meals still had to be cooked and eaten and cleaned up after.

Those outside, however, worried. They checked *Sitting with Fire* several times a day or more. They downloaded Google Earth maps, marking Tassajara with a yellow thumbtack and watching heat detections denoted by yellow, orange, and red dots cluster ever closer to the mark. Many who'd been evacuated recognized the teaching of impermanence in their experience but felt heartbroken and untethered.

It is traditional for monks to wander, as the Buddha did, far from home to seek awakening. The ordination for a Zen priest, *shukke tokudo,* actually means "home-leaving" ceremony. But one receives shukke tokudo voluntarily, after months of sewing one's own robes. Those struggling with being "outside" of Tassajara did not choose to leave their home. For them, both priests and lay practitioners, a symbolic concept was suddenly a real-life teaching.

It's one thing to study impermanence—the fact that there is nothing fixed and unchanging in the world to rely on—and quite another to have that truth thrust in your face by circumstances. Yet this is the point of practice. This is what zazen teaches—not simply how to be quiet and still until the bell rings, but how to let that measure of equilibrium accompany you when you leave the zendo, so that when life rushes in and difficulty comes, you can take a breath and choose your response, instead of being shoved around by thoughts and emotions.

From their temporary refuges at City Center and Green Gulch Farm, evacuated Tassajara senior staff held meetings with displaced students. "I felt I had to be honest, that I was angry and sad, that I didn't have any answers for them if they were looking to me for answers," Maria P. Linsao told me. As work leader, Filipino-born Linsao had been charged with the task of gathering numbers for the students' dentists and next-of-kin info before the evacuation. A forty-four-year-old asthmatic, she wanted to stay but knew she could be a liability, even though she felt strong and capable and had spent a fair share of time with a pickax digging fireline before the June 25 evacuation.

Her sadness and anger didn't disappear. Like the other evacuees, she knew that she was missing a rare opportunity to practice in the middle of a wildfire. But Linsao, who became a priest in 2010, also saw that she could bring her practice to her actual situation. Harvesting kale at Green Gulch one day, Linsao was overcome with gratitude for the chance to be useful in another way. She might not be work leader at Tassajara anymore, she realized, but she was still senior staff. "I need to uphold something here, not out of ego or pride, just a deep responsibility for other beings. I can work here on the farm at Green Gulch, which is actually Zen Center, which is actually Tassajara, so what is it that I'm separating from and making myself suffer for?"

Midday on July 2, Abbot Steve Stücky stopped his car at Ashes Corner, a turnout at a sharp bend in Tassajara Road below Chews Ridge that offers a panoramic view in three directions. He often stopped here—the first and last vantage point from which to glimpse Tassajara both coming and going. Today, however, there wasn't much to see but smoke. The entire sky between the ridge he stood on and the Pacific Ocean was the color of combustion. He'd just driven down from San Francisco, approximately 150 miles away, where the gray of frequent summer fog was flinty with smoke from the state's many fires.

The smoke burned in his throat, but he wanted to stretch his legs after hours in the car, so he walked out on the ridge where on a full moon night in April 1972, a newcomer to Tassajara, he'd helped scatter Suzuki Roshi's ashes.

Stücky never met Suzuki. If told back then that one day he'd be co-abbot of Zen Center, the young Stücky would have been dubious. His path to the abbacy didn't follow a typical course. Though he had been ordained as a priest in 1977—the year of the Marble Cone fire—he'd spent most of his adult life in the "lay" world, raising a family and running a landscape design business, while continuing to practice zazen on his own and with a Dharma group he hosted. He had been informally asked about his availability and declined several times before finally accepting an invitation to become abbot in 2007.

This saying no before saying yes—or saying no to one thing to say yes to something else—is a distinct pattern in the abbot's life. His ancestors were Swiss Anabaptists. He grew up in a firmly Mennonite household in Newton, Kansas. It was at home, he told me, that the tradition was instilled in him of not just going with the flow, of "having a deeper set of values."

From the time he was four years old, he challenged his father's authority and questioned his judgment. His father had what Stücky called "a complex life"—as a minister, college professor and administrator, author, and farmer. "He was a very good-hearted, loving, wonderful person who had this son who was really difficult," reflected the sixty-three-year-old abbot, now father of three, as we talked on a blustery November day at Green Gulch Farm in 2009.

When Stücky was thirteen years old, he was expelled from Sunday school for disrupting the lessons with questions. Instead of just accepting what he was supposed to believe, he wanted to discuss why he ought to believe it. In his twenties, he became a conscientious objector to the Vietnam War (a status made possible by the peace work of his Anabaptist ancestors) and served as a hospital orderly instead of as a soldier. During the 1968 Democratic National Convention in Chicago, he worked in a South Side ghetto as a community organizer and youth counselor. "I joined the rallies at the convention. We occupied the street between the park and the hotel, and when the police charged at us, we just sat down. I was sitting in the street when I was grabbed and whacked with a baton and dragged into a paddy wagon."

Eventually, he found himself disenchanted with what he described as the "righteousness" of the political movement. "We were our own worst enemy in a sense. Even though we had high ideals, we couldn't seem to get out of our own narcissistic way. I began to look at the nature of that in myself and others, which actually led to an investigation of how I perceived anything." Which eventually led him to Zen.

Stücky first shared the details of his life before Zen Center in the abbot's cabin at Tassajara, six months after the fire. He gave the impression not of a rabble-rouser but rather of a peacemaker and rabble-rouser rolled into one—flexible and strong-willed. Like his father, Stücky is both a farmer and a spiritual adviser. He's been working hard since he was given his first tractor at nine years old. As a teenager, he traveled from Texas to Montana working the summer wheat harvest to supplement the family's income. From his Mennonite roots, he carries with him a sense of the value of community and a certain industriousness and seriousness of purpose. From farming, he has learned the importance of taking cues from all directions.

Built like the wood fencing on his grandparents' land, tall, lean, and sturdy, the six-foot-two-inch Stücky knows the edges of his mind. While he claimed there was a time in his life when he was mostly interested in playing the blues on his guitar, Stücky seems to have grown more, not less, playful with age. Deep dimples frame his mouth like parentheses, giving the perpetual faint impression of a smile. Stücky was given the name Myōgen—meaning "Mysterious Eye"—at his ordination by Richard Baker, but he identifies himself as "Abbot Steve." He sometimes ends lectures with a sing-along of the old Leadbelly tune "Relax Your Mind."

From where he stood at Ashes Corner on July 2, Abbot Steve could see the confluence of the Tassajara and Church Creek drainages and the Willow Creek canyon to the south. It was impossible to tell which fire the smoke belonged to, the Indians or the Basin Complex, hard to make out the shape of the fire they were preparing for.

He and Abbot Paul Haller had decided that he should go to Tassajara to check up on things, since Haller was in the middle of leading a three-week period of concentrated practice at City Center, and Stücky knew a bit about fire from farmwork in the summer wheat fields. All it took was a truck's hot muffler to brush the stubble of a cut wheat stalk. If the wind was up, an entire field could erupt into flame.

He planned to stay for a few days, then return to San Francisco to catch a plane back east to visit his daughter. Standing on the ridgeline, he studied the track of the road, cutting across the mountain at a diagonal, its end disappearing into the valley that holds Tassajara, a triangular patch of green.

It could all burn. It had burned before. But he wouldn't call the fire his enemy. "The element of fire is in my own body," Abbot Steve said later in a conversation with a student. "It's not foreign." Neither malicious nor magnanimous, fire is simply fire. The earth and the beings that live on its surface have coexisted with fire for millennia in an interdependent relationship. Fire, he knew, could not be removed from these mountains. Fire belonged in the Ventana, just like the manzanita or the oak trees or Suzuki Roshi's ashes, scattered here in a burst of wind.

On the evening of July 2, the residents met in the guest dining room at Tassajara. Abbot Steve invited them to share how they felt about their situation. Everyone wanted to stay. Some even expressed impatience for the fire to arrive. The Basin Complex had grown almost ten thousand acres in a mere twelve hours, to more than sixty-one thousand acres. Full containment was expected to take a month. Low fog and clouds moving overland from the ocean had kept the fire in check, but temperatures were expected to soar in the coming days, creating conditions less favorable to firefighters and more favorable to fire.

The residents didn't know it yet, but ten miles west, the fire had already flared, jumping the dozer lines and prompting a mandatory evacuation in Big Sur that displaced fifteen hundred residents, shuttered twenty businesses, and shut down a thirty-mile stretch of Highway 1.

Five

GREAT FAITH, GREAT DOUBT, GREAT EFFORT

When you do something, you should do it with your whole body and mind . . .

You should do it completely, like a good bonfire.

—SUZUKI ROSHI, *Zen Mind, Beginner's Mind*

Thursday, July 3, twelve days after the lightning strikes

The air horn sounded, a strange, shrill tone piercing the valley. Then came the planned announcement over the radios: "Fire at the hill cabins!" The residents converged on the equipment shed below the zendo to practice suiting up in jumpsuits, boots, hard hats, goggles, and waist packs for carrying water, a radio, and fire shelter. Then they split off—the pump crew running to pumps at the creek and the pool to charge the standpipe system, the hose crew lugging hoses up the stone steps and rolling them out. The ready-for-anything crew stood by, an extra set of hands, ears, and eyes.

They perspired in the heavy cotton CDF coveralls—hand-me-downs from Stuart, well insulated but less resistant to radiant heat than the Nomex firefighters wear now. Their goggles fogged, and they had to resist the temptation to pull them off. A dry, steely thirst thickened in their throats. Shundo gave the signal that the hose crew was ready, both arms raised like a referee's on a touchdown, and the pump crew opened the lines. CAL FIRE captain Stuart Carlson wasn't around during this drill by the hill cabins—he'd left Tassajara briefly to take his son home and host a Fourth of July party—but the residents backed one another up on the hoses as Stuart had taught them: one person at the nozzle and a second just behind or halfway down the hose length. Over the radio, lookouts flagged the flames: "Roof of hill three! Spotting between the solar panels and the birdhouse!"

It was just a drill, a test of the residents' readiness. Except for the withering heat inside their fireproof gear, none of it was real, but it made Tassajara fire marshal Devin Patel proud to watch how everyone mobilized. "That was a very sweet time," he told me more than a year after the 2008 fire. "We bonded as a community."

A Tennessee native, Devin had been surprised, and not exactly excited, to be given the position of fire marshal. Typically, the part-time job involved testing fire extinguishers and smoke alarms weekly and holding the occasional training or drill. In the early part of the summer, before the fires, it had been hard to recruit people to train on the various fire crews. He'd held only one or two drills. But since the start of the Indians fire, Devin had been attending senior staff meetings, even though he wasn't actually on staff at Tassajara. Now he found himself supervising the fire preparations. "I was walking around doing this management thing, which was funny, because I'd just learned what people should be doing. I was just one step ahead."

At a meeting that afternoon in the dining room, two weeks after the lightning strikes, Devin didn't say much. In addition to him, the group included many members of the core team—director David, head cook Mako, plant manager Graham, head of shop Colin, and fire scout Shundo—as well as Leslie James, who was down from Jamesburg, Abbot Steve, and fifty-six-year-old former USFS firefighter Kim Leigh. Leigh often came to Tassajara during work periods to do painting projects, and David had called him to ask for his help preparing for the fire.

Most of the residents present at the meeting were senior staff. Most were priests. Most had been at Tassajara for a lot longer than Devin's one year. Both Shundo and Mako had served as fire marshal. "They were all pretty active problem solvers. There was a lot of discussion," Devin told me. "I definitely hopped in when I had an idea, but I was the quietest one." At twenty-eight, he was also the youngest.

David wanted to hear from each of them. What is your personal commitment to staying? What factors do you need to take into account in considering whether or not to stay? They went around the room, raising concerns about whether they had the right number of people at Tassajara now, or the right individuals, and about the possibility of a firestorm in the valley.

"I feel safe," said Devin when it was his turn, "unless an expert tells us otherwise."

It was an opinion many in the group shared. David wanted to leave behind a thorough written record of the Basin Complex fire, like the ones he'd been reading from the Marble Cone and Kirk Complex fires. Sometimes he had trouble deciphering his own slanted handwriting, so after the meeting he typed up his notes on the stone office computer.

"The consensus of the group," he wrote, "was that despite the unknowns, we had a lot of confidence in our safety here should the fire pass through, and therefore were all willing to stay. . . . This was, of course, as long as Stuart or Kim or other firefighters themselves felt the situation was safe enough to stay. If they said leave, we'd leave."

While everyone else was out digging fireline and raking leaves, Mako had to cook dinner. She loved being head cook, but as a former fire marshal—and one who had filled the position so thoroughly—she struggled with the juxtaposition. She knew how the pumps worked, where all the standpipes were. Though her body had begun to tire from the physical strain of kitchen work, she wanted to be outdoors, preparing Tassajara alongside everyone else, including her partner, Graham, who as plant manager was charged with safeguarding the water supply, the pumps, the communications systems, and the solar array.

On the one hand, Mako knew that there were cooking fires and wildfires and that both deserved equal respect and attention. It was important—vital, in fact—to fortify the monks for their labors. "But there was also this feeling, everyone's doing the necessary work, and I'm in the kitchen," Mako said later of the weeks leading up to the fire's arrival. There wasn't anything to do about the feeling necessarily, except to watch it come up.

Mako couldn't remember who or what had started an argument between her and Graham, but exhaustion was the likely cause—the duress of nearly two weeks spent in a continuous state of alertness and preparation, waiting for the fire to come. For Mako, there was the added edge of being confined to the kitchen while Graham got to move around and do the "necessary" work. A friction between them had built until it generated enough heat to flare into a full-blown conflict.

When Graham and Mako met in 2003, they had discovered a mutual interest in the martial art aikido. They had much in common. Both had spent summers unleashed in the wild, rural environments of their grandparents' homes—Graham in one of the last remaining old-growth red and white pine stands in Ontario's Temagami region, Mako in coastal New Jersey. Both had a deeply rooted, ongoing interest in studying the mind.

Yet it wasn't unusual for the couple to find themselves in disagreement. There were times when they'd been up most of the night in a fight and still had to go to the zendo in the morning. At Tassajara, a couple in conflict is in conflict in the middle of a very intimate space, with nowhere to go to get away.

As head cook and plant manager, Mako and Graham hardly saw each other during the day under normal circumstances; their days off overlapped only once every three weeks. They'd catch up at night, back in their cabin. But sometimes the couple deliberately spent time apart. During a practice period sesshin—lasting anywhere from five to nine days and conducted mostly in silence—it wasn't unusual for Mako and Graham to live separately or at least carry the silence of the intensive back to their living quarters. "When we're in sesshin we don't really talk to each other," said Mako. "Sometimes we don't interact at all." Such strictures were more for Graham's sake than hers. "He needs more time alone and more space to himself than I do," she said the summer after the fire. "I'm pretty extroverted and have never sought after quiet. It's kind of weird that I'm in a Zen monastery."

During the fire, they were often too tired to talk at night. Sometimes Mako would want to connect, and he would just want to read or need to sleep.

They were both under pressure. "It was smoky down here, so we were constantly not getting enough oxygen. And we were so thoroughly tired," Mako told me later. It was a different kind of tired from the tiredness that comes during sesshin. They hadn't had a day off or been out of the valley in weeks. "Graham got snippy and irritable," she recalled. Something he said, or didn't say, got under her skin. She reacted. "He got defensive. I got angry. It escalated from there."

It was July 3, their anniversary, and by day's end they weren't speaking to each other.

As of July 4, two weeks after the lightning strikes, the Basin Complex fire had not resulted in any fatalities. However, a volunteer firefighter had suffered a fatal heart attack while working a fireline in Mendocino County. And two bulldozer operators were injured when their machines rolled. Often it's not fire that directly threatens the life of a firefighter. It's a rolling rock, a falling tree, a truck tipping over a road edge, too much smoke, an overdose of adrenaline that stops the heart.

But what does happen when a firefighter gets caught in the flames? This is one of the questions author Norman Maclean took up in *Young Men and Fire,* reconstructing the race uphill between a wildfire and fourteen smoke jumpers in Montana's 1949 Mann Gulch fire: "First, considerably ahead of the fire, you reach the verge of death in your boots and legs; next, as you fail, you sink back in the region of strange gases and red and blue darts where there is no oxygen and here you die in your lungs; then you sink into the main fire that consumes, and if you are a good Catholic about all that remains of you is your cross."

Norman's son, John Maclean, uses plainer prose in *Fire and Ashes* to describe firefighter fatalities in a 1953 fire in the Mendocino National Forest in California: "An advance wave of superheated gas entered their mouths and noses and seared the delicate tissues of the nose, mouth, and esophagus involved in breathing, which ceased to function. Deprived of oxygen, the men quickly fell into unconsciousness and died within seconds." It wasn't the fire that killed but the furnace blast of air that accompanied it.

As a firefighter, Stuart had seen what could go horribly wrong. What firefighters call a "slide tray" of haunting images sometimes kept him awake at night.

Once, he'd lit an escape fire on a deer trail to save his crew. "Just like *Young Men and Fire,*" he told me, referring to the Mann Gulch blowup in which the foreman, Wag Dodge, lit the grass ahead of the main fire raging upslope toward his crew to create a safe, burned-out zone. Dodge survived, as did two other firefighters who managed to outrun the fire, but most of the crew perished. They'd thought their foreman had gone mad, adding fire to fire, and many ignored his command to step into the burned area and lie facedown on the smoldering earth while the main fire passed.

Wag Dodge's quick, lifesaving thinking has long fascinated firefighters. Escape fires became standard practice after Mann Gulch. But others outside the firefighting world have been drawn to Dodge's story as well—historians, songwriters, scientists, poets, and those merely curious about his startling access to insight, to knowledge he didn't know he had until it materialized at just the right moment and saved his life. While the fleeing firefighters clutched at the driving thought that they had to run to stay alive, Dodge was able to stop running and open his mind to the wide field of possibilities, from which the solution to his problem dropped into view. Both Dodge's example and current neuroscience attest that a pliant, nongrasping mind is the hallmark of insight. It's also a fine description of the mind in zazen: relaxed yet alert, flexible and porous.

When Stuart ordered his young crew—they were California Youth Authority wards doing time for crimes committed as minors—to follow him into what has come to be called "good black," they did. Helicopters dropped water on their heads. But Stuart didn't tell this story at Tassajara. He wanted to instill confidence in the residents. And everything he saw and heard led him to believe this fire was going to come backing down slow and tame.

When a new incident management team for the Basin Complex fire rotated on duty July 2, the branch director assigned to the area drove down to Tassajara to look around and meet the residents. His name was Jack Froggatt.

David introduced the two firefighters. "Stuart's an old friend of Tassajara. He taught us everything we know," he said. Then he left them alone to talk.

"How long you been with Kern County?" Stuart asked. Froggatt's T-shirt said "KERN COUNTY FIRE."

"Since '84." Froggatt looked to be in his fifties, strong and fit, the gray hair more a testament to a long career in a field of risk than a concession to aging.

"We were always getting sent down to the Kern when I was a crew captain," Stuart told Froggatt, referring to the river sometimes called the Killer Kern. The waterway originates in the Sierra Nevada range near Bakersfield. "One of the fires was in a canyon. It was the steepest climb I've ever done with a fire crew." Stuart gestured to the acutely angled, rocky slopes towering over Tassajara. "You should feel right at home here."

"Glad to have you as a resource," said Froggatt.

The feeling was mutual. Stuart had never met Froggatt before, but he'd met Froggatt's country. And that told him much about Froggatt. He was a veteran, an old hand at rough country. But he didn't swagger around or try to bully anyone. He listened. He asked questions. He seemed, Stuart told me on several occasions, to appreciate what Tassajara is about.

. . .

Until he read a status report from the incident management team that noted the threat to Tassajara, Mike Morales had never heard of the place. After reading more on local blogs, the former CAL FIRE captain who retired early owing to an injury started following the story of the monks' fire preparations. He wrote about the efforts at Tassajara on his site, *Firefighter Blog.*

Morales had been tracking the California wildfires since June on his blog. Chief among Morales's concerns was the lack of resources. "This is the widest spread of resources I can recall," he wrote on June 22, the day after the lightning strikes. Two days later, he observed that there were still only 380 personnel assigned to the Indians fire. "Under normal circumstances CAL FIRE would have 1,500 people swarming this fire." When the number of personnel on the Basin Complex fire jumped to 1,000 on June 29, Morales still wasn't impressed. "All considered this is a very small army for a fire this size. Troops are scarce statewide so it's improbable this one will ever get adequately staffed."

Three days before the lightning strikes in June, Casey Judd of the Federal Wildland Fire Service Association had testified for a Senate oversight committee on the readiness of federal land management agencies—such as the U.S. Forest Service, which oversees national forests like the Los Padres. Judd told the committee that the agencies were not sufficiently prepared for the 2008 fire season. Federal fire programs were increasingly under the management of people with little or no expertise in wildland fire, said Judd, and funds meant for fire preparedness and fuels reduction had been diverted to nonfire programs and projects.

These trends may explain in part why there didn't seem to be enough firefighting resources to go around in the summer of 2008—that and the extraordinary, unanticipated burden of more than two thousand wildfires. But Morales argued that the Ventana Wilderness deserved better. "If the fires meet in the middle on their own, I have no problem. If the fires are being directed to meet, I suggest the forest is a victim of mismanagement." Even after the number of firefighters assigned to the Basin Complex fire doubled in late June, Morales lamented that "two thousand firefighters is about a quarter of the manpower they need to make a dent."

As the projected acreage for the Basin Complex fire continued to climb in early July, Morales consulted GeoMAC, an Internet-based fire-mapping application, alongside topographic maps he'd spread out on his desk. GeoMAC occasionally hiccuped and showed spot fires burning in the Pacific Ocean, but simple geographic common sense told him that if the fire grew, it had to grow inland, away from the coast, toward Tassajara.

"As the week progresses," he wrote on the Fourth of July, "firefighters will find themselves working away from Big Sur proper and farther into the Ventana Wilderness." And they would do so in brutal heat. Temperatures for the beginning of the following week were forecast to bust ten-year records. "Folks at the Tassajara compound," he warned, "have renewed reason for concern."

On July Fourth, an NBC Nightly News *crew drove down the road,* filmed Tassajara residents clearing leaves and testing out Dharma Rain, and interviewed Abbot Steve. The footage aired the following evening as part of a larger report on the California fires, particularly those threatening Santa Barbara and Big Sur.

That evening, at a festive dinner of pizza, ice cream, and fizzy drinks in the dining room, David allowed himself two slices of pizza. He tended to gain weight in the summertime at Tassajara, when leftover guest food was available at the back door of the kitchen for endless snacking. Cherry scones. Pecan pancakes. Double chocolate cookies. He knew well the false comforts of food. When he was ten years old and living with his father again, he had weighed 152 pounds.

For the past few days, the core team had been trying to anticipate various scenarios. David had made a list of the thresholds and contingencies they'd discussed, mostly in the form of questions. What are the "trigger points"—a term firefighters used—at which we evacuate noncore team members? Evacuate everyone remaining in the valley? Take shelter in safety zones? If a CAL FIRE crew is here, who stays and under what circumstances? When do we evacuate: if they do? Or if they tell us to but they stay? When do we bury the Buddha?

They'd been trying to hammer out a system of tiered evacuations in which nonessential people would leave when the fire was close and a smaller group would stay for the fire to fuel the pumps Dharma Rain depended on. But by July Fourth, they'd abandoned that idea and decided to focus on ensuring that there were twenty people inside Tassajara willing to stay and defend it even if the road was cut off.

Counting the fourteen residents who'd initially stayed behind during the June 25 evacuation, plus students who'd returned to help after, residents then at Tassajara numbered around twenty already. Some of those individuals, however, hadn't committed to staying for the duration, as the core team had. Bringing in more people would mean more reinforcements and more time to recover from the constant physical work of the last couple of weeks. One resident was so fatigued that he'd walked into the bronze gong outside the kitchen used to announce student meals and nearly knocked himself out.

After dinner, when the dishes were bused to the dish shack and the food put away, they gathered again around the table in the dining room. An upbeat mood lingered from the special holiday meal. It flattened when David made his announcement: Now is the time to choose. If you stay, you must be willing to meet the fire when it comes to Tassajara. Those concerned for their safety and unwilling to engage the fire should leave right away so others can come.

That Fourth of July evening, the skies were quiet over much of California. Some citizens had heeded the governor's request to forgo fireworks. Normally, July Fourth is a festive night at Tassajara. Residents perform skits and parade down the main path, celebrating the anniversary of Tassajara's official opening day in 1967 as much as the national holiday.

Zen students are more likely to affirm interdependence than independence. Part of Buddhist practice is learning to perceive the ways we are all connected to one another, just as each moment is tethered to the past and the future. Like a stand of aspens, all phenomena emerge aboveground from the same root. People forget this most of the time. They remember in times of crisis, when the habit of disconnection is broken.

This Independence Day at Tassajara, the residents were too tired to put together a celebration. They went to bed early as the forest put on its own display, bathing everything in a smoky orange glow.

The Three-Day-Away fire had been lurking in the Ventana Wilderness for two weeks. Though the fire wasn't holding true to its name, it was still fitting. Many things come in threes in Zen. An old adage advises: Reflect three times before speaking. Monks make three bows (or nine, a multiple of three) during service. They eat from three bowls. They recognize three worlds or realms of existence: the realm of desire, the realm of form, and the realm of formlessness. They vow to abide by three pure precepts—to do no evil, to do good, and to save all beings—and to cherish the three treasures: Buddha (the teacher), Dharma (the teachings), and sangha (the community).

On the steamy afternoon of July 5, the standoff between Mako and Graham was three days old. When Mako left the kitchen after lunch, she ran into Graham inside their temporary lodgings in one of the stone rooms, where it was blissfully cool.

"Do you want a cookie?" she said. She'd brought some from the kitchen.

He answered no with a quick shake of his head.

"I wish you'd talk to me," she said.

She took a bite. The cookie didn't taste sweet, despite the sugar and chocolate chips in it. She closed her eyes and took a breath, reminding herself that she and her partner were still connected, even if she couldn't feel it. Still, it hurt to feel separate. That day, Stuart had returned to Tassajara, bringing his girlfriend, Solange, as his guest. Introducing her at work circle, he was solicitous and sweet, protective, maybe overly so. Shundo, the acting work leader, had sent her to the kitchen. Her presence there made the dissonance with Graham all the more vivid for Mako.

One moment, you're so close you feel you share the same skin, and the next, you're a universe apart. But Mako knew better than to take Graham's silence personally. Whatever was bothering him wasn't really about her. His mood would shift eventually.

"I'll leave this here," she said, setting a cookie on the table.

She petted Monkeybat, asleep on a chair. The cat lifted her head into Mako's palm and purred. Four weeks out from surgery for an intestinal tumor, she seemed to be slowly healing. Mako had sent Monkeybat to Jamesburg during the June 25 evacuation, but as fire preparations dragged on at Tassajara, Monkeybat was brought back in so Mako could take care of her personally.

"See you," said Mako. Graham gave no reply. She opened the door and stepped back out into the smoke and heat.

"There is nothing to pin down, nothing to say," said Dainin Katagiri, a Japanese Zen teacher who helped Suzuki Roshi establish the practice in San Francisco. "The voiceless voice, which comes from the depths of the human life, can't be measured. Yet it is always there. It is what you actually experience. Somehow—in a word, through your body, with your mind—you must express it." Katagiri often lamented the difficulty of giving talks, because words were just as good at creating distance as intimacy. They ultimately couldn't touch the essence of things. Often misheard, mistaken, misquoted, and misused, words could wake us, but they could also entangle us and stir up trouble. Katagiri's first book of lectures was called *Returning to Silence*. The second: *You Have to Say Something.*

Sonja Gardenswartz, who'd been at Jamesburg since the June resident evacuation, wanted to say something. She sat at the computer, a tickle of smoke at her throat. As a member of the senior staff, she'd been part of the communications loop after the fires started until, abruptly, she wasn't. Being cut off from decision making and asked to evacuate against her wishes had activated a familiar pain, a sense she had of falling through the cracks in a place where there weren't supposed to be any cracks. It hurt, yet she knew others were hurting, too. Her suffering was one burning leaf in a forest on fire.

From her place in Jamesburg, she wanted to do what she could to help keep the scattered community together. She couldn't pick up a shovel, so she reached for words, slowly typing up an e-mail to a Google group for evacuated residents. "Well, there are some of us outside the box," she wrote, "but we can draw closer in our own way—the heart of understanding the body mind of the many displaced beings in the world."

The fire wasn't creeping. It was gaining ground at a sprint. To manage the ever-expanding Basin Complex—now covering nearly seventy thousand acres—the incident management team had divided the complex into two zones of operation. In the west zone, near Big Sur, the fire exhibited extreme behavior on July 5, leaping from treetop to treetop in what's called a crown fire. Reports for the east zone, where Tassajara is, noted similar activity, with groups of trees torching simultaneously and "active runs." The incident map of the fire for that day showed the red fingers of fire perimeter lines pointing toward Tassajara from the Tassajara Creek drainage to the northwest and Willow Creek to the southwest.

Yet fire managers on the incident continued to predict that the fire was three days away. They still expected it to creep down Tassajara Creek or over the ridge behind Tassajara, from the west, and that residents would be able to ride out the fire safely. According to branch director Jack Froggatt, who debriefed the crew at Jamesburg that day, the problem wasn't really the fire. The problem was the road. The incident management team wouldn't send crews into Tassajara when the only road in and out of the valley could be cut off for days by the fire.

By then, Tassajara Road had been in a state of "soft" closure since June 25, when a notice from the Monterey County Sheriff's Office went up in Jamesburg. The closure point wasn't manned, however, and the sign didn't deter a tour group from driving down the road on July 5 to visit Tassajara. The carload of four Korean Buddhist tourists and their guide arrived unannounced in the late morning and wandered into the work circle area. David offered them a bath and an invitation to stay for lunch.

"Did you know the road is closed?" Abbot Steve asked the priest from the Carmel Valley temple that hosted the group.

"Yes," the priest replied, smiling. "Road closed. But also open!"

That evening after dinner, Abbot Steve, David, Graham, and Stuart drove to Jamesburg for a meeting with Ken Heffner, deputy supervisor of the Los Padres National Forest. Heffner's secretary had called to arrange it. The sky was neither night nor day above Tassajara Road—a patchwork of ash-colored clouds, scrolls of smoke, and streaks of blue. A weak sun pulsed on the horizon. The gate to MIRA observatory stood open so that engines stationed there could come and go.

"They'll get us out and then tell us we can't go back," David half joked on the drive up. Mostly he was thinking of the way he'd felt tricked by fire officials in prior weeks, but clearly the authorities were capable of drastic measures. News of a citizen's arrest in Big Sur had already made its way down to Tassajara that morning. A resident of an area under mandatory evacuation had taken matters into his own hands when he'd received no help from professional firefighters and lit several backfires to save redwood structures on his family's fifty-five acres on Apple Pie Ridge. When law enforcement officers came to make arrests—on Independence Day—he had turned himself in so that his brother could continue defending the property.

"It's legal," a surprised Stuart had said. "They can't arrest you for that. Maybe the guy didn't know what he was doing." An out-of-control backfire could be worse than no backfire at all. But firefighters in Big Sur privately praised the man's efforts. As a firefighter himself, Stuart knew it could be extremely useful to have locals around to tell you where water sources were or where the roads went, people who knew a place inside out, not just from a flyover or a map. But a home owner watching a fire race toward his house could be hijacked by emotion and act rashly, risking his life and endangering the lives of the firefighters who would feel duty-bound to rescue him. Before the deadly Black Sunday fires in Australia in February 2009, many in the firefighting world were already skeptical about whether that country's "Leave early or stay and defend" policy could be applicable in the United States. When I asked Stuart about the policy after Australia's fires, he did not equivocate. People who successfully stay and defend, he said, are mindful, year-round stewards of the land. But citizen defense should never take the place of trained professionals.

In the living room at the Jamesburg house, Heffner kicked off the meeting, spreading out maps of the fire zone that showed Tassajara Road, with the wilderness boundary scooping around it and Tassajara at the very bottom of the dip. His message was clear and brief, as David and Abbot Steve later recalled: We will not come to your aid if you choose to stay. "The Forest" doesn't do structure protection. The safest thing would be for everyone to leave.

"We appreciate your concern," said the abbot. He shrugged his shoulders slightly, adjusting, settling into the right position for the moment. "But we've made a lot of preparations. We have a sprinkler system installed on the rooftops, and five pumps. We've retained a small staff of twenty able-bodied people who have been training with Stuart here, doing drills and monitoring our water delivery systems to make sure everything is operational. We feel that Tassajara is in a good position." He paused, drumming his fingers lightly on his knees. "Have you been to Tassajara?"

Heffner shook his head. "The safety officers keep us well informed."

"Why don't you come down and have a look? We can give you a tour, show you what we've accomplished. You can see that Tassajara is defensible." It couldn't hurt to ask.

"I won't be coming down," said Heffner. "If you're down there, and something happens, any kind of medical emergency, crews won't be able to get to you if the road is compromised. You could be cut off for days. Your staying risks not only your own safety but also the safety of the firefighters. All I can do is ask you once again to leave."

George Haines, CAL FIRE unit chief for the San Benito–Monterey Unit, also attended the meeting. As his agency's representative on the Basin Complex, Haines operated mostly out of his office in Monterey, but he made frequent visits to the incident command post. After Heffner left the Jamesburg house, the abbot asked Haines whether he would come see Tassajara.

"I'll try," Haines said. "It may take a couple of days, but I'll see what I can do." Haines also told Stuart that he'd attempt to get him officially assigned to Tassajara.

On the ride back, they compared notes.

"Well, what did you think?" Abbot Steve asked no one in particular.

"I don't understand," said David. "They did it in '77 and '99. The road hasn't changed. What's so different now?"

"Ach"—Stuart swatted the air with his hand—"they're just talking tough. You'll see. George will get us help, even if it's just one engine crew. Good guy. He's a man of his word."

They didn't talk about it then, but much had changed in wildland firefighting since Stuart first picked up a Pulaski in the late 1970s. Firefighter fatalities had heightened awareness for safety. Incident managers had become less willing to put firefighters at extreme risk and more likely to pull crews off firelines in explosive conditions. In 2007, federal prosecutors charged an incident commander with four counts of involuntary manslaughter after four firefighters suffered fatal burns on a fire he supervised. His case wound its way through the court system as incident commanders across the country watched—and purchased liability insurance. The old "can do" attitude of firefighters had been tempered by a fresh concern for safety.

In the driver's seat, Graham kept his thoughts to himself. The meeting had left him feeling as though he'd been slugged by what he later called "the blunt edge of bureaucracy." Deputy Supervisor Heffner wasn't a firefighter—he was an administrator. He had tried to assert his authority. His intention seemed to have been to impress upon them that they weren't going to get any help, and since the road could be cut off by fire, they should leave immediately.

But it hadn't had the desired effect on Tassajara's plant manager. If anything, Graham's own resolve to stay was reinforced by seeing how ready "the Forest" was to abandon Tassajara.

David gave a weather report at the morning meeting on July 6, fifteen days after the lightning strikes. Predictions continued to move in an undesirable direction. Temperatures would top 100 degrees Fahrenheit during the week, with winds sweeping the fire due east, toward Tassajara. "Fire is actively moving down the Tassajara Creek drainage and north from Willow Creek. We still don't know which direction it's going to come from," he told the residents.

By then, one of the residents who'd driven down from the city on June 25 had rigged a temporary Internet connection on the stone office computer so they could view Google Earth maps of the fire. The latest one showed the fire advancing from the south-southwest to within a mile of Tassajara, having spread a startling three miles in the past twelve hours.

David recapped the encounter with Los Padres National Forest deputy supervisor Ken Heffner. "The official word is that we shouldn't expect any help. The Forest has changed its policy on structure protection."

"What's their policy now?" a resident asked.

David glanced at Stuart, hoping he might jump in and explain, but he didn't. "My understanding is that they don't do structure protection anymore. They don't want to put their firefighters at risk."

Those who weren't at the meeting the night before exchanged concerned glances. If the USFS wasn't willing to put their professionally trained firefighters at risk, then did it make sense for them to stay there, a bunch of novices?

Having swapped his *hippari,* a traditional Zen jacket held closed by fabric ties, for a brown Tassajara sweatshirt, Abbot Steve spoke up: "We told Mr. Heffner that we didn't feel we were putting people at risk. We've made preparations. We've been training. Our assessment and the assessment of the firefighters who've been here, including Stuart, is that Tassajara is safe. It is defensible."

"Stuart's colleague, CAL FIRE unit chief George Haines, is lobbying for backup for us, and we're hopeful we'll get another crew in here to help when the fire comes through," added David.

"Yeah, even if the Forest Service won't send a crew, that shouldn't stop CAL FIRE from coming down, right?" asked another student.

David looked to Stuart. This time he took the cue. "George is going to do everything he can," Stuart said. "I have complete confidence in that. He's a good man. A man of his word. Don't worry. They know we're down here. They know we're not going to leave. They won't leave us high and dry."

The July 6 morning meeting felt "airless" to Shundo, the constant deliberations over scenarios for the fire's arrival abstract and tedious. As he and Bryan Clark headed up to the solar panels afterward, he was glad to be moving, using his body, letting his mind wander. One particularly memorable image stepped forward: the abbot on his way to the zendo in the predawn haze, wearing his robes, with a blue bandanna over his mouth to filter the smoke.

Clark cursed when they arrived at the solar array around eleven a.m. "We missed it!" That morning, Graham had spotted flames for the first time from Tassajara, looking toward the Tony Trail. But the flames had died down by the time Shundo and Clark arrived. There was only a great, cloudlike plume of smoke bearing down on the ridges to the west. This was the one day they hadn't gone up the Tony Trail. Shundo didn't know whether they would have had a clearer view of the fire from there anyway, but it was disappointing to see only more smoke.

After driving up the road with a few others to get another view of the skies to the west, Shundo returned to the student housing area, where residents had held a drill the prior evening after dark, in case fire entered Tassajara from downcreek, at night. Though the scenario was unlikely, the exercise had not inspired confidence. Water pressure from the standpipe system had been weak, even though the ground trends downhill there. The hose lines, the same color as the dirt path, had been difficult to see.

Shundo folded hoses, drained and ready, accordion-style so they'd be easier to handle. His work could be undone that afternoon when the grounds got watered, but he didn't mind. As with Zen practice, the point wasn't to create some static state of permanent perfection. The point was to be perfectly ready for whatever comes.

Mako stood in the walk-in, surveying the supplies she had to work with. There was still plenty of food: boxes of lettuce, potatoes, leeks, crates of apples and pears, all labeled with the date they'd entered Tassajara. Her mood was lighter than it had been for days. The night before, when she had come back from the drill, tired and dispirited, Graham had finally talked to her. "I don't know what to say to you," he'd said. It wasn't much, but it was something. It opened the door.

She sensed a shift in him, a soft malleability rather than resistance. And she was right. Remembering the moment later, Graham told me, "One of the amazing things about being in a relationship is it affords you the opportunity to do the opposite of your tendency, to just be able to completely drop the self and say, Okay, right now I'm going to see what happens when I take care of this person, drop off that part of me that wants to go away, withhold, have space, or argue more."

Water over fire—that was the symbol on the large water tank just up the road that fed the standpipe system. A fire needed to be wet to be subdued. Anger needed to be cooled. But not always. Sometimes a forceful energy is best met with its opposite, other times with its mirror reflection. Fire could be fought with fire—as evidenced by a backburn. And fear, Mako knew personally, could be met with fearlessness.

When Mako was six years old, her best friend's father molested her. For years afterward, he often exposed himself or masturbated in front of her. From the beginning, however, Mako resolved not to be intimidated. As a young teenager, she deliberately cultivated feeling invincible. She'd tell her parents she'd be sleeping over at a friend's house and then stay out all night, wandering downtown Baltimore, often alone. "There'd be guys hanging out on street corners, and I was just this thirteen-year-old girl, but I'd walk right through them. I would not cross the street." It was exhilarating to tightrope between the fear she actually felt and the appearance of fearlessness she projected. "Looking back on it," she told me later, "it was a façade, kind of like fake it till you make it."

Eventually, when she was about sixteen, Mako confronted her friend's father. "I basically told him off, and that was it for masturbating in front of me or anything like that." The man acknowledged and apologized for his inappropriate behavior. Mako forgave him. One might expect that she never saw him again, but that's not what happened. The two developed an occasional friendship that lasted into Mako's young adulthood. When Mako attended a rape survivors group briefly in college, this fact baffled the other women in her midst. Victims generally don't befriend their molesters, and the fact that Mako did so was viewed with suspicion. But perhaps in an early demonstration of her affinity for Buddhism, Mako was more inclined to let go of harm done than to hold it tightly. Hours spent interviewing Mako left me with the impression that her experiments in fearlessness weren't just a façade. She possesses a genuine aura of imperturbability.

Which isn't to say she is invulnerable. Once, Mako was sitting on the front steps of City Center with a friend who made her laugh so hard that she cried. Another friend who lived there walked by. "Mako, are you okay?" she said. "I can't believe you're crying. I've never seen you cry. I didn't think you *could* cry!" The offhand comment stung. "I can always go back to, I'm strong, I'm competent, or something like that," Mako told me. "But I don't want to be seen as this person who isn't vulnerable."

The fight with Graham had started in part because of her vulnerability. She'd wanted more understanding, communication, mutual aid. Part of her work in their relationship was staying vulnerable, staying with the pain of conflict instead of just refusing to feel it.

She carried a box of potatoes and a box of leeks from the walk-in. She tossed the potatoes into a bowl of water and went to look for a scrub brush. If she had time after making the soup, maybe she could get outside and dig fireline or help tend to the pumps.

On the afternoon of July 6, in high heat but clear skies, Shundo jogged up the trail behind the hill cabins to investigate a report of flames on the ridgeline west of Tassajara. By the time he got to the solar panels, thick gray-and-purple swaths of smoke veiled the ridgeline, but again, no flame. He took some pictures of the skies and airtankers dropping retardant above the junction of Tassajara Creek and Willow Creek to slow the fire's upstream spread.

The following day, George Haines arrived at Tassajara. Haines had worked thirty-seven years in CAL FIRE's San Benito–Monterey Unit, from firefighter to chief, before retiring in 2009. He was an engine operator on the 1977 Marble Cone fire and had been to Tassajara before. After taking a tour around the grounds, he told David, Abbot Steve, and the others that it was definitely defendable. "I saw all the work they'd done, the pumps, the rooftop sprinkler system, the fuel reduction," Haines told me months after the fire. "It was my opinion that it was survivable, and I told them that. I told them it would be ugly, but I did believe it was survivable."

The residents drilled again on July 7, this time at the flats, with better results. Haines happened to be there for part of it. He was struck by how harmoniously they worked together. Later, he told me he wished he could have them as a crew. "They were a fire brigade. It was impressive. It really was."

Before leaving Tassajara, he repeated his promise to try to get professional backup. Bolstered by the fact that he had taken the time to come visit, and by Stuart's assurances, Tassajara's residents had renewed faith that help was coming. Hopefully it would arrive before the fire did.

Faith. Hope. These are not words frequently heard in Zen. When they are used, they mean something slightly different from the usual interpretation. "There's nowhere you can actually plant yourself if you recognize that things are completely flowing and changing and the next moment is unknown," Abbot Steve told me in one interview. "Faith in Zen Buddhism is being willing to live face-to-face with the unknown and have confidence that however that goes is your true life."

There is an old Zen saying, "Great faith, great doubt, great effort—the three qualities necessary for training." The phrase points to the dynamic interplay of mind-states and action at the core of Zen practice. It takes a certain kind of faith just to practice Zen. Not faith in something. Faith alone. Faith in groundless, shifting, unpredictable reality.

Just to make our best effort in each moment is Zen, Suzuki Roshi once said. When you have great faith, make an effort. When you have great doubt, make an effort. "Moment after moment, you should say, 'Yes, I will,'" he told his students, chuckling as he often did during his talks.

On Tuesday, July 8, branch director Jack Froggatt came to Tassajara bearing good news. A fire crew was coming down to wrap the buildings with a brand of reflective, fire-resistant aluminized fabric called Firezat. "They've got fifteen rolls," Froggatt told the abbot and director. "You can tell them where you want it." The crew was from Indiana. Firefighters from all over the country had flocked to California in response to the governor's call for help.

David and Abbot Steve looked at one another, mirroring surprise. Ken Heffner had said something when they met in Jamesburg about people wrapping buildings and evacuating and coming back to find the structures intact. But they'd gotten the impression that the wrap was prohibitively expensive.

"That's great, Jack. And what would that cost us?" asked Abbot Steve, eyebrows arched.

"No cost," said Froggatt. "And if the fire comes through while they're here, well . . ." The implication was that the Indiana crew would be able to help fight the fire.

By noon, David was showing the crew bosses around Tassajara and prioritizing buildings since they didn't have enough Firezat to cover everything. They chose structures that were on the periphery or next to steep slopes and dry brush—or that were particularly vulnerable, like the shop, with its lumber stacks and propane tanks. One unlucky squad headed up the eighty stone steps to wrap the birdhouse and the other hill cabins, while others worked in semishade, wrapping the backside of the founder's hall and the abbot's cabin. They didn't wrap the central buildings—the zendo, kitchen, dining room, or stone office—or the bathhouse. Abbot Steve drafted a letter to Heffner on the office computer while the crews worked, reinforcing Tassajara's extensive fire preparations and the fact that residents did *not* plan to leave. He thanked Heffner for his part in sending the Firezat.

Before Froggatt left that afternoon, he programmed frequencies for the branch of the fire he directed into Stuart's walkie-talkie. "So you can stay in touch," he said. The command frequencies Froggatt shared would put Stuart in contact with the people making strategic decisions, while the tactical channels would keep him abreast of action on the ground.

The mandatory evacuation for Big Sur had been lifted. Residents returned to their homes without the threat of arrest. The fire worked its way east toward Tassajara through the forest, but the arrival of the Indiana crew indicated that maybe Tassajara would have some professional help after all.

The only one with mixed feelings about the crew's arrival was Mako.

When David told her that they would be staying, it meant she somehow had to make the Thai dinner she'd planned—with butterscotch pudding for dessert—feed twenty more mouths.

On Sitting with Fire, *people had begun to debate the wisdom of* residents' staying in the valley during the fire. "If the fire services do not feel safe enough to fight the fire there and they are highly experienced professionals, how is it believable that a small group of volunteers 'can ride out the fire safely if it arrives'?" wrote one blog reader, referring to a July 5 post by Slymon.

Having seen the *Los Angeles Times* article that quoted fire marshal Devin Patel saying, "You can't actually burn down Tassajara. Fire can never touch Tassajara's heart," Devin's father posted a message to his son: "I am proud of what you are doing. Please take very good care of yourself. I love you."

The improvised cyber sangha stretched across oceans and national borders. In Toronto, Graham's parents, Walter and Joanne Ross, relied on the blog for updates between reassuring phone calls. One of those calls was on the afternoon of July 8. Graham told his parents that if worse came to worst, they had a "safety zone" in the rock-walled stone office, stocked with food, water, first-aid supplies, and an oxygen tank—at the time, no one had thought about the tank's potential to explode if the stone office caught on fire. Mako was fine, Graham told his parents, they were both fine. If anything, they were impatient for this fire to come.

Graham's confidence comforted his parents, but they couldn't always expect to hear his voice, even when there wasn't a wildfire to prepare for. Tassajara has three phone lines—a radio phone and two satellite lines. The radio phone is unreliable, the satellite connection staticky and subject to an awkward transmission delay. A demanding monastic schedule and the fact that up to 120 people shared just three phone lines meant that even under ordinary circumstances Graham didn't call Toronto as often as he would have liked to. The Rosses didn't try to talk Graham out of staying, in part because he reassured them that Tassajara was safe but also because they knew they couldn't persuade him.

But two of the nineteen residents at Tassajara on July 8 did evacuate that day. In the case of one of them, a loved one's concern ultimately convinced her it was time to go. And David had requested that those who didn't want to be there for the duration leave now so willing people could be brought in to replace them. Neither of the two residents who departed on July 8 were comfortable with the fact that those making decisions on their behalf hadn't established a clear trigger point for evacuating all of Tassajara. "For their own sense of safety, some people wanted us to clearly delineate the point at which we'd all leave. A lot of us on the core team felt that it was hard to say," David told me later. "We wanted to respond to events as they arose rather than draw a line in the sand." How could they make a decision now about a moment they didn't yet know?

In Zen, "don't-know mind" is the only kind of mind that is true. When you practice don't-know mind, you let go of the need for knowing and acknowledge how little you can ever actually know. This is hard work. Humans don't particularly want to admit the limitations of highly developed cognitive function. But not knowing and knowing are actually not so far apart. Like faith and doubt, they're intertwined. "Not knowing is most intimate" goes an oft-quoted teaching from a ninth-century Zen master.

On the morning of July 9, eighteen days after the lightning strikes, David launched Google Earth on the stone office computer. They'd had nothing like this during the Marble Cone fire, he knew from reading the logs. Phone communication had been knocked out for weeks. The only information they had on the fire came from what they could see with the naked eye. That fact made it all the more amazing now to David that he could zoom in on an image of Tassajara and see new fire detections picked up by satellite or infrared-sensitive pilotless planes called drones. Clusters of red dots scattered over the ridges northwest of Tassajara, marked by a yellow thumbtack. Of the ten new detections in the last twelve hours in the Church Creek valley, the closest appeared to be about a mile from Tassajara Road. David counted fourteen ignitions up Tassajara Creek and eight in the Willow Creek drainage, south of Tassajara.

Don't-know mind doesn't mean willful ignorance. It was better to know where the fire was, that it was making its approach. They still didn't know which arm of it would reach Tassajara first. They just needed to stay calm, alert, and ready for anything. Add "Think clearly" and "Act decisively" to those imperatives and, taken together, they make up one of the Ten Standard Orders every firefighter has to know by heart.

Six

FIRE IN THE CONFLUENCE

When we know something and rest in that knowing we limit our vision.

We will only see what our knowing will allow us to see. In this way experience can be our enemy.

—ZOKETSU NORMAN FISHER

Wednesday, July 9, eighteen days after the lightning strikes

By the morning of July 9, the Basin Complex fire had charred more than eighty-six thousand acres—an area roughly the size of sixty-five thousand football fields—at an estimated containment cost to date of nearly twenty-eight million dollars. The six a.m. report from the incident management team noted "poor overnight humidity recovery" as a cause for concern, the lack of moisture in the air likely to add more blackened acres.

Around nine a.m. that morning, Shundo Haye and Bryan Clark set out for the peak of Hawk Mountain. It was already stifling—too hot even for Shundo, who usually relished Tassajara's heat. On the shadeless, steep trail that climbs fifteen hundred feet above the solar panels, his heart thumped, his legs dragged, his fingers stiffened and swelled. "It was the hardest climb we'd done," Shundo told me later.

At the top, through the haze, they observed a fat plume of smoke rising from the ridge separating Church Creek and Tassajara Creek. They stood looking at it for a while, catching their breath. Neither stated the obvious—now the fire had only to work its way down into the Church Creek drainage and make an uphill run on the opposite slope to reach Tassajara Road. But how long would that take? This fire wasn't in a rush, or at least it hadn't been for the past couple of weeks.

After a minute or two, Shundo's heartbeat calmed and his breath no longer came in gulps. But he felt as if he'd run a marathon—in a pair of borrowed sneakers; he had somehow neglected to bring his own to Tassajara and wore Colin's old cross-trainers.

Their mission that morning went beyond scouting. They'd carried up some Firezat for covering the radio phone antenna, one of Tassajara's few links to the outside world. The signal traveled by line of sight from mountain to mountain, but there wasn't a clear line of sight in the Ventana. The ridgelines intersected and bisected one another at eccentric angles. The radio phone's functioning had always been patchy at best, but they would do what they could to protect it.

Graham had announced at the morning work meeting that a repairman was arriving later that day to switch the satellite phone—the source of Tassajara's other two phone lines—to a different signal source. "The forest is on fire," he'd said straight-faced, "so they thought they'd come do some maintenance." The timing couldn't have been worse, but if they didn't make the switch now, they'd lose the satellite link entirely. Tassajara would be even more isolated than it already was.

Shundo and Clark took the rolled remnants of Firezat from their packs, covered what they could of the radio phone antenna, relay box, cable, and replacement battery boxes on the ground, and secured it with tape. By necessity, the antenna stood in a prominent, vulnerable place, poking up from an exposed ridgetop. If fire stormed uphill, as it had in the Esperanza fire, the wrap would do little good.

Shundo had heard some firefighters at Tassajara say that the doomed crew should never have been on that ridge. But Tassajara wasn't on a ridge. It was down in a valley, cut through by a creek whose cold waters he planned to soak in when he returned from the peak. That was his habit on the hottest summer days even when there wasn't a fire.

The night watches, the miles spent running trails in Colin's Nikes, the smoke, and the waiting were all wearing on Shundo. Yet there was nowhere he'd rather be. He'd talked to his ex-wife on the phone. She'd told him someone had suggested on the blog that they rotate new people into Tassajara to spell those who'd been preparing for the fire. Shundo had shot down the suggestion as nonsense. Why would they leave now, when they'd learned so much about fire, about pumps and hoses and working together like a fire crew? They were in a groove.

After all this time, and with the fire finally in sight, Shundo couldn't imagine leaving. His ex-wife had teased him, pointing out his attachment. Shundo didn't deny it. He'd lived in the city and practiced with sirens and homeless people and stinking exhaust. He'd lived at Tassajara and practiced with the biting blackflies and no Internet and no toast—his favorite—for breakfast. But he'd never had a chance before to practice in the realm of fire. He wasn't sure he knew what that meant, but he knew it meant something. He could feel the energy of the community's shared concentration beneath his tired feet, the falling away of the inessential, the crucible of the unknown. He could see that the fire was a field test for Zen practice.

In his journal, Shundo had tried to describe a feeling of complete and fundamental integration, the way the residents' task connected them to the land, to one another, to themselves, to the essence of all things. "We become elemental," he'd written. What would they become, he wondered, when fire reached the valley? They wouldn't fight fire; they'd meet it. In one hand a fire hose, in the other the *vajra,* or diamond, sword of what is called the bodhisattva vow—to save all beings before oneself. It's a pledge that can never be completely fulfilled, yet anyone who formally takes Zen Buddhist precepts, whether priest or lay practitioner, vows to refuse his or her own liberation from suffering until every other being is enlightened.

One of Zen's most beloved bodhisattvas is Manjusri, the bodhisattva of wisdom. Often depicted sitting on a lion, holding a sword in his right hand, Manjusri symbolizes insight, a clear-eyed, deep knowing that transcends conceptual and dualistic thinking. Sometimes his sword—used to cut through delusion—is on fire.

But bodhisattvas come in many forms—like the firefighter who gives up his vacation to help his friends prepare for a wildfire. Shundo felt safe at Tassajara in part because Stuart did. "He'd been there and done it before," Shundo told me later. "We really depended on him." Unlike the various fire officials who'd given the residents a talking-to, painting vivid worst-case scenarios to scare them, Stuart didn't seem overly concerned about the road being cut off—he'd driven it many times, and like Shundo and the other residents, he knew that the road was always a risk, fire or no fire. If someone had a heart attack at Tassajara, it would take at least an hour just to get that person to an ambulance at Jamesburg. One time a hiker had broken a femur and had to be airlifted to a hospital. Risk was always present, whether acknowledged or not.

"It's not pretty, but that should do it," Shundo told Clark as they finished the wrapping and inspected their work.

Shundo watched his footing carefully on their descent. He'd ground the soles of Colin's trainers to a smooth, slick finish in the last couple of weeks. Still, the way down went much faster than the way up—the opposite of fire.

When they passed the wrapped solar panels and reached the first patch of shade at the hill cabins, Shundo took a long drink of orange-flavored Gatorade. There were cases and cases of it now at Tassajara, brought in by the fire crews. The residents had pronounced it the official drink of the fire. It had gone warm in his pack, but he drank it anyway, then headed straight for the creek.

The routine nightly task of ensuring that all kerosene lamps are extinguished, called "fire watch" at Tassajara, is an adaptation of a centuries-old practice in Japanese villages. Nonetheless, most Zen temples in Japan have burned to the ground not once but several times. This is due in part to building materials—most temple structures are wooden—and to the traditional use of fire for light and cooking. At Soto Zen founder Eihei Dōgen's own monastery, Eiheiji, where Suzuki Roshi's son Hoitsu Suzuki is now the head teacher, the temple gate is flanked by six-hundred-year-old cedar trees, but none of the current structures are more than a few hundred years old.

Especially during the tumultuous fifteenth-century Onin War in Japan, many temple fires were started intentionally—by monks in rival sects. While contemporary Buddhism in the West carries strong pacifist sensibilities, in medieval Japan warriors meditated in the morning, then headed off to battle with sharp swords in their belts. Zen found a home among the samurai. Says G. B. Sansom in *Japan: A Short Cultural History*: Zen encouraged "a useful type of practical wisdom, and thus no doubt made it easy for clever Zen teachers to deal with military men who like simple answers to difficult questions."

In one legendary sixteenth-century episode, the abbot of a temple near Mount Fuji sheltered enemy troops of the warlord Oda Nobunaga and refused to turn them over when Nobunaga demanded it. In retaliation, Nobunaga forced the monks into the gate tower and set it on fire. The abbot is said to have turned to the monks and offered these words from the *Blue Cliff Record,* a compilation of koans, or teaching stories: "Calm meditation doesn't require peaceful surroundings. If the mind is clear, fire itself is cool."

But just as wildfires sweep the forest and promote new growth, temple fires created opportunities for sculptors, builders, and those skilled in art restoration. Despite the loss of relics, and sometimes lives, newer structures often surpassed those that preceded them. Creation and destruction are not leagues apart. They are, rather, in league, arising together. And Buddhism's own edifices, no matter how glorious, are not free from impermanence.

Yet it would be a mistake to think that acceptance of impermanence and the practice of nonattachment, another guiding Buddhist principle, requires allowing a monastery threatened by fire to burn. "There's nonattachment," Abbot Steve told me after the fire at Tassajara, "but there's also not turning away. Nonattachment doesn't mean you separate yourself from things."

At the core of Zen is the practice of taking care. It starts with your own body and extends outward to all phenomena and beings—to the sangha, or community, the temple objects, buildings and grounds, and, ultimately, the land and its natural processes, including fire. It's a particular kind of caring, free of rigid expectation, free even of hope.

Not to say the residents at Tassajara didn't hope to save it. They did. Tassajara is a living record of Zen in America. Suzuki Roshi's generous spirit supports every floorboard, peeks from behind every door. To lose the place where he walked around laughing and encouraging, the buildings where he shared the teachings that have touched so many lives, would be heartbreaking.

But hope can be held too tightly. Zen cultivates a mind that doesn't tether itself to any fixed view or perspective—the belief that the buildings at Tassajara must be saved or, by contrast, that physical structures aren't important and worth saving. Hope is fine, as long as it doesn't lead to inflexibility. "When you're living in the present moment, you're not so involved in hope or invested in a particular outcome," said the abbot. You do what needs to be done simply because it needs to be done, accepting that your actions may not bear the fruit you intend—and that this does not render the actions themselves fruitless.

A clever Zen teacher might say that standing back and letting the monastery burn belies a kind of attachment to the idea of nonattachment, that trying to save it when it could all burn anyway is true nonattachment. In trying to save Tassajara from the fire—or your own life from disaster—you can't be sure you will. In fact, you can lose everything you love in a moment. And that's not a reason to give up. If anything, it's a reason to turn toward the fire, recognizing it as a force of both creation and destruction, and to take care of what's right in front of you, because that's all you actually have.

Around one thirty p.m. on July 9, residents and the members of the Indiana fire crew gathered in the shade for a group photograph in front of the gatehouse. Shundo, fresh from his dip in the creek, handed off his camera to someone else to take the picture, which looks like a post-vacation snapshot. The mood is relaxed, collegial, as if they'd just finished an expedition together and were now back at home base, celebrating. No one in the photo knew how quickly and dramatically things were about to change.

In the photo, David squats in the first row, in front of Abbot Steve, who stands behind him. Stuart sits on the grass with his legs out straight, boots crossed, at the opposite end of the front row from David, with his arm around his girlfriend. The core team is scattered around, monks interspersed with firefighters—a bit hard to tell apart unless you know the people. Only the abbot and the director, at the edge of the group, wear hipparis. Members of the Indiana crew, which included a couple of women, wear dark pants and T-shirts, like most of the residents.

"When other crews came," Mako told me later, "they looked like they were about to jump into the wilderness and fight fire, but the Indiana crew didn't look like that at all." They weren't wearing heavy-duty fire gear. They didn't have radios, maps, and other firefighting accessories strapped to their packs. They wore sunglasses and baseball caps, not goggles and hard hats.

Earlier, when the Fenner Canyon inmate crew had arrived at Tassajara, one of the firefighters had looked around and asked Shundo, "Where are the monks?" The inmate was confused because they weren't in robes.

Whether priest or student, Tassajara residents generally put on formal robes between two and three times every day in the summer. A priest's robe called an *okesa,* sewn together in an intricate patchwork pattern inspired by rice fields, wraps around the body and over one shoulder. Newly ordained priests spend months learning how to do things they used to do with ease, such as bowing, now swaddled in a lot of extra fabric. Some senior priests, like Abbot Steve, wear brown robes to signify that they have received Dharma transmission—reception into the lineage of Zen teachers and authority to pass on the teachings. But it had been weeks since anyone had changed out of work clothes; a few hadn't entered the zendo at all. Their work and their meditation were preparing the grounds for fire. Wearing robes while doing heavy labor is not a sensible choice, and Zen is at its core a practical path.

That morning, a reporter and photographer from the *San Francisco Chronicle* had come down the road. The reporter seemed interested not only in the fire, but also in the practice of the monks. In the published story, he quoted one resident's comment likening clearing brush for a firebreak to the practice of zazen, "where you clear the mind from external thoughts burning through."

While the *Chronicle* reporter waited for a chance to talk with Abbot Steve, absorbed in conversation with branch director Jack Froggatt, the post-lunch repose of the group portrait transformed into an orderly haste. The Indiana crew had been instructed to evacuate immediately. The fire had reached the preestablished trigger point of the confluence of Tassajara and Church creeks and now had an easy path to Tassajara Road.

Froggatt explained the news to Abbot Steve only after he'd initiated the Indiana crew's departure.

"So they won't be staying for the fire after all," the abbot said matter-of-factly.

Froggatt shook his head, a deflated expression on his face. Months later, he told me that he may have implied that there was a possibility the crew could get stuck in Tassajara and be able to help. "But we wouldn't be there by choice," he insisted. "I was told that wouldn't happen." As their minimal gear evidenced, the Indiana crew wasn't a hotshot, or Type 1, crew—with the most rigorous physical requirements and training; they were a Type 2 crew, drawn from a mix of federal, state, and local government agencies. Froggatt himself had seen the terrain around Tassajara from a helicopter, when there was a lot less smoke in the air. There was no place a pilot could safely set down to pick up people in a medical emergency. So he'd ordered the crew to pack up their gear.

When Froggatt said it was time to go, the Indiana crew immediately stopped stapling up the Firezat wrapping. They left behind fragments of unused material and half-wrapped buildings, including the gatehouse where they'd just taken the group portrait. "They grabbed their backpacks and tools and they were out of here in what seemed like ten minutes from the time they got that order," Abbot Steve said later.

After the Indiana crew left, Froggatt stuck around, planning to escort the satellite technician back up the road when repairs were completed. The *Chronicle* reporter checked in with his office on the radio phone, the one operational phone line. His boss told him to get out of the valley, but he and his photographer didn't leave right away. They wanted to document the scene unfolding at Tassajara, perhaps struck by the calm that pervaded despite the sudden departure of the firefighters. The reporter interviewed Abbot Steve as residents practiced rolling out hoses in the work circle area.

"We'll be moving more vigorously than usual," Abbot Steve said, hands on his hips, not a shred of detectable doubt in his voice. "And we'll be watching those tendencies to get overexcited. We'll stay calm and alert. We'll be ready."

Fire is not a stranger, he went on, smiling, seemingly unperturbed by the sudden loss of hands on deck. "We're not really fighting the fire. We're meeting the fire, letting the fire come to us." Instead of confronting the fire as an enemy, he explained, they would "make friends with it, tame it as it reaches our boundaries."

Colin drove the Isuzu up the road and pulled over at Lime Point, just below where he'd seen the cloud that turned out to be smoke on the day of the lightning strikes. That was nearly three weeks ago. It seemed like the right thing to do now, as the last crew of firefighters pulled out of Tassajara—to get his own eyes on the fire. And it had the added benefit of getting him out of talking to a reporter.

At one time, Colin had wanted to be a writer himself. He wrote short stories as an English major at the University of Michigan but dropped the habit when he began to sense that he was hiding out behind his own writing. "I didn't even need a Twelve Step program to quit," he told me with a wry smile the summer after the fire.

Colin didn't need a Twelve Step program to end what he calls his relatively short "drinking career," either, a time that overlapped his military service. He sobered up on the road after realizing he'd probably die in a motorcycle accident or kill someone if he didn't dry out.

In the Marines, he took heat for being too much of an individual. Now he's a Zen priest and lives in a community where the self's very existence is called into question. At first, he didn't make a connection between being a soldier and being a monk. Slowly, he saw the resemblance. "Both are about letting go of the self. One wants to crush it. The other just wants to release it."

At Lime Point on July 9, the clouds overhead offered a kaleidoscope of fire color: red and purple, orange and black. For weeks, the fire had simmered just shy of the confluence of Tassajara and Church creeks, in the Tassajara Creek drainage. Now smoke trails spiraled from farther downstream. The fire had crossed into Church Creek. It had already burned an area where there are caves etched with handprints and drawings of the Esselen Indians.

Farther up the road, looking west toward that area, there is a massive sandstone formation weathered into the shape of two hands pressed together as in prayer. The same image, held in high esteem by the Esselen, adorns the interior walls of the caves. Tassajara residents call the site *gassho* rock, after the hand gesture that is also a staple of Zen.

But Colin didn't drive any further. He'd seen all he needed to see.

"I thought, This thing's taking off," he told me later, standing at Lime Point, the brim of his baseball cap pitched down to block the midday sun. He also thought: Stuart should see this.

Throughout their fire preparations, it had seemed important that the same people do the scouting. Consistency was critical to properly measuring the fire's progress. Shundo hiked; Colin drove up the road—when he wasn't boarding up windows and eaves with plywood to keep sparks from entering and igniting a building or helping Graham troubleshoot the pump near the stone rooms that had been acting up. But as Colin looked through his binoculars and tried to see anything but smoke, he remembered what the fire captain had told him: "The difference between a professional firefighter and you is I know what to be afraid of."

On his way back to Tassajara, Colin met the departing crew from Indiana on the road. He'd begun to suspect that some of the firefighters flowing in and out of Tassajara were sightseeing more than anything else, but these men and women, like the inmate crew, had done real work. "The cabins were wrapped up like Christmas presents," Colin recalled. Their engines pulled over at a wide spot so he could pass. Hands reached out the windows, waving. It was a strange sensation, to keep going in the opposite direction from those who knew what to fear.

Around two p.m., while Colin was up the road, Shundo hiked over the hogback ridge on the west end of Tassajara, above the flats. Visibility was poor from there, so he jogged partway up the Tony Trail. He saw plenty of smoke. It was hard to tell where it was coming from exactly, but he wasn't particularly alarmed. He'd seen similar smoke plumes most afternoons, when the fire rose up with the day's heat before dying back down again at night. The departure of the Indiana crew troubled him more.

Having covered close to five miles of trail that day already, Shundo returned to Tassajara and jumped in the creek again. On his way back to his cabin for a fresh set of clothes, he met up with Colin, returning from Lime Point. He and Colin had a running joke that they traded places—usually, whenever one was back at City Center in San Francisco, the other lived down at Tassajara.

"It's taking off," Colin said, standing at the foot of the steps to the hill cabins.

"I couldn't really see much," said Shundo. "Just a lot of smoke."

"How was it over the hogback?"

"Smoky," said Shundo, his eyes tearing up, irritated by sweat and sunscreen. "And bloody hot. I think your shoes are melting," he said, lifting a foot to show Colin the treadless sole.

Colin laughed, but the brief levity didn't fully penetrate his features or linger on his face. He looked across from where they stood in the work circle area, where eighty steps led up to the hill cabins and the trail to the solar panels, radio phone antenna, and satellite dish, and above that Hawk Mountain, where Shundo had hiked earlier that morning. "That satellite guy still here?"

"Don't know," said Shundo. "I've only just got back."

Colin drank some water, then pulled his bandanna back up over his mouth for protection from the smoke. "I'm gonna go out there," he said, gesturing in the direction of the hogback with his chin. "Then I'll check in with Stuart."

"Right," said Shundo. Sweat trickled down his brow as it sometimes did when the zendo was hot and he was in robes. The urge to wipe it would arise, and he'd have a choice. Brush it away or simply do nothing? The choice for how to respond was always there, and there wasn't a right or wrong answer. When he simply had to move, he moved. Other times, he let a droplet of sweat, or a tear, simply follow its own course.

"I'm going to rest up," he told Colin. "I'm knackered." First, he washed out two sets of sweaty clothes in the laundry area. Then he went to his cabin, lay down, and promptly fell asleep.

Up on the hill with the satellite technician, Graham answered a call from David on his walkie-talkie, asking about the status of the satellite switch.

"Umm, still in progress," Graham said. He looked up at the sky, a constantly changing canvas of smoke and sunlight and helicopters with water buckets swinging beneath them.

"Jack wants to drive up to Lime Point so he can keep an eye on the fire. Any idea how much longer the switch will take?" David asked.

Graham looked at his watch: It was after three p.m. "Not really," he said, regulating the amount of frustration he allowed to surface in his voice.

When the Indiana crew had pulled out after lunch, the technician had wanted to go out with them, but Graham had persuaded him to stay. If he left Tassajara without implementing the switch, they'd be down to just the unreliable radio phone. But the satellite switch, which was supposed to be straightforward, had gone curvy. For the past hour, they'd been adjusting the position of the dish and testing the connection, unsuccessfully. Now the technician wiped his damp brow with his sleeve. He punched some numbers into a handheld device and muttered in frustration.

Neither of them wanted to be up here on this hill under the intense sun, breathing the smoky air. There were any number of places Graham would have preferred to be. But Tassajara needed the phone. It wasn't the technician's fault his company had sent him into a burning forest on a job. Playing goalie on a hockey team as a kid, Graham had to stop whatever came flying at him from going in the net. He didn't get to pick the shots. Now, as Tassajara's plant manager, he needed to see the repair through.

"Tell Jack I'll take the tech out when we're done," Graham radioed David. "I'll make sure he gets safely over the ridge."

Shortly after this radio contact, David picked up a message from Jamesburg on the answering machine in the stone office. Los Padres National Forest deputy supervisor Ken Heffner had called, with his boss, supervisor Peggy Hernandez, at his side. They reiterated that they would not provide the support of professional firefighters on the ground and requested again that everyone evacuate Tassajara immediately.

David transcribed the message in his slanted handwriting and left it on the desk instead of putting it in his pocket with his notebook containing important phone numbers and whatever else he needed to remember. There was nothing new or surprising in it and therefore no need to carry it around.

So this is spotting, Colin thought. He climbed over the hogback, looked up Tassajara Creek, and saw the fire advancing downstream, throwing embers with the wind behind it. On big crown fires or fires driven by warm winds, flames can drift for miles. This wasn't miles, but the way wind and flame cooperated to move the fire astonished him. Above the bandanna he wore to mask the smoke, the exposed skin of Colin's face prickled in the heat.

Asked what a Buddha is, Dōgen said, "An icicle forming in fire." He evoked the metaphor of fire for the urgency of the endeavor to wake up, instructing his disciples to practice as if their heads were enveloped in flames. The way it looked to Colin from the hogback, Tassajara's head was about to catch fire.

He called Stuart on his walkie-talkie. "I'm at the hogback. It's spotting down Tassajara Creek. It's coming."

Finally, sitting with fire was about to become meeting fire.

"Okay, everybody, let's suit up and meet down at the flats." Stuart's voice over the radio woke Shundo from his nap around three thirty p.m. "I thought it looked like death," Shundo wrote later in his journal, of the view looking toward the hogback from the front of his cabin. Five minutes later, he was at the fire shed below the zendo with the rest of the residents, pulling on their fire suits, hard hats, goggles, packs.

There were too many people in the narrow shed. Shundo grabbed his gear quickly and moved outside to get dressed. His feet, still tired from the morning's hike, protested as he shoved them into the heavy leather fire boots.

"Is this a drill?" someone asked.

"I think it's an activation," replied another. This was the real deal, and its energy was palpable as they tried to move quickly and efficiently but without haste.

A spike of adrenaline made it challenging. You hear "Fire!" and you instinctively want to run. But running is the last thing you ought to do. Running means you're either already in a bad situation or you're about to be. Walk, Stuart had told them, and always know what's behind you.

Above the hogback, thick, swirling plumes of smoke spun through the sky. Smoke-saturated sunlight cast a crimson glow down to the valley floor.

June 25. Residents say good-bye at the work circle after being ordered to evacuate. Only fourteen would stay behind.

June 28. Simon Moyes sets up Dharma Rain on the bathhouse roof.

July 1. CAL FIRE captains Dave "Spanky" Nicolson (far left) and Stuart Carlson (right) confer over maps with Tassajara student fire marshal Devin Patel.

Water pumped from Tassajara Creek fed the Dharma Rain sprinklers throughout the fire.

July 2. Resident Bryan Clark looks up the Tassajara Creek watershed from Hawk Mountain. Almost two weeks after the lightning strikes, flames had not been spotted yet from within Tassajara.

Tassajara director David Zimmerman (left) gives Basin Complex fire branch commander Jack Froggatt (in yellow) and Abbot Steve Stücky a tour of the residents' fire preparations on July 2.

July 9. Head cook Mako Voelkel and fellow residents leave Tassajara during the final evacuation. But Mako and four others would return within the hour.

July 10. Flames descend from Flag Rock, above the zendo, into Tassajara.

A dragon of fire near the confluence of Tassajara and Church creeks. This photo of the advancing fire front was taken at dusk on the evening of July 9, a few hours before flames closed the road, cutting off access to Tassajara.

Graham Ross, Mako Voelkel, David Zimmerman, Steve Stücky, and Colin Gipson—"the Tassajara Five"—posed for this portrait after facing the flames for six straight hours.

July 14. Abbot Steve Stücky and Colin Gipson clean the Buddha after unburying the statue from the bocce ball court. This 2,000-year-old Gandharan relic had previously been restored after being damaged in the 1978 zendo fire.

Cartoonist Tom Meyer's take on what it means to be a fire monk.

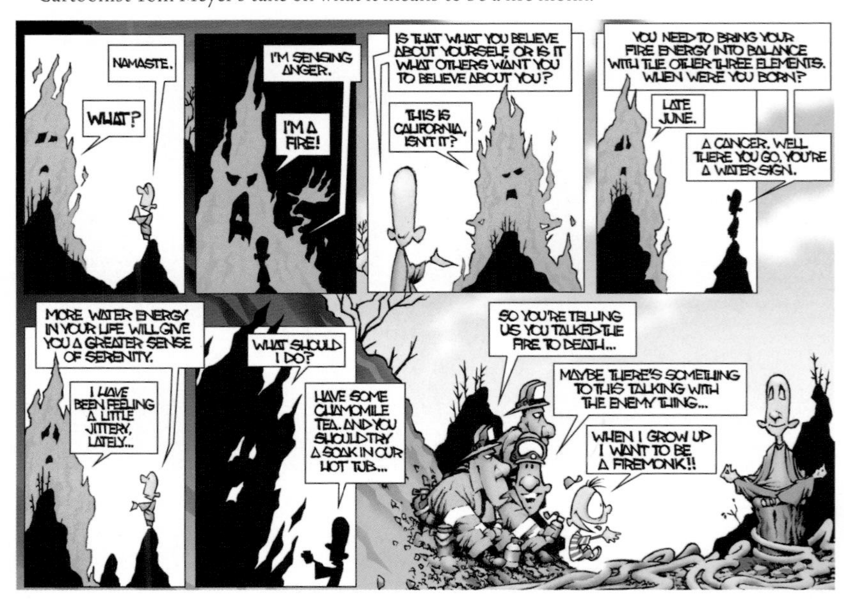

July 26. Sixteen days after the fire's passage, Shundo David Haye hikes the Tony Trail, surveying the bare ridges and burnt brush left behind.

This wooden plaque, called a *han*, hangs outside the zendo and is struck to call residents to meditation.

Stripped of vegetation four days after the 2008 fire, Tassajara Road appears even more isolated and exposed than usual.

Tassajara Road in May 2009, nearly one year later. This photo was taken from Ashes Corner, where five priests turned around during the final evacuation to stay at Tassajara and meet the fire.

Stuart stood in the middle of the activation, disbelieving what he was seeing—not in the sky, but on the ground: a tangle of hoses, some swollen with water before the hose crew had them under control. Charged with water, the hoses were difficult or even impossible to lift. Some lacked nozzles. People bumped into one another, worked at cross-purposes, wandered around in confusion. One hose even broke.

Stuart had instructed them to get on the hoses and wet everything down. If the fire came over the hogback, they could obstruct its path by saturating the entry to the rest of Tassajara. He didn't expect Zen students to be as polished as his own seasoned fire crew. But what the fire captain saw now made him cringe. He decided to hike up past the Suzuki Roshi memorial to the hogback to look at the fire himself. If this fire was coming quickly, they couldn't afford to be clumsy.

"Stuart, I have George Haines on the phone," said David over his walkie-talkie, calling from the stone office.

Stuart watched as one resident backed another up on an open hose, but with her legs in an unstable, wide stance. If her hose partner lost his balance, they'd both topple over, and the hose would whip and writhe.

"Okay," Stuart said. He didn't like the sound of David's voice. It was not a voice about to bear good news.

"He says he personally met with the IC and his deputy. They won't budge. They won't send a crew," said David, relaying Haines's message.

"Not one engine?" Stuart asked.

"Copy. Not one engine."

If this were CAL FIRE's operation, Stuart thought, a whole strike team would be on the way. He wouldn't have the sinking feeling he had in his stomach right now, like the time he was seventeen, surfing Moss Landing near the Monterey Peninsula in February, looking over his shoulder at waves with eighteen-foot faces. After throwing him off his board and running him like a rag doll through the washer, the ocean had spit him out on the beach, semiconscious. He didn't ride big water anymore. Now, if the surf looked great but the locals were on the cliffs drinking coffee, he joined them for a cup.

"Tell Chief Haines I said thank you for trying," Stuart told David.

After a long pause, David's voice came over the walkie-talkie again. "He says he is sorry he couldn't deliver. He asked how many people we have here now. I told him twenty two." David had a list in front of him of the residents and volunteers at Tassajara on July 9, with names and numbers of next of kin.

On an engine crew, Stuart's "span of control" was limited to five firefighters. Twenty-two? he thought. Did they really have that many?

Sometimes you don't know how much you are depending on something until all possibility of its attainment vanishes. After signing off on the walkie-talkie, Stuart shouted to the crew at the flats, "That's it! We're done here! *Basta!*"

They looked around at one another, confused. Weren't they activating? Wasn't the fire coming? Why stop?

"I'm going up to the hogback to get a look," Stuart told resident fire marshal Devin Patel. Then he headed for the ridge.

Standing next to Shundo, her partner on the hose crew, Mako shook her head, dismayed. If Stuart had lost confidence in them, she couldn't blame him. There were people there who shouldn't be, she'd thought to herself as the activation unfolded—or rather, unraveled. "It wasn't hysteria," she said later, "but it definitely felt like people weren't doing what they were trained to do." And a couple of people were new and not fully trained yet—they'd just arrived to replace the two residents who'd decided to leave on July 8.

But what had just happened wasn't a real demonstration of their preparation or abilities. Sometimes even when you followed a recipe to the letter, Mako knew, it didn't turn out. Ingredients varied, as did the number of stirs with a spoon, the mood of the cook, the moisture in the air. She'd seen days when the kitchen crew just couldn't harmonize, no matter how they tried. Dishes broke. Bread failed to rise. Sugar was measured out instead of salt.

Their drills had never been perfect. According to Shundo, though they had lots of new gear, there was always something "a bit homemade" about the resident fire crew's execution. The portable pumps wouldn't work—Mark 3's are notoriously cranky, even in the hands of trained professional firefighters—or they struggled to hear each other on the radio. But they'd steadily improved. "It was never superhoned," Shundo admitted later, "but we were doing our best."

But if their best looked this bad, and the fire was just over the ridge, heading for Tassajara, he hated to think what their worst might look like.

Just below the hogback ridge, Colin looked upcreek with former firefighter Kim Leigh, his partner on patrol. They made a natural, complementary pair. One had joined the Marine Corps straight out of high school and later become a Zen priest. The other, drawn to Buddhism through an interest in its art, went into firefighting in his early twenties to avoid becoming a soldier.

As a conscientious objector, Leigh had found some irony in the militaristic nature of professional firefighting—it evoked much of what he'd been trying to avoid. He remembered being helicoptered into remote lightning-ignited fires on a CDF Ecology Corps crew. "They'd drop us off, and then they couldn't find us," he told me in October 2009. "We'd flag them down with whatever colorful thing we had." Eventually the Ecology Corps became the California Conservation Corps and program staffing switched from mostly conscientious objectors to volunteers without much wildland fire training. "People would come in fresh and go to a fire. We needed bodies, so we'd bring them. It was an on-site training situation, challenging at times, and dangerous."

Now a working artist, Leigh often went to Tassajara during the transitional period between monastic practice and guest season to help with painting projects. He'd had to think about it when David had asked him to come help the residents prepare. His wife had had a car accident. She was fine, but the car wasn't. He was in the middle of preparing for an art exhibition. And it had been many years since he'd worked a wildfire. But he said yes. "If your neighbors call you and say their barn is on fire, do you say, 'Sorry, I'm busy'?"

From the moment he'd arrived he'd felt welcomed into the circle, impressed with the presence of mind of the residents. Back when Leigh was a firefighter, there weren't any women on the crew, so he was particularly struck by how inspiring it was to work alongside them. "They bring something the male energy doesn't seem to arrive at," Leigh told me.

Standing on the steep trail that cuts across the slope below the hogback and looking up Tassajara Creek, Leigh saw what looked like a series of small volcanoes erupting. As fire crept up ravines, trees torched into columns of flame.

"Stuart should see this," said Colin.

Leigh nodded.

Colin raised Stuart on his radio.

"I'm already on my way," came the reply.

One hundred thirteen degrees Fahrenheit: That was the predicted high Stuart had heard for the following day. He could feel the atmosphere working its way up to that troubling number. Stuart was used to being uncomfortably hot inside his fire gear. But as he climbed above the Suzuki Roshi memorial site and crossed onto the backside of the ridge facing Tassajara Creek, he felt the distinct additional heat of the fire, like a blast of warm air from an open oven door.

He joined Colin and Leigh at their post. Leigh was sitting down, resting his legs. Colin stood beside him, looking through his binoculars. But Stuart didn't need binoculars to see what he estimated to be sixty-foot-high flames in the Tassajara Creek drainage, about a mile upstream. He looked at Leigh and saw confirmation on the former firefighter's face: This was no creeping fire. This fire was exploding, with only the hogback to cross before it entered Tassajara.

"Is everyone still out at the flats?" asked Colin, unscrewing the cap on his water bottle and taking a drink. He hadn't seen the activation, nor had Leigh.

Stuart nodded and left it at that. "I want to look at this from Lime Point."

"I'll go with you," Colin volunteered. "I've already been twice today. Do you mind, Kim?"

"Not at all, Buddha buddy," said Leigh. "Buddha buddy" was his nickname for his patrol partner, whom he later described to me as "the kind of person you'd want around if your plumbing broke, house caught on fire, and dog ran away all at the same time."

As Colin headed back toward the memorial and the trail down to the flats, Stuart hung back a moment.

"They won't do it," he told Leigh. "They won't send a single engine crew."

Leigh sighed. Back in his firefighting days, the feds and the state tangled over fire management. Clearly that hadn't changed. The USFS had the home team advantage in the Los Padres. It didn't matter whether CAL FIRE wanted to send in resources or not. The final say wasn't theirs.

"I don't want any of these young people getting hurt." Stuart gestured toward the other side of the ridge. "They're not prepared for this," he said, glancing back at the fireworks up Tassajara Creek.

The two had often consulted with each other in days prior, as the only people with professional firefighting experience at Tassajara. Though both were volunteers, Leigh's role was clearly subordinate to Stuart's—a few years on a ground crew a long time ago didn't match the breadth and depth of a veteran fire captain's experience. But he was the closest Stuart had to a colleague at Tassajara.

"Does this look like a fire you want to fight?" Stuart asked.

Leigh shook his head and sucked in a breath.

A fire captain—or anyone in a management position on a wildland fire—is constantly assessing and reassessing, making plans and changing strategies according to the realities on the ground and in the air. Risk moves. "Before I go into a questionable situation where I'm going to take a calculated risk," Stuart told me in our first interview, "I turn around and look at who I have with me. I know what their capabilities are, their strengths and weaknesses. I think, Do I want to do this? Generally I've got young people in their twenties with me on an engine. Do I want to explain to their spouses and families why they're in the burn center, or they're dead? And for what?" he asked, then answered his own question. "For trying to save a frickin' house that can be rebuilt." He had a simple motto: *When in doubt, chicken out*. They were words he'd learned from an old World War II vet when he'd first signed up with CAL FIRE, and they'd served him well.

Stuart had been genuinely confident in their readiness to meet the fire. His confidence had drained away with the coastal fog, as temperatures had spiked, further drying out the fuels in the fire's path, and winds had kicked up, creating potentially explosive conditions. Now, as Stuart saw flames the length of a hook-and-ladder truck turned on its end, the fire captain looked over his shoulder and asked himself, Can they do this? Do I want to?

"I'll make this run to Lime Point," he told Leigh. "You'll be my eyes?"

"You got it."

Colin had waited at the point where the trail rounds the ridge, as if intuiting that Stuart might want a word alone with Leigh, firefighter to firefighter. When he saw Stuart coming, he started moving again, so they descended the trail without conversation. A few minutes later, they followed the fork in the trail that passed behind the yurt. At the flats, the Tassajara fire crew bided time after the called-off activation. Some were standing, some sitting. Most had pulled off their hard hats.

If people stayed here to fight this fire, they were going to need guidance. They hadn't signed up to be firefighters. They were Zen students. Hardworking, calm, and composed, yes, but that didn't mean that if it really got hot, someone wouldn't panic and flee up the road or make any number of dangerous missteps. Firefighters learn how to function in chaos. How would a bunch of well-meaning Zen students handle the heat?

These were Stuart's thoughts as he headed up the road to Lime Point around four thirty p.m. on July 9. He wanted another view of the fire. On the one hand, he hoped it would look better, tell him something different. On the other, he just needed to confirm what he already knew inside.

Seven

BUDDHA IN THE BOCCE BALL COURT

In nature, adaptation is important; the plan is not.

—LAURENCE GONZALES, *Deep Survival*

Wednesday, July 9, four thirty p.m.

Standing at Lime Point, Colin couldn't see flames through the smoke. But he could hear the fire roaring through the valley below. It sounded like wind whipping through pines or, oddly, like white water pitching through a canyon.

"Is that the fire?" he asked, pretty sure he knew the answer.

Stuart nodded.

Colin adjusted the brim of his baseball cap, boiling in his jumpsuit over jeans and a long-sleeved T-shirt. Tufts of smoke rose from the ridge where the fire had run into the Church Creek drainage and headed east toward the road and south toward Tassajara. "It's taking off," he said.

Neither David nor Stuart said anything. David worked his jaw back and forth as if chewing gum, a habit when concentrating. He rubbed his eyes, which were stinging from the smoke.

Stuart's radio squawked again. Colin recognized Jack Froggatt's voice, requesting a medevac on the fireline for a thirty-year-old firefighter suffering from heat exhaustion. He thought Froggatt said his location was Church Creek Ranch, a place every bit as isolated as Tassajara, and that surprised Colin. Was Froggatt or one of his firefighters all the way down there? But more surprising, and unsettling, was Stuart's uncharacteristic silence.

Ever since he'd arrived at Tassajara, Stuart had joked about lounging with his feet up on one of the pine room porches and dousing the creeping flames with a cold beer. Sometimes he joked that the stone office, stocked with oxygen, water, and MREs (meals, ready-to-eat) donated by the fire crews, would be their Alamo. Stuart had stopped using the phrase after the native Texan Colin set him straight: "Do you know everyone died at the Alamo?"

But on the ten-minute drive up to Lime Point, they'd heard a red flag warning over Stuart's radio. The forecast for the following day, July 10, predicted temperatures above 110 degrees Fahrenheit and 25–30 mph fire-stoking, down-canyon winds.

Stuart hadn't exactly been upbeat when they'd started up the road to Lime Point, Colin noticed, but the red flag warning seemed to have pushed him over some edge. He looked stricken, and he wasn't saying much.

The air smelled scorched and his eyes burned, but David didn't think the fire looked much different from Lime Point. He squinted toward the Wind Caves, a wall of rock scooped out and sculpted by wind and water and time. How could it already be July and he hadn't walked there yet?

Things were definitely heating up. The Indiana crew's hasty departure and the red flag warning were ample evidence of that. But David's experience with this fire had trained him not to immediately heed the dramatic pronouncements of people in uniform—and demonstrated the truth of the Buddha's teaching not to believe something simply because you have heard it. Rather, taught the Buddha, "after observation and analysis, when you find that anything agrees with reason, and is conducive to the good and benefit of one and all, then accept it and live up to it."

Still, David didn't know how to measure a fire's progress or anticipate its next move. He depended on Stuart for that. Standing at Lime Point, he could tell Stuart didn't like what he was seeing. He seemed agitated, which was understandable. But David felt ready. Tassajara was ready. If the fire was ready, then let it come.

In this moment, he didn't feel fear. Being first an orphan and then a gay man in a straight society had instilled in him a quiet resilience and steady determination before practice had taught him how to find it in any circumstance.

"Okay. Let's motor," said Stuart, climbing into the Isuzu's front passenger seat. David took the seat behind him.

They didn't say much for the next few minutes. But halfway back to Tassajara, the matter-of-fact voice of branch director Jack Froggatt came over Stuart's radio: "The fire's making a run for the ridge."

David's eyes met Colin's in the rearview mirror. If the fire climbed to the ridge, it would surely cross the road. For weeks, the USFS had pointed to the one route in and out of Tassajara—and thus the lack of evacuation alternatives—as the reason for their reluctance to risk a professional crew. The very feature that made Tassajara desirable as a place for a monastery—its remoteness—also made it a liability.

"If Zen Structure Group decides to evacuate, how long do we have before the fire reaches the road?" Stuart asked, using the official designation for the people still at Tassajara.

Why is Stuart asking about evacuation? David thought. Who said anything about leaving Tassajara?

"Two, maybe three hours," said Froggatt. "Is Zen Structure evacuating?" He sounded as if he doubted what he had heard.

David checked the rearview mirror, hoping to catch Colin's eyes again, but he had them trained on the road. The struts on the Isuzu creaked and groaned on every rut. The engine whined in low gear.

Stuart paused before raising his radio to transmit his answer: "Affirmative."

"Everyone's coming out?" Froggatt asked.

David felt suddenly breathless. He shook his head no, though no one had asked him a question.

"Affirmative."

"Wait!" David cried. "Stuart, no one said we're evacuating!" His skin felt tight, his muscles locked around a rising swell of frustration and confusion, a feeling that time had just skipped forward and left him behind.

Stuart didn't respond. He kept his eyes forward on the road.

"Call when you're ready to exit," said Froggatt. "I'll call air attack to hold the road."

"Copy." Stuart lowered his radio until it rested in his lap.

For a second, David considered clawing the radio from Stuart and calling Froggatt back himself to straighten out the misunderstanding, but instead he took a deep breath and noted the bottomless, dropping feeling in his belly. He had to find a way to slow time by being in it. He had to inject his voice where it was not wanted.

"We have *not* decided to evacuate," David said again, enunciating each word, thinking, You are not in charge here! "We need to talk this over with everyone. Stuart? Are you listening?"

Stuart didn't turn around to face David. "Things have changed," he said, his voice uncharacteristically flat. "We have to leave now. We just have to leave."

In the weeks that fire had been chewing through the surrounding forest, David never really knew how the different agencies managing the blaze were related or whom he could trust. Though others on the core team, Mako and Graham in particular, felt Jack Froggatt gave them the straight story and that he genuinely liked Tassajara and what it was about, David wasn't sure whose interests Froggatt represented.

But Stuart didn't work for anyone on the fire. He always said what was on his mind—for better or for worse. He was a longtime friend of Tassajara. Now that trusted friend, the one with the expertise who'd told them repeatedly Tassajara was defensible, had determined it wasn't safe to stick around. Without consulting them, he'd set their evacuation in motion.

They all heard David's announcement over their radios—*the acti*vation group at the flats, waiting for their next cue; Shundo and Devin, who had hiked over the hogback for a look at the fire up Tassajara Creek; a skeleton kitchen crew, preparing supper; Abbot Steve, on his way to the work circle to intercept the three returning from Lime Point: "Everyone on the core team please come to the stone office immediately."

Abbot Steve ran into Stuart first, near the gatehouse across from the zendo.

"We're leaving," the fire captain told the abbot. He lifted his gaze to the smoke-washed sky above the half-wrapped gatehouse.

"What?" Abbot Steve peered at Stuart through frameless eyeglasses, projecting a naturally confident, cool demeanor despite Stuart's urgency.

"You don't like this, do you?" Stuart shifted on his feet.

"No, I don't." In the week since Abbot Steve had arrived at Tassajara, they'd been doing everything they could to stay there safely, not to leave it. The abbot knew the activation had not been exemplary. He was there and had witnessed the confusion of hoses and roles, the nervous lack of focus. But that alone couldn't have so drastically shifted Stuart's commitment to staying. "What did you see from Lime Point?"

"The fire's approaching the road," Stuart explained. "They're sending air support to keep it clear. We have ten minutes to get out of here."

The fire reaching the road might be a trigger point for the fire service, Abbot Steve thought, but it wasn't a trigger point for him. Just a few days prior, he'd talked with a reporter on the bridge just above where Cabarga Creek spills into Tassajara Creek in the rainy months. Summer guests and residents often relax on its benches made of long, smooth slabs of wood. "If the fire comes to visit us at our front steps," the abbot had said as sunlight splashed the head student's cabin behind him, "we'll meet it." The sun had set and the moon had risen several times since he'd made that assessment, but it had not changed.

"This isn't the agreement we had, Stuart," he said. "It's not how we make decisions here."

A lone Steller's jay squawked on the hill behind the gatehouse—one of the many that usually patrolled Tassajara looking for handouts and crumbs. Most of the wildlife seemed to have cleared out in advance of the fire.

Stuart sucked in a breath and turned his gaze in the direction of the hogback, the low ridge where earlier he'd seen fountains of flame spilling down the canyon toward Tassajara. He shifted his weight from side to side and blew out the intake of air, shaking his head. "We have to leave," he repeated.

Stuart was all motion, but the abbot held his body still, his movements frugal, precise. "We have a designated safe retreat, Stuart. We have our sprinklers and pumps to take care of. You yourself said—"

"It's a different fire today than it was yesterday," Stuart interrupted. The wind rattled the wrapping on the gatehouse. "They're calling for red flag conditions. We're alone here. I've got no backup. We don't have the capacity to do this by ourselves—not in these conditions—and I don't want to be responsible for what could happen. We have to leave."

"We need to discuss this with the core team," said Abbot Steve, reiterating what David had told Stuart on the road.

The abbot turned back toward the stone office, walking past the small altar where, ordinarily, incense is offered daily in the work circle. Stuart, incredulous, trailed a few steps behind as they passed the kitchen. On a typical summer day, sounds of pots banging and knives chopping—one meal's cleanup and another's preparation—would float from the windows. Now it was quiet. Only one or two people were needed to prepare a simple dinner for the twenty-two who remained.

The reassuring murmur of Tassajara Creek drifted through the windows of the open-air student eating area, where Abbot Steve had sat tangaryo his first practice period at Tassajara. That was before the zendo burned, and he remembered exactly where his seat had been, facing the creek, near the door. His legs had felt every kind of pain—throbbing, tingling, cramping, aching, even burning—but he'd sat through it all, watching how the mind tries again and again to refuse to feel what is unpleasant, unwanted.

Now, simply watching his own response was not an option. According to Stuart, this fire had become a different fire. That was entirely possible—every fire was different from one moment to the next, just like everything in the universe. Despite the less-than-perfect activation, Abbot Steve thought they were ready. The words he'd said earlier to the reporter were still true. He didn't feel a change within himself corresponding to Stuart's shift.

Stuart had said he didn't want to be responsible for what could happen, but in Abbot Steve's view that responsibility fell to the core team. If they left, as Stuart said they had to, the pumps drawing water into the standpipe system and pushing it through Dharma Rain would run out of fuel. The sprinklers would sputter and stop on the rooftops. The fire would pour into that vacuum. Even the stone kitchen would burn, as the old zendo had, the fire consuming the cookbooks and the wooden shelves that held them and warping the steel sinks and hanging steel racks used to cool freshly baked loaves of bread. Everything that could would burn.

Abbot Steve was relatively new to his position. At the ceremony installing him as abbot, he'd taken a vow: "Having entered this path, I cannot turn aside." His first concern now was for everyone's safety. But his position gave him another responsibility, not lower or higher, but equally present: to tend to the practice and bring forth the teachings of the Buddha.

It was responsibility in its broadest sense. To take care of Tassajara included taking care of the creek and forest, the temple buildings, the bodies and minds of every resident and guest. The guardian of the temple—a foot-tall wooden figure with a furrowed brow and a stick balanced behind his bowing hands—had already been taken out to Jamesburg. The remaining residents and their embodiment of practice were the guardians of the temple now.

. . .

The same rock walls and concrete floor that made the stone office a safe haven also offered a respite from the heat. Abbot Steve positioned himself behind the counter, Stuart at the counter's end, gripping the edges of the countertop. David stood near the front door. The rest of the core team perched on a few pieces of wicker furniture and wooden benches moved earlier from the student eating area.

The intensity in the room was almost audible, like the low buzz of an electric current. The abbot began by informing the group of the reason for their meeting: the fire captain's recommendation that they evacuate immediately. "We need to understand our situation and make a decision. Let's hear from Stuart first."

Stuart repeated what he'd said out by the gatehouse, speaking quickly, in a voice pitched with urgency: "We have to leave. Conditions have changed. This is a much more dangerous situation than before. The fire's coming in strong. It's not creeping anymore. We aren't getting any help, and I don't want to be responsible for you in these conditions. We have to leave. We have to leave now."

"I told Stuart we had to discuss it first," Abbot Steve added.

"We don't have time to discuss!" cried Stuart. "They're diverting airtankers from somewhere else to hold the road for us!"

The abbot's eyes met the director's. They had come to know each other well over the past year and a half. They'd talked about their Mennonite roots and the respect they shared for its principles of hard work and humility, though neither practiced the religion. But there was also a deep trust between them—in David's words, a sort of "empathetic resonance"—based on their shared experience of Zen practice. If Abbot Steve hadn't been at Tassajara, David, as director, would have been responsible for their decision making in this moment. He was relieved that he wasn't. He stood silently by the door, confident that Abbot Steve would find a way through the confusion to the right words. David didn't think he could—he was too angry, and when he got angry, he tended not to speak.

Shundo was the first to say something, the image of the amateur activation still fresh in his mind. "We agreed we'd do what Stuart recommended."

"We did say that," Colin said quietly, almost to himself.

Devin nodded. In his mind, this was a scenario they'd discussed—a clear trigger point for leaving—and Stuart had pulled the trigger.

"What about Dharma Rain?" Graham asked, sitting on his hands, a tightness in his voice, a blush in his cheeks from the sun. As plant manager he knew that though the systems they had in place were good, they required human attention. "The pumps can only run for three or four hours before they run out of fuel. Someone needs to be here to fill them."

Sitting upright and alert next to him, Mako nodded vigorously. It was unusual for Graham to speak before, or more than she did. But there was nothing to add. He'd said the most important thing without saying it exactly: *If we leave now, Tassajara is finished.* She glanced up at the ceiling above their heads. When 40 percent of it is on fire, they'd been told, it's time to get out and jump in the creek with your fire shelter.

"We don't have time for this!" Stuart pursed his lips to release a stream of air, shaking his head. "We have to evacuate. Right now!"

Abbot Steve laid his hands on the fire maps on the countertop. The Three-Day-Away fire. That's what they'd been calling it for almost three weeks. Did anyone really know how to predict the movements of a fire? he wondered. He sensed the passage of time, moving much too slowly for the fire captain yet too quickly for the group being asked to abandon their temple and home. Later, he described feeling "extreme concentration, a deep awareness of the consequences of our decision"—like a diver on a high-dive board, about to leap into space, knowing every movement counts, even the movements inside the mind.

It was true that they'd agreed to follow Stuart's advice—before Abbot Steve arrived at Tassajara—and that conditions had worsened weatherwise. It was true that the heart of Tassajara couldn't be burned, and buildings did not matter when compared with a human life. But something else was also true. At a question-and-answer session at Green Gulch Farm after the fire, Abbot Steve would observe, "If you look at Tassajara on the map, and you see only one way in and out, and you don't really know Tassajara . . . it looks like this is a very dangerous, risky place to be. Sometimes a close, intimate perspective is critical in understanding what to do, and sometimes you need to step back and have a wide view."

In fact, having both perspectives is best. Dōgen wrote: "Put your whole attention into the work, seeing just what the situation calls for. Do not be . . . so absorbed in one aspect of a matter that you fail to see its other aspects." When you wash the rice, see the sand in the rice and the rice in the sand. One aspect of Zen practice is learning not to stick to any fixed view—or sense of situation or self. Zen also teaches the cultivation of "skillful means," the ability to approach a situation with flexibility and respond appropriately, with an eye toward encouraging awakening, in oneself and others.

Abbot Steve looked up from the stack of fire maps. "Okay," he said. "I guess we need to go."

He said, We need to go. But inside the contours of his own mind, he started plotting how to stay.

*The meeting lasted five minutes, maybe ten. After the abbot an*nounced his decision, there was a long moment in which no one moved. It was as if they didn't know what to do next. They had no form for this.

"Can I go ring the bell?" asked Devin, thinking of the rest of Tassajara's residents, who weren't privy to the core team's conversation. No one said anything, so he said, "I'm going to go ring it," and left the stone office to sound the railroad bell, the residents' cue to drop whatever they were doing and report to the work circle immediately.

"Should we bury the Buddha?" Mako asked.

"Yes," said Abbot Steve. "Quickly."

Outside the office, Mako asked Bryan Clark, a member of her kitchen crew, to remove the Buddha from the zendo altar. In heavy fire boots, Clark, Shundo, and a summer student ran past the shoe racks onto the strictly shoeless wooden platform that wraps around the building and stepped into the zendo from the rear door, behind the altar. The Buddha faced the other direction, gazing toward the creek, marks of its previous encounter with fire undetectable in the dim zendo light. With wire cutters placed for just this purpose at the back of the altar beside the matches and incense, they snipped the wires securing the statue. It took the three of them to lift the Buddha, carved from a chunk of dark gray metamorphic rock called schist.

They placed a yoga mat under the Buddha and folded blankets over him at the bocce ball court just after five thirty p.m. Whenever a Buddha is installed on an altar or removed from one, the statue's eyes are brushed open or closed in a formal ceremony. After gathering whoever happened to be around as witnesses, Abbot Steve performed an abbreviated eye closing. Graham, making a last check of all the pumps, walked by, saw the ceremony in progress, and thought, Good, that's being taken care of, one less thing to worry about. Abbot Steve wouldn't remember what he said to the Buddha exactly. Others who were present recalled something like "You're going to sleep for a while." But Mako remembered something more—part request, part apology—the abbot saying to the Buddha: "You'll see what happens here." Then Kim Leigh and Colin shoveled dirt back into the hole.

Leigh had seen the plywood over the hole in the bocce ball court earlier but hadn't realized what the hole was for until he found himself in the middle of the eye-closing ceremony. "It was very quick and urgent," he told me later. "Lots of energy was flying around, but they took the time to do this sacred thing."

Why hadn't the residents taken the Buddha out to Jamesburg, as they had the other ceremonial objects and statues and the recipe binders? The Buddha should stay put, they'd decided early on. To take him up the road would have felt like removing a ship's keel. He would be safe at Tassajara, tucked into the earth.

. . .

Letting go of the idea they'd held collectively for nearly three weeks—that they'd be there when the fire came through—the residents enacted the one scenario they'd never discussed or drilled for: leaving Tassajara entirely.

Ten minutes of orderly chaos passed as the community scattered to attend to whatever individual tasks still needed doing and fetch personal belongings before meeting in the parking lot. In the stone room she and Graham shared, Mako stripped off her fire gear. She put on a pair of sandals, grabbed her backpack, and tucked a distressed, meowing Monkeybat inside a pillowcase, an impromptu carrier. Colin threw his bag in the lumber truck, figuring he would drive it out so it wouldn't burn—they would need it if they had to rebuild Tassajara. Shundo recovered a small statue of Kuan Yin, the goddess of compassion, sitting on the back of the zendo altar—he'd noticed it there when they went to get the Buddha—and handed it to Stuart's girlfriend for safekeeping, the statue's, hers, and theirs. In the parking lot, the resident charged with making sure they were all accounted for consulted her clipboard and directed people to their assigned vehicles. Abbot Steve had radioed her that he wanted to be the last to leave, alone, in his own car.

Stuart had positioned his Toyota pickup at the top of the parking lot so cars could queue behind him. The fire captain's countenance had shifted from extreme frustration to provisional relief. Just before six p.m., five cars had lined up behind Stuart's truck: Shundo had four passengers in the Isuzu. Behind him were Tassajara's two Suburbans. The first one, driven by Graham, held five passengers, including Mako and Devin. The other also held five, plus a driver. Colin tailed the second Suburban, alone in the lumber truck. Abbot Steve stood beside his Honda CR-V, last in line. Including Stuart and his girlfriend, the resident with the clipboard counted twenty-one heads. Everyone was present but the director.

"David, where are you?" she asked over her walkie-talkie.

After a brief delay, he answered, "I'm on the phone with Paul." Paul Haller, Zen Center's other abbot.

Some in the cars thought, Must this conversation happen now? A few speculated that Haller, who had installed the standpipe system after the Marble Cone fire, might try to talk David out of leaving. Haller could be a fierce teacher, in the confrontational style of the old Zen masters. He'd once shouted at Shundo in a student-teacher interview that Shundo was wasting his time—and Shundo is not the only one with such a story. Haller grew up poor in Belfast, Ireland. His Dharma name, Ryushin, means "Dragon Heart/Mind."

After a few minutes, the resident responsible for counting heads raised David again on the radio: "David, we're all waiting for you."

"I'll go get him." Mako set Monkeybat on the front seat and jogged to the stone office in her sandals. Abbot Haller had ordained both her and Graham, giving them the same Dharma name, Unzan, or "Cloud Mountain," though unintentionally. She wanted to talk to Paul herself, to make sure he knew what was happening. She and her teacher had had many pre-dawn *dokusans,* one-on-one encounters in which teacher and student, sitting cross-legged on the floor facing each other, a bit too close for comfort, discuss the student's practice or some aspect of the Dharma. Again and again, by flicker of candle-light, Haller had shown Mako to herself, helped her touch what in Zen is known as "big mind."

Big mind is an awareness that includes all existence inside its own. From cells viewed through a microscope in a neurobiology lab to trees torching in the Ventana Wilderness to satellites arcing through space, capturing images of fire thousands of dark miles away—all are recognized as the self, and the self as threaded to all existence. With Haller's help, Mako had learned that Zen wasn't just mind tricks, as she'd once thought. It wasn't about fooling yourself or anyone. It was about facing the reality that we are not separate from anything in the world. Not from fire, not from one another, not from our own minds. All things arise and cease together.

But what she wanted from her teacher now was one of his fierce shouts. She wanted him to do something, say anything, so they wouldn't have to leave Tassajara.

After the core team meeting had ended in the decision to leave, David had sat at the desk where for weeks he'd called an ever-changing list of information lines and fire management contacts. He'd dialed the Jamesburg house and told Leslie James they were evacuating, and no, he didn't have time to explain. Then he'd grabbed his radio and walked to his cabin to get his duffel. When he'd realized that the green bandanna he used to shield his lungs from smoke was still in the stone office, he'd doubled back to get it—and to make sure they hadn't left behind anything essential. The phone rang as he walked in the door.

"David, why are you leaving?" Abbot Haller's Irish vowels, the rich register of his voice, resonated over the patchy phone line.

Haller had once been director of Tassajara. It was his job then, just as it was David's now, to take care of Tassajara's guests, staff, and grounds. It was a simple enough question, and David understood where it came from. Haller had first come to Tassajara as a resident just after the Marble Cone fire in 1977. He knew of the legendary commando trips students had made from Jamesburg under cover of nightfall to resupply, refuel pumps, and remove valuables, in the days before a small group had returned to stay and fight the fire. During the weeks of preparing for the Basin Complex fire, Haller had told David on more than one occasion, "They can't force you to leave, you know."

Now, Haller's question was deeply disturbing: Why were they evacuating? They had planned to be here. They had never planned to leave. So why were they leaving?

"I don't know," said David. "I don't know myself."

A voice came over David's radio again, requesting that he come to the parking lot. David asked Haller to hold on and set the phone aside to say he'd be right there.

He typically loathed being late—and rarely was. Now, he refused to be rushed. In fact, all awareness of time had fallen away. The hours of the morning had slid into the hours of the afternoon, and he couldn't account for them. They'd waited weeks for this fire. Now it was here and he didn't understand why they were leaving. He couldn't explain it to Haller, because it didn't make sense to him.

David picked up the phone again. "I mean, how did this happen?" Haller asked.

"Stuart ordered it," said David. "He says it's not safe to be here anymore."

"Ordered it," echoed Haller, turning over the words.

"We had a meeting. We decided—Steve made the final call, and I guess we all agreed—that we should follow Stuart's recommendation." Even as he chose the word, David realized a recommendation isn't an order. Had Stuart ordered them out? It had felt like an order, but by what authority? And they hadn't really agreed so much as deferred to the two experts in the room—one in fire, the other in the Buddha's practice.

"I see," said Haller. He could hear within David, by nature diligent and conscientious, an unspoken conflict between doing the right thing by Stuart and doing the right thing by Tassajara.

"I think that as director, David felt an enormous responsibility," Haller told me later. "Tassajara is the jewel of Zen Center. And here he is, holding a pivotal role in its survival." While David's memory of this phone conversation is scant, lost to the tension of the moment, Haller recalled that they agreed that Stuart needed to do what he was doing even though it seemed contradictory. "We respected it. But we weren't fully persuaded by it."

Just as they were ending the call, Mako burst through the door. "Let me talk to Paul."

David promised to call Haller back as soon as the caravan reached Jamesburg, handed Mako the phone, and slung his bag over his shoulder. A blast of warm air greeted him when he opened the stone office door. It was warmer than it should have been at almost six p.m., even on a hot July evening.

Feeling slightly queasy, he put one foot in front of the other, but his body resisted the motion of going forward. Some part of him knew that it was time for evening service—for chanting, bowing, and making offerings of food and light so that all beings might be nourished and awakened. But there would be no evening service. He hadn't been inside the zendo in weeks. He had packed his priest robe and sent it up the road.

He walked the gravel path beside a patch of lawn bordered with lavender, rosemary, sage, and thyme. He ducked under wisteria vines twisting through the trellis, passed the flat bronze bell that calls residents to meals, and climbed the steps to the work circle. Tassajara seemed hushed, strangely empty. From the time Zen Center had purchased it in 1966, except for a few hours during the 1977 fire, there had always been someone at Tassajara. Even in the depths of December, when many residents took a two-week break between monastic practice periods, a few always stayed, and former residents often came to practice again in the profound quiet of the winter canyon.

David looked up into a charcoal gray and orange sky, then glanced at the zendo to his right, at the empty shoe racks on the wraparound wooden platform, the motionless, silent bell and drum. When he was six years old and driving away from the children's home with a temporary family, the sky overhead seemed to contain every kind of weather. He remembered storm clouds and lightning, bright white clouds and patches of blue, even a rainbow. He had vowed to himself then that someday he would find his true home. He had, eventually—not in a place, but in the practice of paying attention.

This moment is home. In a sense, it is the only true home you will ever have. And still, David thought, Tassajara is the place where this practice lives. How many people had come here and walked away changed, touched by the stillness and silence, the possibility of living differently, with an unguarded heart? The transformation had something to do with the place where it happened, this remote, narrow valley. Could they really leave it now to burn?

The sprinklers rained on the rooftops. The residents had done everything the experts had told them to, preparing Tassajara so that when the fire came, they'd be safe and ready. They'd designed and installed Dharma Rain. They'd raked. They'd swept. They'd dug fireline. They'd drilled and briefed and debriefed. They had planned to stay and meet the fire. Now, after weeks of Stuart's consistent confidence and despite the fact that Abbot Steve had said he couldn't imagine leaving Tassajara under any circumstance, both waited for him in the parking lot with the rest of the evacuees.

His radio squawked again: "David. Mako. Are you coming?"

He could hear Mako's footsteps behind him, faster than her usual purposeful stride. He pushed the talk button: "Yes." He would go, even as every molecule of his being protested.

Mako caught up with him, arms swinging at her sides. David sensed that her haste had more to do with wanting to talk to Graham than with any desire to leave Tassajara. Like him, Mako hadn't said much during the evacuation meeting. But he didn't need to hear her say it to know that she didn't want to go. At Tassajara, you learn how to read your fellow practitioners through your senses. You know the sound of their footsteps on the floorboards of the zendo, the way they open and close a door, the clicking sound their jaw makes when they chew. You know them the way you know family—perhaps more completely. Your eyes have learned to see and your ears have learned to hear, without filters or labels.

David walked out the gate, to the line of idling vehicles. At the end of each summer guest season, the residents held a gate-closing ceremony, reading the names of all the people who had worked at Tassajara over those months and supported the practice. But there would be no closing ceremony today, no time to mark everyone who had come to help since the fires first started a month before. Airtankers droned overhead. He felt the fire's closeness. He glanced back and wondered, Would he be the last to see Tassajara as it looked now?

Eight

THE LAST EVACUATION

Human life is messy. It's out of our control. It's like we're walking around in total darkness with a little speck of light which is called "right now."

—LESLIE JAMES

Wednesday, July 9, six p.m.

*A line of vehicles queued up behind Stuart Carlson's car at Tas-*sajara. The residents had made their decision—in part because of a decision they'd made earlier: to heed the counsel of the expert in fire and evacuate. That didn't stop it from feeling, in the moment, like a terrible misstep. For many in the line of vehicles pointing up the road, it wasn't even their choice; they were merely following the lead of others.

David was supposed to get into the Suburban with Mako and Graham, but he tossed his bag in the backseat of the abbot's car instead. "Did you want to talk to Paul?" he asked.

Abbot Steve shook his head. "I'll talk to him later."

Over the walkie-talkies, a resident took a final head count, calling out names and asking for confirmation.

It pained David to answer yes to his name as Abbot Steve shifted the

CR-V into gear. Both abbot and director initially kept their thoughts to themselves, yet each was aware of a shared backward pull as the car moved forward. Both sensed that they had much to talk about and that it was good they were in the car together. Yet they wanted to take their time, to go at their own pace, not at the urgent clip set by Stuart.

The vehicles ahead churned up dust. They drove slowly, in rare radio silence, closing windows and waiting for gritty clouds to clear. Manzanita bushes and hardy scrub oaks gripped the road's steep shoulder. These plants had taken seed and clung to life with fierce tenacity, using whatever earth and light and water they found to survive. But fire would mow them down in minutes.

A month before, fire had cremated the body of a long-term Green Gulch Farm resident and friend of Abbot Steve's who'd died. Abbot Steve had been at Tassajara leading a retreat and missed the ceremony. His friend's death had been expected. But if you really took to heart the words of the Heart Sutra, chanted daily in Soto Zen temples, no death could come as a surprise: "Form does not differ from emptiness, emptiness does not differ from form. Form itself is emptiness, emptiness itself form. Sensations, perceptions, formations, and consciousness are also like this."

Every moment is a life-or-death moment, Abbot Steve had realized through Zen—"Every act is the last time this happens," he told me. And because he had grown up close to nature's rhythms, working fields and tending animals, he understood that cycles of burn and regrowth are natural and necessary, that landscapes like the Ventana have coexisted with fire for millennia.

"How are you feeling?" he asked David.

"It feels wrong. We shouldn't be abandoning Tassajara." With these words, the knot in David's gut began to loosen. He was aware of the facts. But it wasn't a matter of weighing the facts—the disadvantageous change in the weather, the observable features of the fire, Stuart's judgment born of experience against his own lack of fire knowledge. David just trusted the truth of his own experience at that precise moment, and that truth shouted, Don't go!

"Maybe we could go back," he added.

The abbot nodded, adjusted his hands on the wheel. "I don't want to alarm the others," he said. His bushy eyebrows shrugged upward as they often did in conversation. "We'll need to find a way to tell them."

About a mile and a half from Tassajara, where the road widens at a switchback, Stuart pulled over so the convoy could pass him and he could take up the rear. Abbot Steve pulled in behind, honked, and waved back, declining to move ahead. Stuart got out of his car and made vigorous gestures for the CR-V to pass, but Abbot Steve just shook his head. Eventually, Stuart gave up and got back into his truck ahead of the abbot's car. "It was a who's-in-charge-here moment," Abbot Steve recalled afterward. In his mind, who was in charge couldn't have been clearer. "There was no way I was going to let Stuart get behind me."

The captain is the last to leave a sinking ship. "But Stuart was never the captain," said Abbot Steve. "It's a whole different thing, being abbot of Zen Center as opposed to being a guest here, a consultant on the fire." The abbot wasn't at Tassajara when the core team had first agreed to take the fire captain's advice and follow him out if he said it was time to go. "I wasn't in on that," he told me later with a slight smile, pushing his glasses up the bridge of his nose. "I would never have made that agreement."

About ten minutes after leaving Tassajara, around six fifteen p.m., the convoy passed Lime Point. Here, they could look out the car windows into the Church Creek canyon. A bruised, prematurely dark sky hung like a heavy curtain over the ridge, blocking the setting sun. Flames backing downslope on this side of the Church Creek divide needed to climb across the valley and uphill to reach the road. If the fire burned down the Church Creek canyon, toward the confluence with Tassajara Creek, it would enter Tassajara over the hogback, near Suzuki Roshi's memorial marker.

David wondered if they should radio the others and let them know they were thinking of returning. But there were problems with that approach. First, Stuart would hear it. Would he try to prevent them? Somehow the core team needed to be able to have a conversation, some sort of process, and they couldn't do it over walkie-talkies.

Many nights over the past couple of weeks, David had lain awake repeating, I don't know, I simply don't know, silently to himself. He dreaded the thought of causing someone else to suffer because of a decision he'd made, and as director he'd made many decisions since the start of the fires. He'd gathered information and consulted with the core team, but most of the time he just had to trust his instincts and let go, embodying his Dharma name, the part that suggested where he should point his effort: Complete Surrender.

"My sense of responsibility meant that I had to carry others," he told me later. It was something he'd learned to do early, in response to his parents' inability to care for him and his brother. During the fire, he had to be strong and decisive even when he didn't know what would happen next or whether the choices he was making were good ones. Complete surrender and full responsibility. Was it possible to hold both?

As they drove past Lime Point and climbed toward the place where some of Suzuki Roshi's ashes had been scattered, David looked out the passenger window at an old bathtub slumping into the hillside. How many times had he driven past this landmark in seven years? Too many to count. A drinking trough left over from the road's horse-drawn carriage days, the tub carried whatever water the season brought, gushing in the wintertime, barely damp this time of year.

As you drove in to Tassajara, the bathtub signaled that you were getting close. But as they drove out that evening, it meant they had to find a way to turn around soon.

Graham pointed to some smoke in the distance and scoffed, "We're going because of this?" The fire didn't look any different from when he'd escorted the satellite tech up the road a couple of hours ago. He grumbled, "If Paul were here, we wouldn't be leaving!"

When I spoke to Graham and Mako about this moment later, they couldn't agree on which one of them had actually made the comment about Abbot Paul Haller. In any case, it was a momentary slip, a lashing out that had more to do with frustration than with their actual experience of Abbot Steve. They just didn't understand why he had agreed to evacuate and believed that Haller simply would have refused. Abbot Steve's arrival *had* changed the decision-making dynamic, Graham told me later. Before, David consulted the core team and they decided what to do together. But Abbot Steve had basically driven this decision. And now they were leaving Tassajara to burn.

Monkeybat meowed. Mako tried to soothe the cat, scrubbing her head around the ears through the pillowcase.

"We'll find a way to get back in," she said. On the phone, Haller had reminded her that just because they were leaving Tassajara now didn't mean they could not return. That's what residents had done in 1977—they'd evacuated when ordered to by the USFS, leaving sprinklers whirling on the rooftops. First a few people had sneaked back in to refuel the pumps, and then a full crew, including poet Jane Hirshfield, had returned just before fire closed the road.

Mako's words seemed to bounce off Graham. He had one hand on top of his head as if to hold it in place, his lips pressed tightly together. The mood was markedly different in the back of the Suburban. Four residents, clearly relieved to be leaving, talked happily about eating at the Running Iron, a bar and grill in Carmel Valley Village, and where they'd like to go for vacation now that they weren't going to be fighting fire.

At Ashes Corner, branch director Jack Froggatt stood on the side of the road. When the convoy reached him around six twenty-five p.m., Shundo Haye stopped and talked to him for a moment and then drove around the corner and continued up the road to the ridge.

When Graham and Mako's vehicle reached Froggatt, Graham cut the engine. Mako handed Monkeybat to a resident in the backseat, and she and Graham climbed out of the Suburban. "I remember feeling happy it was Jack," Mako told me later, "someone familiar."

It was windy on the ridge, hot and smoky. The airtankers thundered through the valleys a few hundred feet away, sometimes disappearing below the level of the road.

"Hey, Jack, what's going on?" said Mako.

"I'm surprised to see you." Froggatt stood with his hands on his hips, looking sideways at them, a quizzical expression on his face. He'd shed the dark reflective glasses he'd worn earlier that afternoon.

Mako and Graham looked at each other.

"If you leave, you know you can't go back," said Froggatt.

"We were looking for any little opening," Graham recalled later, anything that would allow them to stay.

Maybe we don't need to be on the road going out, Mako thought. It was an ah-ha moment, the moment when a clear path opens and you take it.

Colin had pulled up to Ashes Corner in time to catch Froggatt's re-mark. Those behind him stopped as well. Now five of the six vehicles leaving Tassajara were parked along the road—the Isuzu driven by Shundo had gone ahead. It was half past six. As the abbot and director walked up to Froggatt and the others, a few more evacuees spilled from the two Suburbans. Some stayed put inside the vehicles to avoid the smoke or because they were tired and ready to move on.

"Let's keep it moving, folks," said Froggatt, a roll of fire maps tufting from the side pocket of his black utility pants. "We want to get you out safely." The fixed-wing airtankers he'd ordered to protect the road stitched noisily through the smoke, dropping loads of water.

What he'd said to Mako and Graham was true. Froggatt was surprised to see them, because they'd never planned to leave. But he was also relieved. It meant he wouldn't have to worry about them any longer. Sensing the group's hesitation, he now encouraged everyone to keep heading up the road. A ridgetop with fire beneath it, as the disaster on the 2006 Esperanza fire had tragically proved, is not a place to linger. There'd been a red flag warning issued then, too, with high winds and perilously low humidity, before the burnover that killed five firefighters.

"Are you the last ones out?" Froggatt asked.

Abbot Steve nodded and looked out over the valley from the ridge. Dark, forested ridgelines cut straight up and down at nearly perpendicular angles. A searing, blustery wind blew down the canyons from the northwest, driving the flames both toward Tassajara and uphill toward the road. Smoke drifted up from the valley floor and waltzed with the wind into a black opal sky.

Wind had also blown fiercely the night a group of students scattered Suzuki Roshi's ashes under a full moon in April 1972. Abbot Steve was among the disciples who felt their way on a short rocky trail that extends along a ridgeline from Ashes Corner out to a peak. "A big gust of wind came up and, poof," he told me later, fingers spreading, palms drifting apart, "it took the ashes." Mitsu, Suzuki Roshi's wife, had said, "Ah, Suzuki Roshi like wind." Abbot Steve had tasted the grit of the ashes on his tongue.

Words he had written for the occasion of his installation as abbot in 2007 could well have been penned for this moment on the smoky ridge above Tassajara, airtankers rumbling through the canyon, beating the fire back from the road: "Our practice of zazen gives us backbone. Tough, sturdy, resilient. Soft as silk, tempered like fine steel."

He thought of his wife. She would understand why he needed to do what he was about to do. She trusted his judgment. He thought of Haller, his Dharma brother and co-abbot. "I knew that I'd have Paul's support," Abbot Steve told me later. Part of that confidence came from knowing Haller. Both had studied under the same teacher and received Dharma transmission in 1993 at Tassajara. But part of it came from the question Haller had put to David in the stone office: Why are you leaving?

On the ridge, the abbot turned to the branch director. "What happens if we don't go?"

Stuart stood to Abbot Steve's right, looking as if he couldn't believe he was hearing this question. He let out an exasperated chuckle, then peeled off from the conversation and walked a few yards up the road.

Froggatt's face was less forthcoming. The branch director kept his emotions tucked away, out of view. "I can't make you leave," he said. "But once you pass this point, I have to stop you from going back in until we know it's safe."

By definition, being in the path of a moving fire front is not safe. You could be overrun by fire or overcome by smoke. You could be crushed by falling trees, rolling boulders, explosions. A firestorm could suck all the oxygen from the valley. A crown fire, leaping from treetop to treetop, can reach 2,000 degrees Fahrenheit, releasing the energy of an atomic bomb every fifteen minutes.

But even a seemingly minor mishap could become life-threatening at Tassajara, Froggatt knew, because once fire compromised the road there would be no way in or out. "I could have attempted to prevent their return, since they were no longer on their property," Froggatt told me afterward, "but I am not a law enforcement officer, and the best thing to do was to try to convince them that returning was not a good idea. I felt strongly that their lives would be at risk."

An airtanker roared overhead, then banked along the ridge, dropping a few thousand gallons of water into the Church Creek valley.

"We need you all to keep moving," said Froggatt, waving his hand up the road.

Abbot Steve turned to David. "Let's call the core team together."

This chipped Froggatt's neutral demeanor. "We just spent fifty thousand dollars keeping the road open for you so you could have a meeting?"

Someone else was yelling at them from a vehicle that had driven down from another post: "Go! Go! Get moving! Now!"

"That was your decision," said the abbot. Fifty thousand dollars was a lot of money, but, as he said to Froggatt next, walking down the road a ways so the core team could meet in private: "We didn't ask for that."

"You feel this wind now?" Stuart asked Colin. They stood on the uphill side of the bend, with an up-valley view of the fire, while Abbot Steve talked with Froggatt. A hot wind raked the road. "It's going to be like this and one hundred thirteen degrees tomorrow. You don't want to be down there."

When I asked Colin to describe what the fire looked like from Ashes Corner then, he couldn't remember. He was looking closer in, at Stuart. "I didn't know what was happening for him, but I could feel it. I could feel fear. What arose was, Maybe there's something to be worried about here. I'm thinking, He's been through this a million times, why would he be scared?"

At Ashes Corner, Colin overheard the conversation between Abbot Steve and the branch director even as he talked with Stuart, his senses trained to take it all in. But what registered the strongest, what he remembered best, was the concern he saw on the fire captain's face.

Everyone who'd been at the stone office evacuation meeting now gathered around the abbot. The huddle did not include all of the core team members—Shundo had continued obediently past Froggatt and driven on up the road. Those present briefly discussed whether they ought to wait for Shundo, but there wasn't time. And they thought maybe he'd driven out of radio contact.

"I'm going back to Tassajara," Abbot Steve told the five people circled around him, making deliberate eye contact with each as if meeting them in dokusan, one-on-one. "What I hear from Jack Froggatt is that we might not be able to get back in if we leave now, but I feel that Tassajara can be defended. I can't make the decision for you or request that you stay under the circumstances. You have to decide for yourself what you want to do."

Abbot Steve already knew David's answer.

Practically in the same instant, Mako and Graham said they wanted to return. As former fire marshal and plant manager, they knew the systems that would be critical for protecting Tassajara.

Next it was Colin's turn. After a moment's hesitation, he confirmed that he would return, too. Despite what Stuart had just told him about what a furnace it would be in the valley when the fire came through, he felt he had to go back. He was head of the shop, and these were his friends. He didn't think he'd be able to look them in the eye again if he let them go back alone.

After Colin said he'd return, the group focused on the only member of the huddle who hadn't spoken yet, fire marshal Devin Patel.

"I'm going out," he said.

Devin's girlfriend, a guest cook, waited in one of the Suburbans. She'd returned to Tassajara just the day before with another evacuee primarily to help in the kitchen. But Abbot Steve suspected that Devin's desire to continue with the evacuation had just as much to do with Stuart's recommendation that they leave. "He took his cues from Stuart," the abbot said later. "He depended on his experience."

Abbot Steve respected Stuart, too, but he didn't base his own evaluation of the situation or his own state of mind on the fire captain's or that of the few firefighters on the road, shouting, "You've got to go! You have five minutes! You no longer have five minutes! The road is going to burn up any minute!"

Proud of Devin for choosing his own path, Abbot Steve nodded once. "I was concerned about putting pressure on people to stay," he told me. "The fact that Devin said no meant that it was possible to be in that meeting and not stay."

A few residents who had left their vehicles and heard the exchange between the abbot and branch director Froggatt asked Abbot Steve if they could go back, too. But Abbot Steve turned them down. Each of the four returning with him had attended regular fire briefings and decision-making meetings. He didn't feel he could ask others to assume the same risks when they didn't have the same information and experience. Moreover, five was a solid, manageable number. Though the abbot didn't know this, five was the maximum number of firefighters on one of Stuart's engines—more than that, and you risk losing track.

Abbot Steve had looked at the core team and seen something different from what Stuart had seen: not inexperienced firefighters, but seasoned practitioners of calm mind, prepared to deal with uncertainty. "We had confidence in beginner's mind," he told me when we spoke about this moment later. On one side there is what you think you know, the abbot explained, but on the other, there is simply trust in staying open, "the willingness to remain completely present and not turn away from the unknown—an extension of our zazen practice."

He walked back up the road to Froggatt, whose cheeks tensed with impatience.

"Five of us are staying." Abbot Steve chose the word *staying* deliberately. To him, they weren't going back. They'd never left Tassajara, because it was all Tassajara. They'd merely gone up the road a bit.

Froggatt simply nodded. No surprise this time. He turned to a colleague, a safety officer standing nearby. "Make sure we've got their names." Then he walked off, talking into his radio.

Things can change quickly on a fire, in either direction. "I've been on fires where one day we were in dire straits and the next day it snowed on us. The only fire out there was the campfire keeping us warm," Stuart told me in one interview.

On July 9, the moisture-starved air and soaring temperatures had transformed the fire threatening Tassajara from a creeper into a fierce and unpredictable force. For Stuart, the dots had aligned into the profile of a treacherous situation, prompting him to call for the evacuation. Now, as the group huddled around the abbot on the road, he watched a plume of smoke drifting toward the ridge with the northwest wind and mentally traced the footprints of his decision.

First there was the botched drill—hoses unrolled and pumps primed without nozzles, people running around as if on a scavenger hunt. Then he'd seen fire shooting upward sixty feet, reverse waterfalls of flame over the hogback, after learning that Chief Haines couldn't hustle up an engine crew for Tassajara. Haines had relationships with the people managing the Los Padres National Forest. But the USFS was in charge, and the agency had said, Not on our turf.

"It was their fire," Stuart lamented later. "If it was ours, things would have been different. I used to be a patriot of the U.S. Forest Service, but Forest Service policy was the problem here. If I had had one good engine crew, there's no question, I wouldn't have left Tassajara."

When Froggatt had shared the frequencies used by the Basin Complex incident command staff, Stuart was initially grateful for access to fire information at its source. "But things got dicey for me when they started referring to me as the Zen Structure Group resource. Suddenly I was on the radar. That put a ton of pressure on me," he said, adding, "It was pretty shrewd on their part. Tag, you're it." He'd been made official.

Standing in the middle of the failed drill, hearing he couldn't count on professional backup, Stuart had realized he'd be in charge of twenty monks. Or worse, maybe he wouldn't. Would a crew of Zen monks follow his orders? This moment on the ridge seemed to hold his answer. From years on fires, he'd learned there are fires you want to fight and fires best left alone. The fire he saw heading toward Tassajara wasn't a fire he wanted to fight, not with a novice crew of Zen monks trained to continuously question everything.

When I spoke with Stuart for the first time several months after the fire, he sighed with a palpable regret, looking back on the evacuation. He had glanced over his shoulder on July 9, as he always did when about to take a risk, and he'd seen people he cared for, mostly young, unaccustomed to following orders, and untested by fire. "The firefighters on my engine know what they're seeing. They know what to fear. . . . I was the only professional firefighter down there." He sounded almost hurt, recalling the loneliness of his position. When asked whether Froggatt ordered the evacuation, he quickly answered no, then added, "He highly encouraged it. You know, I trusted Froggatt. He's a good wildland firefighter. He liked what Tassajara was about. But when he and I had that conversation on the radio, he wanted us out."

Stuart insisted that he made the right decision at Tassajara with the information he had at the time. But as he recalled the moment when the core team huddled up at Ashes Corner, his expression turned mournful. He knew they'd decide to go back. When they came up to say good-bye, a wave of doubt rolled over him. Had he let them down? The firefighter in him wanted to return with them.

As the five prepared to turn around at Ashes Corner, he nodded toward his girlfriend in the passenger seat of his truck and said under his breath to Graham, "If it weren't for Solange, I'd go back with you."

He turned to Colin. "If it gets really bad," he advised, "get an inch-and-a-half hose at the front and back of the stone office, turn it on, and hunker down. If you just can't stand it, jump in the creek with your shelters."

When the abbot and director reached Stuart, David thanked him for everything he'd done for Tassajara.

"You're really mad at me, aren't you?" Stuart asked.

"It's just a different decision. This is what we feel we need to do. It's our decision," Abbot Steve said, his voice clear, buoyant. He clasped Stuart's hand and shook it. "You are not responsible for whatever happens."

Stuart knew the abbot intended these words to release him. They didn't. If anyone died inside Tassajara, he would wish he'd died along with them.

But Stuart dredged up a smile. Now that they were going back, better to bolster their confidence and remind them of the essentials than to dwell on all the things that could go terribly wrong. "Stay together. Don't get spread out," he told them, resting his palm on David's shoulder. "Never lose contact with each other."

There were quick good-byes, hugs, good-luck wishes, bows. Mako arranged for one of the departing residents to take care of Monkeybat in Jamesburg. As Graham pulled their belongings from the Suburban and tossed them into the lumber truck, Froggatt stepped in close.

"Those pumps running?" he asked.

"Yep."

"Got enough fuel?"

Graham nodded.

"Just keep your wits about you," Froggatt said softly.

It felt like another acknowledgment that their choice was solid. "Like we were doing the thing he would have done," Mako told me later.

Just past six thirty p.m., Abbot Steve turned his CR-V around. Colin followed suit with the Ford. As blades of flame knifed through the smoke in the canyon below, two vehicles carrying five monks headed back down Tassajara Road.

Nine

NO LEAVING, NO GOING BACK

Whatever you feel is right at the edge of your familiar world, that's the edge of your bodhisattva vow, the edge of your deep intention to wake up with what is.

—ABBOT STEVE STÜCKY

Wednesday, July 9, six thirty p.m.

In the vehicle Shundo Haye drove, someone had suggested that they ride away from Tassajara in silence. From the time they'd pulled out of the parking lot, they'd watched smoke billowing in the canyons and listened to the low drone of the airtankers without a word. When they'd reached the second overlook, Stuart Carlson had waved them past, making theirs the lead vehicle on the road.

Shundo said later that Stuart's pleading with them to leave Tassajara had "flipped something" in his head. All along they'd been learning the politics of the fire world—"the to and fro, who could override whom, along with what the fire can do." Now that the promise of help had been cut off, and along with it Stuart's confidence, it seemed the proper thing to do to evacuate. Maybe this was easier for Shundo than the others because he no longer lived at Tassajara, he speculated. He'd come down from San Francisco just to help. He hadn't expected to be here this long, hadn't even brought the proper footwear.

When they'd reached Jack Froggatt at Ashes Corner, Shundo had continued around the bend, climbing toward the ridge. It wasn't long before he'd noticed that no one was behind him.

After a few more kinks in the road, the Isuzu reached the ridge more than three thousand feet above Tassajara, the site of the informal finish line for the monastery's "No Race"—a noncompetitive five-mile run/walk/saunter up the road held every spring before guest season starts. They all got out of the car to watch trees flaring into flame in the canyons below and wait for the others to catch up.

When David radioed Shundo and told him some of them were reconsidering the decision to leave, it didn't fully register. What was there to reconsider? They were on their way out. Froggatt was stationed on the road, clearly intending to see that they left. "I didn't think I needed to be part of the conversation," Shundo told me. "I wasn't invited to come back and be part of it. It just seemed like they were having this discussion, and my assumption was everyone would follow along."

When a CAL FIRE chief scolded them to continue on, Shundo rallied everyone back into the Isuzu. A few minutes later, a resident radioed from one of the Suburbans and told Shundo some of the core group had turned around.

"I didn't have any feelings about it at that stage," Shundo said. "I thought, I'm driving the car. I'm going to Jamesburg. In my head I was set on the idea that everyone was going out, for better or for worse. That was the decision."

*"It went, I'm in, I'm in, I'm in . . . I'm out." When it was fire mar-*shal Devin Patel's turn to choose, he'd opted not to join the group going back to the monastery. Their decision to return to Tassajara alone when the

professionals had told them to evacuate had struck him as rash, perhaps even foolish.

As he left Ashes Corner after the five turned back, everything about his own decision felt solid. Devin felt calm, centered, and eager for some rest. His mother, whom he'd called daily to reassure, would be overjoyed to learn that he was leaving the forest. He could spend time with his girlfriend. They could take a break together and make up for the nearly three weeks they'd spent apart since the earlier evacuation, tough on a new relationship.

Of everyone on the core team, Devin felt most connected to Shundo. As former fire marshal, he was helpful and supportive when Devin had questions about equipment or protocols. Both had spoken up in support of Stuart in the hasty preevacuation meeting in the stone office. Now, listening to Shundo say he was driving on toward Jamesburg over the radio, Devin sensed a continuing alignment.

All the time he'd been on the core team during the lead-up to the fire, he'd perceived himself slightly apart from the group, closer to the rest of the students, who didn't have the authority or visibility that staff members did at Tassajara. He'd never shared what he saw as the prevailing headstrong attitude: They did it in 1977. We can do it now! Though Abbot Steve was a compassionate, gentle leader, and Devin never felt discounted by the group, every member of the core team was a priest but him. They'd dedicated their lives to Zen practice and, by extension, to Tassajara. They'd all expressed a wish to stay at Tassajara no matter what. Devin had often found himself being the voice of caution in meetings, reminding everyone that no building was worth anyone getting hurt or, worse, killed. He didn't actually think Tassajara would burn. "And I had this idea that if it did, good things would come of it," Devin said later. Like a proliferation of wildflowers after a fire, those who loved Tassajara would come forth, band together, and build it again.

More than a year after the fire, Devin told me that he saw the turnaround moment on the ridge as "the final narrowing down to the real core group." He said his decision still felt as right as it had on the ridge. "There was no consideration. It was instantaneous. I still don't feel like it was even a choice." The rest of the drive out was less tense, but mixed emotions swirled around inside the car: relief to be leaving, confusion about the split-off, concern for those returning, fear, awe, love. Such a mélange of feelings was hard to put into words. Perhaps Monkeybat said it best, letting out an occasional piercing meow.

"Bring dinner," Leslie James had told David. She didn't have supplies to feed twenty-some Tassajara evacuees at Jamesburg.

When David called just before six p.m. on July 9 and said they were all leaving Tassajara, Leslie was understandably thrown. She'd been present at a meeting with Abbot Steve and the core team shortly after the abbot's arrival, where they'd gone around the room and each had affirmed a willingness to stay. She recalled Abbot Steve saying that he couldn't imagine a situation in which he would leave Tassajara unattended. What had happened to cause such a shift?

But Leslie is not the kind of person who needs to understand why something has happened in order to see what needs doing in the present moment. She has a rare designation—she is not a priest, but she has received Dharma transmission. She doesn't wear brown robes—hers are green—but she is a fully acknowledged senior teacher, in a lineage of transmitted understanding that can be traced all the way back to the Buddha.

There would be time later to find out what had happened. First, Leslie needed to find something to feed the evacuees when they arrived, because she had a feeling they'd forget to bring food. She also needed to call neighbors to round up places for them to spend the night.

By seven thirty p.m., there was another crisis unfolding in front of the Jamesburg house. A California Highway Patrol (CHP) officer had parked his car across the road and was stopping residents on their way back from a community meeting with fire officials and refusing to allow them to return home.

The locals argued with the officer. They hadn't been given any kind of warning. Some of them had left children and animals at home. One resident (and mother) was so irate about the closure that she ended up in handcuffs.

While Leslie was outside, watching the cars back up on the road and soothing distressed neighbors, the convoy from Tassajara pulled in from the other direction. As the daylight dimmed, seventeen people—fourteen residents, plus Stuart, his girlfriend, and Kim Leigh—stumbled from the vehicles, hungry, tired, in a kaleidoscope of emotional states. They retreated into the Jamesburg house, instinctively avoiding the drama out front.

Eventually, the local volunteer fire department stepped in to help sort things out, and the CHP officer realized he'd established the roadblock in the wrong place. He moved his patrol car down the road to the Los Padres National Forest boundary. The neighbors drove home as the last light drained from the sky, and all was quiet again in Jamesburg. At least outside.

Inside the house, Leslie made sure that residents whose fretting parents had called—like Devin's mother, who'd already seen a post about the evacuation on *Sitting with Fire*—called their parents back. A mother of two adult children herself, Leslie knew the anguish of a parent's worry. Over a cobbled-together pasta dinner, the evacuees tried to relate what had happened that afternoon. There wasn't one coherent story to tell. It was more like a dozen people working on a puzzle, everyone reaching for pieces and putting them in where they saw a match. Some gaps persisted, and some pieces couldn't be found.

Stuart and his girlfriend stuck around for a while. "He was very calm and contained, but he was pretty upset," Leslie recalled shortly after the fire in a videotaped interview for a Zen Center documentary, *Sitting with Fire,* named after the blog. Stuart hadn't left Jamesburg yet when David called from Tassajara to say they'd made it back safely, and they'd been thinking, maybe five people might not be enough: Would any of the evacuees be willing to return to Tassajara? Maybe sneak back in during the night, as residents did in 1977?

Leslie relayed the question to the people gathered in her living room, sitting on the furniture and cushions on the floor. The question highlighted the bleak fact that five people couldn't cover all of Tassajara effectively and maybe not safely. But to go back in now was also dangerous, and illegal.

"Are they serious?"

"This is crazy!"

"First they won't let me go with them. Now they want me to go back?"

Former firefighter Kim Leigh, who'd stood on the hogback with Stuart before the fire captain decided to pull them all out, stayed quiet but felt a twinge inside, an urge to grab his pack, sneak back down the road, and join the five who'd returned. "I knew from my own experience fighting fires that you had to have an unfaltering sense of concern and responsibility. They did. They were completely together, completely unified."

The group in Jamesburg was unified, too. Everyone who'd evacuated—including, ultimately, Leigh—agreed that they wouldn't return to Tassajara without permission from the fire service, even if it meant that for the time being, the five at Tassajara would be there alone. Leslie reported this to David over the phone and told him that Robert Thomas and Greg Fain, president and treasurer of Zen Center, were on their way from San Francisco now, intending to drive in to Tassajara.

Just as Stuart didn't know how dependent he'd been on the hope for backup until that hope was extinguished, some evacuees realized how much anxiety they'd been carrying around only when they set foot in Jamesburg and felt it shed from their muscles like snow from a roof in the sun. When you're in the middle of something, you're just in the middle of it. It's when the environment or circumstances change that you become aware: Oh, that was fear I felt.

Zazen grounds you in your experience. My own teacher often calls zazen "total dynamic activity." It may not look like much is happening, but *everything* is happening—breath, posture, thoughts, sensations, a quality of attention that is unlimited and alive. Since June, the residents had had little time for formal zazen. Many of them had hardly entered the zendo since the fire preparations began. It was all they could do to have several minutes of silence at the start of work meeting in the dining room and a short service after. Fire marshal Devin Patel wished that they hadn't dropped the meditation schedule and the forms of practice so completely. "It would have been great to have a Dharma talk, or meet in the zendo," he told me.

But actually, the residents never stopped doing zazen—even though they weren't in the zendo, wearing robes. Their zazen moved from the zendo to the bare paths and the rooftops wet with Dharma Rain.

After a while, Stuart said good-bye to the group at Jamesburg. He had to drive his girlfriend home, try to get some sleep, and report back to work the next morning at his station.

"I'm just so glad you're all out," he told them. "You did some great work down there, and you're safe now."

*Shortly after the evacuees arrived in Jamesburg, Zen Center pres*ident Robert Thomas appeared, after driving down from City Center with Sonja Gardenswartz—who had evacuated, unhappily, on June 25—and Simon Moyes, one of the four former residents who'd arrived in the middle of the confusion of that first resident evacuation. Moyes had spearheaded the engineering of Dharma Rain, then left Tassajara, intending to return after attending a wedding.

Thomas already knew that some people in the evacuation convoy had turned around and gone back to Tassajara; Leslie had called his cell phone to tell him. But to his surprise, people in Jamesburg asked him what had happened. Most had little idea, since they weren't among the core group that had met in the stone office. Nor did they know how those who went back had come to their decision. They wanted to know, Did the request for five to return come from City Center? Did Abbot Haller talk them into going back?

Thomas didn't know, but he intended to try to get to Tassajara. He wasn't sure what he would do there, exactly. He'd had no firefighting training. But as president of Zen Center, and as someone who'd lived at Tassajara, he felt he had to be there.

In his interview for the *Sitting with Fire* documentary, Thomas spoke of

Tassajara as a sort of headwaters: "It became a reference point for my life, for every moment of my life." He'd gone there a confused young man and found himself being turned toward a different way of being, not quite by his own will. For the then thirty-four-year-old, disaffected Thomas, this was a new sensation. After days tending to kerosene lanterns during the work period between guest season and the monastic training period, he'd decided Zen practice wasn't his cup of tea. But as Thomas was leaving Tassajara, a priest stopped him on the path, bowed, and thanked him for his efforts. Though Thomas didn't know it at the time, that priest was Sojun Mel Weitsman, then an abbot of Zen Center. And the simple gesture of acknowledgment changed Thomas's life. A few footsteps later, he knew he'd be back. He eventually spent six years at Tassajara. He met his wife there.

Shortly after Thomas's arrival in Jamesburg on July 9, the phone rang. It was Abbot Steve, calling from the stone office. "We've been talking here, and we don't think you should come in to Tassajara," he told Thomas. "You haven't had fire training. For your safety, everyone's safety, it would be better if you didn't come down."

The room had hushed. People who knew it was the abbot on the line wanted to hear Thomas's side of the conversation.

"I appreciate your concern," said Thomas, "but I'm coming in. I'm just stopping in here at Jamesburg. I'm coming in to Tassajara." As Zen Center's president, Thomas wasn't looking for the abbot's permission. "I think I had a lot of force behind my voice," Thomas told me later. "Maybe Steve felt that."

In a tense telephone conference call a few days before, Thomas had pushed Abbot Steve and other senior members of Zen Center's leadership to ponder some difficult questions: What exactly are we doing here? Are we asking people to fight the fire? And if so, what if the fire comes and somebody dies? He'd been assured that the safety of the students was the first priority, that they'd been told repeatedly that Tassajara could be defended, and they had a place to take shelter if necessary.

"I said, 'We can't be asking people to risk their lives to save Tassajara,'" Thomas remembered. "'I hope that's what we're saying here.'"

To Thomas's relief, everyone on the call agreed: Clearly, no one should risk his or her life for Tassajara.

Abbot Steve talked Thomas into waiting to drive in until they could check fire conditions on the road. Thomas promised he'd stay in Jamesburg until they called with an update.

Earlier that evening, even before the convoy had pulled out of the parking lot at Tassajara, Chris Slymon had posted news of the evacuation on *Sitting with Fire*: "We do not know how long Tassajara will remain empty but the current red flag warning does not end for a couple of days. Fire crews have told us of strong winds at the ridge. These winds together with the extreme temperatures and little or no recovery in humidity overnight produce ideal conditions for the fire to move faster than we had hoped . . . We appreciate that this news may cause concern but please do not call the Tassajara or Jamesburg numbers as we need the phones."

When the convoy arrived at Jamesburg, its passengers startled and confused by the turnaround on the road, Slymon didn't post an update. But someone else put the word out in an anonymous comment on the blog around nine p.m. that night: "For those of you who don't know . . . There are 5 people still inside Tassajara. The last car turned around and decided to stay."

Within the hour, a Zen student who had attended a meeting about the evacuation at City Center in San Francisco responded with an attempt to allay fears. He reminded blog readers of the fire preparations that residents had completed and the training they'd received—and noted that "these are long-term, senior practitioners making these decisions." But the word was out: Five people had gone back in to Tassajara in the midst of an evacuation just as the fire was heating up and drawing close. Only two were named—the abbot and the director. Worried friends and family responded with frustrated posts like this one: "If I cannot find out where my son is another way very soon, rest assured, I WILL call. PLEASE contact the families of those who stayed, & tell the evacuees to call home."

. . .

*Back in the stone office, the five who'd returned to Tassajara iden-*tified their immediate priorities and established a schedule for night patrols. It quickly became clear that they would be spread thin. "I remember making the recommendation that we keep ourselves in the central area, given how far the flats is. It would be so easy to get cut off," Colin told me later.

After David called Jamesburg to float the possibility of a few more able-bodied residents sneaking back down the road, Abbot Steve called Abbot Haller. The five also discussed the complex web of conditions that had led to Stuart's sudden push for evacuation and their own decision to return. "Stuart didn't want to see anyone get hurt. He had made a decision about the twenty-two of us that were here," David told me later. While the abbot shared Stuart's concern for the residents' safety, "Steve made a decision about the total well-being of Zen Center. He was holding a larger picture."

They ate well that evening, a dinner planned for four times as many people: pasta with avocado, cherry tomatoes, and asparagus, and strawberry shortcake for dessert. The mood was purposeful as they set about wrapping the stone office door and windows with leftover Firezat. They'd discovered by then that only one of the two satellite lines switched earlier that day was actually operational, and David didn't know what lay ahead of them, but in some ways it didn't matter. What mattered was that they had not abandoned Tassajara. He felt a sense of relief, a communion with the unknown. Making this effort felt right. He had faith in their ability to be fully present for whatever showed up.

That didn't mean there weren't also moments of great doubt.

For David, one such moment came while on patrol, standing on the bridge over the creek bed named for Tom Cabarga—a 1977 resident who foresaw the potential for the then-unnamed stream that flows past the zendo to surge to flood levels the winter after that year's wildfire. It was just past dark, around nine o'clock, when David looked up Cabarga Creek and spotted a mountain of flame through the trees.

At approximately the same time, Colin was up the road at Lime Point, watching the fireworks below. It glowed a beautiful, terrible orange, as if the sunset had spilled from the sky into the valley. And this upside-down sunset sounded like a blast furnace.

"This line from *Jaws* came into my mind," he recalled later. "It's the first time Roy Scheider sees the shark. He's so stunned he backs into where the captain is and says, 'You're gonna need a bigger boat.'" We're no match for this fire, Colin thought. We don't stand a chance. "But we're trapped at that point. The one thing they hammered into us over and over again was, When it gets down to it, don't get on the road. If you get trapped in a chimney, you're burned. We'd had our chance to leave."

An hour later, Mako and Graham drove less than a mile up the road on patrol before they had to turn around because the surrounding mountains looked like active volcanoes, spouting flames. They called Jamesburg to tell Thomas: Do not come in over the road tonight.

Abbot Steve called his wife, Lane Olson, after dinner. As concisely as he could, he told her about the day's unexpected events. Ever since Abbot Steve had arrived at Tassajara, he'd been updating her on their preparations. And she'd been following the blog.

When I spoke with Olson months after the fire, she described her husband as "an amazingly capable person. He's just so stable. It's that Mennonite farmer background. He never panics." She recalled how he and his brothers told gruesome stories of near-miss accidents on the farm. Their father had lost part of two fingers, and a younger brother had to extract his own foot from under a piece of heavy machinery. Once, worn out from a day's work, Abbot Steve fell asleep while driving and woke up as his brother jerked the wheel. The car spun around several times before they regained control and continued down the road, hearts pounding but unharmed. "Farmers are a lot closer to death than the rest of us," said Olson.

So are Zen students, Olson knew, a practitioner herself. *Everything changes:* Every living thing must also die. *Everything is connected:* Life and death are completely intertwined, never separate. *Pay attention*.

Given her confidence in her husband—and her trust that whatever decisions he made were the best decisions in the moment—Olson wasn't terribly worried. It wasn't until she checked *Sitting with Fire* and read the concerns others were voicing that she started to get a sense of the very real danger and to wonder, Are they safe? Is this going to be okay?

Abbot Steve's patrol shift was from three a.m. to seven a.m., so after talking to Olson, he went to bed and tried to sleep a little. Now that they numbered only five, he would be without a partner. He awoke a few hours later. In the hazy, half-moon, middle-of-the-night darkness, he made several trips up the road, driving beyond the bathtub between Lime Point and Ashes Corner. "At that point, I could see the whole face of the mountain in front of me was on fire," he said later. "And down below Lime Point—quite a ways down—was in flames. Then the wind shifted, and I felt a hot wind and thought I had better turn around." Because they'd seen how it could linger in an area for days, he thought the fire might still be a couple of days away from Tassajara, but that it had probably crossed the road farther up.

He went up the road again just after sunrise, around six a.m. on July 10. He drove as far as Lime Point. He thought he saw a fog bank to the west, and the sky was peaceful, a muted watercolor of cloud and smoke and dawning light. The airtankers and helicopters weren't flying yet; it was pleasantly, surprisingly quiet. "Fire was just down the slope from Lime Point, below the road, fifty yards down. It still hadn't crossed over into the Cabarga Creek watershed," he told me.

But before Abbot Steve could update Thomas in Jamesburg to say he still didn't recommend traveling on the road, David radioed from his communications post in the stone office.

"They can't get in. There's a CHP officer at the forest boundary. He's got a gun, and he says no one is going down the road."

Ten

RING OF FLAME

A patch-robed monk is like a snowflake in a red-hot furnace.

—*Blue Cliff Record,* CASE 69

Thursday, July 10, nineteen days after the lightning strikes

Robert Thomas woke around four a.m. on the floor in the living room at Jamesburg, having slept maybe four hours. His eyes felt gritty, his limbs stiff, his mind full. The night before, after he'd gotten word from Tassajara that there were flames near the road and he shouldn't attempt to drive it, he'd spent a long time talking with Leslie James and a few others, sifting through the options. The house was quiet and they'd had to keep their voices low—most of the people who'd evacuated Tassajara that day had gone to bed early. It was still dark and quiet when Zen Center treasurer Greg Fain's watch alarm went off. Fain had arrived in Jamesburg around eleven p.m. the night before. Along with Thomas and two others, he'd planned to rise before daylight to try to make it over the road.

Leslie was awake, so she came out to the living room to talk with them before they left for Tassajara. "I think we had a longer conversation than we wanted to," Thomas told me later. "Light was starting to come at the edge of the sky, and I felt like we'd have a better chance if it was completely dark."

They talked about what they'd say if they got stopped. Thomas wanted to keep it friendly and low-key. They wouldn't say they were officers of San Francisco Zen Center or former residents of Tassajara. They weren't wearing robes or anything that identified them as priests. Fain's signature eyeglasses with thick black rims and white cowboy hat made him look more Buddy Holly Meets the Lone Ranger than monk.

Fain and Thomas left Jamesburg at approximately four thirty a.m. It would be just the two of them. The others had decided not to go. They drove about three and a half miles up Tassajara Road before they got blasted by a spotlight on a CHP vehicle parked horizontally in front of the Los Padres National Forest boundary.

"Stop!" an officer's voice boomed. "Stop your vehicle!"

They stopped, got out, and walked toward the officer, who had stepped out of his cruiser with a hand on his pistol, as if to remind them that whatever their business was, he had the final say.

Instinctively, they put their hands up to show that they were empty. "We're just trying to get back to Tassajara," said Thomas, squinting in the spotlight's glare, trying to step out of it, though he couldn't. It seemed to cover everything.

"Road's closed." The officer was alert, awake, his voice crisp and clear. "Nobody's getting by me."

Fain tried then: "Officer, we really need to get to Tassajara. We left and now we're just trying to go back." It was true, if slightly slanted. Neither Thomas nor Fain had lived at Tassajara for several years. But Fain had helped install Dharma Rain in June before he had to return to the city to attend to Zen Center's finances.

The officer shook his head. There wasn't a flicker of interest in his face. "You're not going in, guys."

"We just want to—"

"Nope. Turn your vehicle around and go home. We're not having a conversation about this."

Their faces pale and white in the spotlight, Thomas and Fain looked at each other, bewildered, for what seemed like a long time. Then they turned around and went back to their car. "I remember feeling kind of small and helpless," Thomas told me. "But anything we would have said wouldn't have worked with this guy. As far as he was concerned, it was over before it started."

Day finished shrugging off night as they retraced their route to Jamesburg. Fain stewed behind the wheel, struggling to accept the fact that they weren't going to get into Tassajara, that five people, including the abbot, were alone down there.

"Well, I guess that gets us off the hook," said Thomas, trying to inject some levity to counter their dejected mood.

Much as he was disappointed, Thomas found himself accepting the situation. "We'd spent so much time the night before deliberating. Then we get there and there's really nothing to talk about. It's just not an option." The truth was, he didn't know how helpful he could have been in Tassajara. "Part of me just felt like I was doing what I should be doing," he told me later. "But another part of me didn't know why I was doing that, or that I could offer much."

When the officer said no, those divisions fell away. It's clear now, Thomas told himself, I'm going to support Tassajara from Jamesburg.

*Shundo woke up in Jamesburg just as Fain and Thomas were re*turning. Fain wanted to get back to the city—with Zen Center's revenue from Tassajara choked off by the fire, he had work to do as treasurer. Shundo arranged to ride with Fain back to San Francisco.

The night before, after the Jamesburg house grew quiet, Shundo had mulled over the evacuation, how what happened seemed like random chance but also bore the familiar imprint of his personality. He wasn't one to question authority. It had never occurred to him that when final evacuation orders came, someone might stand up and say no.

Looking back, Shundo felt he would have made the same decision to carry on even if he'd participated in the conversation at Ashes Corner, but it was hard to say for sure. If he'd ridden with Graham and Mako, that might have shifted his inclination to follow Stuart's lead. Instead, Stuart had thanked Shundo in Jamesburg for backing him up.

When David had called Jamesburg to ask whether some people would be willing to come back in, Shundo had had another chance to return. He hadn't taken it. "If you wanted to have a strong response or formed group, then we should have had a different thing happening at Ashes Corner, not just some people deciding to go back in," Shundo said, describing his thinking at that moment. Shundo had chosen not to return to Tassajara, yet he knew five people was not enough. Never mind fighting fire, how were they going to manage being up all night and all day scouting and patrolling?

Before Shundo left Jamesburg the morning after the evacuation, he talked with Jack Froggatt, who stopped by to brief Jamesburg on current conditions. "He repeated the likely weather, which made everything worse, said there were fires at three places on the east side of the road now, and said it would be four days minimum before anyone went in. I resigned myself to going back to the city," Shundo wrote in his journal.

They left Jamesburg around ten a.m. The field at the base of Tassajara Road had been converted into a helibase. "It looked like a circus or fair setup, with a big sign at the gate," Shundo told me, and helicopters and fire vehicles parked here and there. As they headed west toward Carmel Valley Village, they saw signs everywhere, handwritten expressions of gratitude for the firefighters tacked to trees and telephone poles.

Eventually they descended into the Salinas Valley's lush growing fields dotted with migrant workers, then merged into the unruly stream of freeway traffic. A few hours later they arrived in San Francisco, and Shundo felt glad to be in the fog zone for once.

He got to City Center at lunchtime and was bombarded with questions.

"There was so much relief to hear what was going on. That's when I really sensed how much people felt excluded. For people in the city, it was all playing out in their imaginations." Often, with limited information, they imagined the worst.

Shundo had been one of a select few inside events at Tassajara. But now, back in the Bay Area fog belt, he was also outside. And he had to imagine, to worry.

It was Thursday, July 10, nearly three weeks since the June lightning strikes. The red flag warning issued by the Monterey Bay office of the National Weather Service (NWS) had predicted that a ridge of high pressure would build over California, that low daytime humidity and poor overnight moisture recoveries in the region, combined with gusty winds, would create "explosive fire growth potential."

But by the morning of July 10, the fog approaching the Golden Gate Bridge in San Francisco was also drifting onshore farther south, in Monterey Bay, in a more typical summer pattern, when spiking temperatures suck cool, moist marine air inland at lower elevations. Weather observers in both coastal Monterey and the interior Salinas Valley noted the presence of fog and a temperature dip in their July 10 daily logs. Abbot Steve felt the fog's cooling influence when he drove up Tassajara Road on his morning patrol.

Forecasters at the national Storm Prediction Center and local NWS offices, and incident meteorologists and fire behavior analysts in fire camps, make their best effort to predict weather and anticipate its potential effect on a fire. When meteorological warnings are missed, catastrophes happen. Firefighters can die because they didn't get a weather report.

"Weather is the wild card," says NWS forecaster Chris Cuoco in *Fire Wars,* a *NOVA* documentary. Cuoco knows well just how critical weather information can be on the fireline. In 1994, he sent out an urgent red flag warning that was never received by firefighters on the South Canyon fire in Colorado. Winds created a chimney effect and fourteen young people died because they were someplace they probably would not have been had they heard the forecast.

"We have National Weather Service personnel out there with their trucks and equipment on fires now, people with PhDs. And these guys are usually right," Stuart told me. Though relative humidity did drop into the single digits on July 10, the predicted high winds and temperatures that played so heavily in Stuart's decision to evacuate Tassajara never materialized over the Santa Lucia Mountains. For the first time in days, the weather turned in the firefighters' favor.

With Dharma Rain running—and people around the world visualizing the monastery bathed in a protective mist—Tassajara itself felt more like a rain forest than a sauna. For now, the threat of severe weather conditions had died down, but the intense heat of the past few days had helped the fire gain momentum. It continued moving toward Tassajara, burning through the dried-out forest with nothing to stop it—no broad river, no rain. Cooler conditions may slow a fire, but they don't put it out.

The names of the five inside Tassajara were announced on the Zen Center's Web site and the *Sitting with Fire* blog on the morning of July 10. Slymon also posted news that the fire was approaching the road "along a broad front" but hadn't yet reached Tassajara. "They do not plan to fight the fire and they are receiving a steady flow of requests not to try to do anything heroic," he wrote.

So what did it mean, not to try to do anything heroic? In the weeks leading up to the fire at Tassajara, even as the residents drilled and learned to handle the hoses, the assumption was always that they wouldn't engage the fire directly. They'd keep the pumps running and the buildings wet and put out spot fires where they could, but they wouldn't try to stand up to a forest fire. They'd size up flames they could do something about and flames they ought not get in the way of and act accordingly. But simply being willing to put themselves where no firefighters would seemed a courageous leap to many.

Slymon's early morning post on *Sitting with Fire* on July 10 drew dozens of comments instead of the usual handful. One of the first came from Jane Hirshfield. She'd left Tassajara in the second evacuation at the end of June after offering her experience in the 1977 Marble Cone fire to guide the fire preparation efforts. Now, with the fire closing in on Tassajara, in the midst of orchestrating her elderly mother's move out of the New York City apartment she'd lived in for forty-six years, Jane checked the blog every spare minute from her home near San Francisco. "There was a radar beam between my heart and that canyon."

About an hour after Slymon's morning update, Jane posted a message encouraging readers of *Sitting with Fire* to get on the phone and call their senators, representatives, anyone who might be able to get resources to Tassajara. "I'd also like to say (perhaps going out on a limb here) something I am not hearing articulated—support for the decision of the five to return. I think their presence makes much more likely that further assistance will come from CAL FIRE, and I think their going back in to Tassajara is nothing short of awesome. . . . I trust their judgment, and I trust that the safety zones at Tassajara are well sufficient to keep them free of harm."

The night before, after word had gone out that everyone had evacuated, the phone had started ringing at Jane's house—those who'd been there in 1977, now in their fifties and sixties, were calling to say, Did you hear? Tassajara's empty! Jane spoke to Ted Marshall, the resident fire chief at Tassajara and her partner at the time of the Marble Cone fire. If it weren't for the fact that Marshall had had a recent heart attack, he'd have gone down to Tassajara himself. "A howl went up in many hearts," Jane said later. "I thought Tassajara would be lost."

When Jane opened her laptop on the morning of July 10 to see what news it held, what relief, what gratitude, she felt upon seeing that five had gone back. She was also stunned. Five? Only five? That's not enough! She wasn't surprised, however, to find out who they were. Each of those five would have been on her list if she'd been charged with deciding who stayed, who went. And not because she'd seen them fight fire before and trusted their expertise.

She'd simply watched the four who were there at the start step forward and ask, What's actually happening here? How can I respond? They didn't need to know all the answers to act. Each had shown a suppleness of mind, learned on the meditation cushion, that could be brought to bear on any circumstance.

It was this suppleness, Jane suspected, that had motivated them to turn back. "It's a quality of being so present, so fully in the moment, that mammalian self-concern simply vanishes. You're not worried about yourself. You're too busy being part of the moment, taking care of it, responding to it. That's not exactly courage, it's something else."

Over the course of the morning, Jane monitored *Sitting with Fire*. Blog readers chimed in with encouraging words and wishes for the safety and well-being of Tassajara and the small group of people protecting it. Many of the posts came from former students, guests, and members of affiliated Zen communities. Some who posted, however, like Mike Morales, had heard of Tassajara only at the start of the fire, from media coverage.

Morales, former firefighter and the founder of *Firefighter Blog*, had steadily voiced concerns about whether adequate resources had been assigned to the Basin Complex fire. He'd been watching the situation at Tassajara, too, and reading *Sitting with Fire*.

In the late morning of July 10, Morales posted an entry on his own blog entitled "The Battle for Tassajara Hot Springs." Unless the weather changed unexpectedly, he speculated, the five remaining at Tassajara could expect the fire to test their preparations. "The fire looks to be within .5 mile or closer to them at the moment. I don't want to second-guess Basin Complex fire command and I won't, but it seems to me this compound deserves some resources. The monks and other residents have cooperated fully with fire representatives and have prepared the grounds carefully, even under supervision to an extent. The Center serves as a spiritual center for many. The occupants are decent guardians of the land and need help."

Morales also made a prediction—later, he'd call it a challenge: "I personally believe the cavalry will come riding to the rescue before things really heat up."

Jane e-mailed Morales, asking if he had any contacts in active fire service who might be sympathetic to Tassajara's situation. She wouldn't have called preparing for the fire a "battle," but she agreed with Morales's prediction that help was on the horizon. Based on her experience in 1977, she had no reason to doubt that. But she also wanted to make sure help arrived.

You didn't just sit around waiting to be rescued. You did everything you could to be rescue-worthy. The cavalry might ride past Tassajara if it didn't stand a chance. "If this happens," she'd told the residents in June, meaning if Tassajara was to be saved, "it will happen because we do it."

At half past five in the morning on July 10, Mako lay in bed for a moment after waking, imagining she could hear the wake-up bell. Sometimes the creek offered a jangling rattle that sounded just like it, or a knock that could be mistaken for the mallet striking the wooden han outside the zendo, as if it had absorbed the sounds of the valley and could play them back.

But it wasn't the wake-up bell. There was no one at Tassajara to ring it. They'd gone from eighty-something to twenty-something to just five people, with the last drop a precipitous one. No one who remained needed the bell to wake up, if they'd slept at all.

If she listened closely, she could detect something that wasn't creek sound: Dharma Rain, draping a watery veil over the rooftop. They'd decided to run the system all night. And she heard the engine throttle of the five-gallon Mark 3 portable pump serving as a backup for the malfunctioning permanent pump near the stone rooms and as a supplement to the pool pump.

The head cook yawned herself awake, stretching her limbs. Her wrists had hurt before the fire ever started, from washing and lifting large pots. She had cramps in her feet and calves, the beginnings of plantar fasciitis. Her body needed a break, and instead she kept asking it to do more.

Graham stirred but didn't open his eyes. Mako swung her legs over the side of the bed and shivered when the soles of her feet hit the cold slate floor. She got dressed, gray pants and a brown short-sleeved T-shirt, and slipped into her clogs on the porch. Because they'd run the sprinklers continuously since the prior evening, the valley was damp, misty, even cool. Mako pulled on a sweater and walked to the kitchen to make everyone breakfast.

The skies behind Flag Rock and Hawk Mountain no longer looked like volcanoes as they had the night before. Backlit by the rising sun, the peaks were tinged with a mellow reddish gold. It would be another couple of hours before the sun climbed over them and poured into the valley, heating everything up. Maybe it was already waking the fire.

She flipped on the light in the kitchen, smelling metal, wood, spice, grain, and the trace of something human, the yeast of bodies working in collective effort. During the winter interim, when there might be just a handful of people on retreat at Tassajara, she and Graham usually left to visit one of their families. She couldn't remember ever being at Tassajara when there were so few people here, or being the only woman. It felt odd—not pleasant or unpleasant, just peculiar.

She poured some milk into a stainless steel pitcher and started washing fruit to make a smoothie. She heated water for tea and coffee. She found some cereal in the upper shack and scooped it into wide plastic bowls to set out for their breakfast. Ordinarily cold cereal was an infrequent treat at Tassajara, but they'd been eating a lot of it since the start of the fires.

In his *Instructions for the Zen Cook,* Eihei Dōgen quotes an old expression, "The mouth of a monk is like an oven," and tells his disciples to remember this well. An oven makes no distinction between what goes into it, simple or complex, prepared with common or rare ingredients. It accepts everything equally. Elsewhere, Dōgen introduced the similar teaching of the cultivation of "parental mind": an attitude of care and concern for everything one encounters—appetizing or unappealing—akin to a parent's tenderness toward a child.

It's called parental mind, but anyone can access it, as Mako did when her parents' marriage ended. Helping her mother navigate the divorce, Mako began to feel compassion for the Japanese woman who'd left her culture and country and moved to America, changed her name to Patricia, and given her kids Western names, but who had never formally learned English. It was then that Mako changed her own given name, Lisa Jane Voelkel, and took her mother's Japanese name, Masami, shortened to Mako, which means "True Grace."

Nowadays Mako didn't see her mother much, once a year at most. They'd traveled to Japan together a few years back. While Mako wanted to visit temples and be fitted for priest robes, her mother wanted to shop. Patricia Voelkel dreamed her daughter might be a doctor or professor. Instead, she was a thirty-six-year-old monk, childless, with mostly unused degrees and a few boxes of possessions. There wasn't much overlap in their lives. At the moment, her mother was in Japan. Mako hadn't told her about the fire, not wanting to alarm her.

Mako's mother had renounced many of the outward markers of her identity when she married Mako's American father. Later, Mako recalled, her mother had felt deprived and cheated; she'd mourned the identity as something lost. But practice had showed Mako that the more she clung to a sense of self as something to guard and protect, the more she felt obstructed. Happiness came in loosening your grip, letting your solid identity—your expectations and assumptions about who you are—go into the oven's mouth and burn up in the fire of practice.

Or in a wildfire.

Breakfast was ready. Mako carried what she could to the stone office. The fire could be anywhere, she thought. Right now flames could be flickering up the trunks of trees. Or it could slow down again and hang out nearby for three more days. Mako didn't think it would. She got on the walkie-talkie and called everyone to take this opportunity to eat what the warmth and light of the sun and the cool, damp earth had together made. Because who knew when the next meal would be.

The morning might have felt cool to Mako, but when the five gathered for breakfast in the stone office, it was already approaching 80 degrees Fahrenheit up on Chews Ridge. Typically, it is pleasantly cool in the early hours during the summer. The monks often wear long-sleeved layers until midmorning.

The group discussed their priorities for the morning as they ate, then dispersed around Tassajara, taking care of whatever needed attention. Mako hiked up the hogback to scout the fire. Colin loaded up a garden cart with refueling supplies and tools and covered it with Firezat so they could wheel it around Tassajara to the various pumps. "We had fifteen gallons of gas in there," he told me later. "That would have been colorful if the cart caught fire." Graham checked the fuel levels on the pumps, topped them off where needed, and rechecked his backup supply of extra parts and tools in case any part of Dharma Rain or one of the pumps malfunctioned. Abbot Steve lay down to rest, as he'd just come off patrol. David checked their supplies in the stone office, made calls, and retrieved the latest information on the fire.

Overnight, the fire had gained a little more than 400 acres, bringing the total acres burned to 90,114. There were still nearly a thousand firefighting personnel on the east zone—the majority of them from CAL FIRE. The fire was definitely not sleeping in. Crews worked to contain a spot fire outside the control lines—the "big box" fire managers had drawn around the Basin Complex—just a few miles south of Tassajara. The morning report from the incident management team noted more spotting, "torching" trees, and "slope-driven runs"—signs of active fire behavior, unusual during cool morning hours—and aggressive fire spread toward Tassajara Road.

There was fire in pretty much every direction except directly east of Tassajara, so the five still couldn't be sure from which orientation it would come. All they could do was continue what they'd been doing for weeks: stay ready. Not for a certain kind of fire, a fire they could anticipate, but for whatever kind of fire showed up.

A feeling prevailed of battening down the hatches on a vessel tacking into rough weather. Even the birds were quiet—having either hunkered down or, in the case of the canyon wren pair nesting in the eaves of the founder's hall, left their nests. The group at Tassajara didn't fret because there were only five of them, though it was clear now that's all there would be for a while. They just did the next thing and the next thing, continuously. They did what they could and didn't dwell on what they couldn't.

Around eleven a.m., Mako and Colin hiked up the Overlook Trail, which loops up and around the steep backside of Tassajara, to scout the fire. The day before, a few people had carved out the beginnings of a fireline up there, but the trail was still narrow most of the way and laced with poison oak. The wind blew strong but indecisive—angling the July-dry grasses covering the slope one way, stopping abruptly as if taking a breath, then flattening them in the complete opposite direction. A dark plume of smoke churned above Flag Rock, directly across the Tassajara valley from where they stood.

Mako took a quick video. Playing it back for me later, Colin noted the sound of the portable Mark 3 pumps beneath the gusting wind and remembered how pervasive the sound had become. In the moment, he hardly noticed it. His attention was focused on the heat and the crazy wind, the fire sucking itself into the valley. He remembered the look on Stuart's face when he talked about the forecasted wind speeds as a turbo engine for the fire.

The plume over Flag Rock shifted as they watched, from purple to charcoal gray to black and back to purple again. It was not one color but all of those colors, boiling together. They'd already seen another dark plume to the northwest, close to the summit of the Tony Trail. Normally, Lime Point is an obvious white band in the road from the Overlook, but they couldn't even see it. The road was muzzled in smoke. Beyond that veil of smoke and farther up Tassajara Road, MIRA observatory's caretaker Ivan Eberle was on his roof around then, photographing four-hundred-foot-tall flames advancing toward MIRA despite 10–15 mph headwinds.

On the Overlook Trail at Tassajara, the only place the sky wasn't full of the breath of fire was behind Mako and Colin, toward the Willow Creek area south of Tassajara.

"Mako, we should go—we don't want to get caught out here," said Colin.

"Okay." Mako dodged the poison oak as they descended the trail and emerged in a meadow just downstream from Tassajara, anchored by a tall old oak.

To get back to Tassajara, they crossed the creek on several large boulders set there by students. Sometimes in the spring the creek was so high that the rocks were submerged and you needed a walking stick to cross safely. The sticks were stacked for the taking against a tree on the Tassajara side. But they didn't need them anyway. The stepping-stones were well exposed, their tops dry, in the midsummer creek. They could step across them without even getting their feet wet. Their footsteps left prints in a fine layer of ash coating the stones.

*Around eleven thirty a.m., when Colin and Mako were on the Over*look, Abbot Steve woke from his nap and decided to drive up the road again for a look. At the Church Creek trailhead, about a mile from Tassajara, he was startled by flames spotting among the Coulter pines and scrub oaks, not very far from the road itself. The fire was much closer than he'd estimated just a few hours before. Ground squirrels, wood rats, and other rodents were hightailing it across the road in a rapid exodus from the burning area. Not wanting to get cut off, Abbot Steve turned his car around without getting out and hurried back to Tassajara.

According to Graham's watch, it was just before noon. He'd climbed up to the solar array after checking on the east end of Tassajara and observing the same wind patterns Mako and Colin had noted on the Overlook Trail: eerie reverses and ash drifting horizontally, sliding off the rooftops in sheets and eddying under the eaves. The wind was warm and weighted. From the hilltop where the solar panels slanted toward the sun, Graham saw black plumes behind the Overlook ridge. He got on his walkie-talkie. "Where is everyone?"

Mako responded first. "Colin and I are on our way to the stone office."

Abbot Steve also answered and described what he'd seen. "The fire is at the Church Creek trailhead. Looks like it might come down the road. I'm coming back now."

David said he was at his communications post in the stone office.

What a relief, everyone accounted for. But what Graham saw next, as he descended the steps from the solar array, stunned him. Where Mako and Colin had just been hiking, there was now a wall of fifty-foot flames dancing in every direction, cresting the ridge. Graham got back on his walkie-talkie and reported that they were surrounded, with the closest flames coming downhill behind the office, about three hundred feet from the creek.

It was twelve forty p.m., past lunchtime, though they hadn't had lunch. They scattered to restart the sprinklers and pumps from one end of Tassajara to the other. To allow the pool to replenish and to conserve fuel, they'd turned off Dharma Rain that morning, planning to run it as they had been, twice a day, to saturate the grounds. "For all we knew, it could have been another few days before the fire came in," Mako told me later. After returning to the central area, along with David and Colin, she started covering the wooden deck behind the stone office with leftover Firezat wrap. "I was thinking, This is our safe zone, and we better make it more safe. I'm there with the staple gun, *chika chika chik*."

But Colin disagreed. "We don't have time for this," he said, and left the stone office to suit up and station himself at the shop to protect the lumber and other building supplies, the propane and gasoline tanks. They had four hundred gallons of gasoline stored at the shop, which is built around a live sycamore tree, and four propane tanks holding a thousand gallons each. If the fire reached these combustibles, he didn't want to contemplate the consequences. After he'd left the Marines, he'd worked for a few years doing security at embassy construction sites, including in South Africa. It was during apartheid, and bombs were frequently detonated in shopping centers and restaurants. He had some sense of what it was like to feel an explosion rumble through the ground beneath your feet, and he didn't want to know that particular sensation more intimately. "I just fell back on, The shop is our number one priority," he told me later.

From the shop, Colin saw flames charging downslope behind the stone office. Over and over, they'd heard that fire ran uphill and crept down. But this fire wasn't doing what the firefighters had said it would. It was moving as if the best fuel were down in the canyon. He tried to warn the others over the radio, but the bandanna over his mouth muffled his words and no one understood him.

When Colin's transmission came through, Abbot Steve and Graham were out at the flats. They'd decided to walk out to the area to wet it down, but by the time they got there, balls of flame rolled downslope from the hogback. Flames chewed through the trees and spit out branches, which tumbled downhill in a daisy chain of fire.

Graham stood by the standpipe as Abbot Steve tried to sort out a confusion of hoses from the called-off activation. "I could see a quick-moving, rolling smoke ball, glowing orange, coming our way," Graham recalled later as we stood at the edge of the flats. "I started seeing flame through the branches, hearing the fire."

Residents had been told repeatedly by firefighters not to get too spread out or let themselves get isolated. Graham was well aware of the distance between the flats area, since he and Mako lived there together, and central Tassajara—a brisk five-minute walk he made several times a day. "We should get out of here," he said calmly but firmly.

Abbot Steve agreed. The two walked back toward the stone office as the skies clenched into fists of flame around them. Then Mako's voice broke over the radio, high and breathless—flames were blazing down both Hawk Mountain and Flag Rock.

. . .

She'd come around from the backside of the office just in time to see the fire reaching the two peaks opposite the office and to grab her camera.

In the video, dark clouds swim through an orange sky. Wind ruffles the shadows of trees. Flames swat at the cliffs surrounding Tassajara. From Hawk Mountain, where the radio tower and satellite antenna are, across the slope above the hill cabins to Flag Rock, all is fringed with a dragon spine of flame. "Wow, this is totally incredible," Mako breathed as she panned the camera. Her recorded voice is not so much fearful as full of wonder.

She didn't turn around to film the flames lapping down the hill toward the creek from the Overlook ridge where she and Colin had stood less than an hour earlier. Her video is only sixteen seconds long. Long enough to think: I should probably be doing something else.

The summer's elusive guest had finally arrived. They'd been waiting for this moment for almost three weeks, imagining scenarios, educating themselves, guessing which direction it would come from. But they'd never imagined there would be only five of them to meet it. And they hadn't imagined it would arrive on three sides simultaneously, plowing downhill as if trying to make up for lost time.

The surprise in Mako's voice, seeing the fire come so fiercely and from every direction, is clearly audible. But she had the presence of mind to pick up her camera to document the moment of the fire's arrival—and the presence of mind to put it down.

Inside the cocoon of the wrapped stone office, David's head ached from the smoke and a restless night spent sleeping on the floor in the office, to be near the phone. The two aspirin he'd taken hadn't kicked in yet. He'd spent the morning on patrol, making sure that nothing had been left vulnerable to floating embers during the previous day's rushed evacuation. Then he'd helped to wrap the office windows and moved flammable back porch furniture away from the walls. With images of the fire whirl video he'd watched at MIRA still fresh in his mind, he wanted their safe zone to be absolutely safe.

Every thirty minutes he'd checked the phone inside the office for new fire information. As flames crested the ridges surrounding Tassajara, David had called Jamesburg with an update. Stepping outside now, he saw himself that the fire was arriving not in one discrete front, but in a ring of flame. Like an *enso*—a circle drawn in one brushstroke that symbolizes enlightenment—inked with fire. Fire wasn't just "descending" on Tassajara, he wrote later, it was "converging" on it.

But the five people at Tassajara did not converge, circle up, or even talk about what they should do next. There wasn't a moment when they all stood together as they had in the emergency meeting in the stone office or huddled on the road, to collectively make a decision. Yet they had to make a decision, to either bunker in their safe zone as the fire passed through the valley or make a stand to try to defend Tassajara.

Here was another pivotal moment, from which so many possible outcomes could spin, the kind of moment that might be held up to the light afterward. If all goes well, it might inspire and amaze. But if something goes badly, it would be the precise moment people point to, saying, Here's where they made the wrong choice. Here's where if they hadn't done X, then Y would never have happened. A moment like the one five firefighters faced in the Esperanza fire.

The five Zen priests at Tassajara weren't in the habit of dividing choices into right or wrong, good or bad. They'd practiced seeing everything that happens as part of a continuous and always completely unified stream of events. Each moment flowing like the creek, from what came before into what comes next, all of time moving together.

The Greek philosopher Heraclitus said that you cannot step in the same river twice. A Zen master might add cheerfully: You cannot step in the same river because there is no river, there is no actual you. The river and you and your stepping are in a dynamic and interrelated state of constant change. Maybe it is the river that steps into you. Maybe there is only stepping, no one to step or thing to step into.

In Zen, you can't really make a "wrong" decision. But you can't make a "right" decision, either. You can only respond moment to moment in a way that feels the least harmful and deluded, the most compassionate and true.

Suzuki Roshi liked to quote a passage from Eihei Dōgen about *shoshaku jushaku,* Japanese for "one continuous mistake." In a talk from *Zen Mind, Beginner's Mind,* Suzuki Roshi explained that the words were meant to encourage: "According to Dōgen, one continuous mistake can also be Zen. A Zen master's life could be said to be so many years of *shoshaku jushaku*. This means so many years of one single-minded effort."

It's the effort that counts, Suzuki Roshi told whoever came to listen, the sincere commitment to wake up, wherever you are, moment by moment. No one can ask more of you.

As a ring of flame looped around Tassajara, David felt a palpable beat of hesitation, a flickering thought that maybe they'd gotten themselves in over their heads. But then, as individuals, and as a small sangha within the sangha, they acted. They made an effort. They moved toward a river of fire.

They didn't so much make a decision as manifest, collectively and without words, a mind already decided. They didn't need a decision tree or cost-benefit analysis or even a plan. They just got to work, doing something extraordinary with the mind they cultivated in their daily practices and activities. On another day, it might have been a bell that needed ringing, a soup that required stirring, a broom that needed picking up. At one o'clock on the afternoon of July 10, it happened to be a fire hose.

Eleven

MEETING FIRE

Fire is simply fire. It has no sense of morality, has no persona, does not wish to do good or bad, is neither deliberately enemy nor friend.

—DOUGLAS GANTENBEIN, *A Season of Fire*

Thursday, July 10, one p.m.

Nothing Mako had read when she was fire marshal prepared her for the actual experience of witnessing an advancing fire front. "It had this feeling of being ferocious and unrelenting and aggressive and just, you know, consuming," she told me later, making explosive gestures with her hands. The entire sky boiled above her head, a canopy of fire. Thirty-foot flames tore down the mountains into Tassajara. Holy crap, she thought, I'm going to die.

A wildfire has a head, a tail, and flanks. The fire blasting over Flag Rock, Hawk Mountain, and the Overlook ridge seemed to have two or three heads, maybe more. But then this head of fire met the moisture hanging in the air from Dharma Rain and transformed into fingers of flame before their eyes. Maybe they didn't have to hunker down in the stone office after all. Maybe all of Tassajara wasn't going to burst into flame at once, so that only the Buddha would be left, buried in a moonscape of blackened tree trunks and soot-smudged rocks.

Maybe they could do something.

The five remaining at Tassajara didn't have the experience of trained firefighters and were in violation of some of the established guidelines for staying safe in the field—what are known as the Ten Standard Orders and Eighteen Watch-Out Situations, or more simply, "the Ten and Eighteen." They didn't post a lookout. They didn't have a plan or clear assignments. No one was in charge. But they'd mastered one order: "Be alert. Keep calm. Think clearly. Act decisively." And they had two essential safety tools in abundance—readiness and attention. "We didn't set up a command structure," Abbot Steve told me later. "We set up a communications structure."

Each of the five carried a small two-way Motorola walkie-talkie. They used them throughout the day to check in with one another, to announce their whereabouts, and to ask for help when they needed it. But during the next few hours, they had no direct contact with Stuart or Jack Froggatt or anyone else working the Basin Complex fire. This meant, according to firefighting guidelines, that they were in a "Watch-Out Situation"—they couldn't see the main fire and weren't in contact with someone who could.

Some fire managers insist that the Ten Standard Orders are fundamentally non-negotiable, never to be broken. Ted Putnam, wildland fire investigator and longtime meditator, disagrees: "You only think you can follow them if you have never observed your own mind in meditation." In *On the Fireline: Living and Dying with Wildland Firefighters,* one former seasonal firefighter wrote that the Ten and Eighteen "are too much to ask of ground-pounding crewmembers engaged in the controlled chaos that is firefighting. These rules are 'ideally possible but practically unattainable.'"

Ideally possible but practically unattainable sounds a lot like the vow to save all beings that residents at Tassajara (and Buddhists everywhere) make on a daily basis. That the vow cannot be upheld does not mean it's not worth making. The five at Tassajara may not have been trained in the Ten and Eighteen, but they knew intimately the importance of having signs on the path that point the way toward what is often called "right effort." And they also knew that you shouldn't hold on to any rule too tightly. Reality doesn't follow directions. The fire you want or expect will not be the fire you get.

On the pine room rooftops, the sprinkler heads sputtered and hissed; they weren't moving much water. So while Mako wet down the deck and trees behind the stone office to protect their safe zone, David opened a hose line on the stone and pine rooms, some of Tassajara's oldest structures, which sit creekside, just upstream of the office.

It had bolstered his confidence to watch the fire reach the moist valley slopes and slow down—as if the Buddha's hand, sometimes depicted touching the earth in a simple gesture of steadfastness, had halted the flames. The fire now moving down the steep hillside below the Overlook Trail in isolated clumps wasn't directly threatening the stone and pine rooms, but what if it hopped the creek on a floating ember, started the rooms on fire, and spread to the office?

Lashing the rooftops with water, David felt intensely alive. The necessary actions at last were clear: The fire's here. Put water on it. In fact, put water ahead of it. Far better to wet the buildings down now and prevent their catching fire than to try to put them out once they were ablaze. The fire hoses were heavy and difficult to move, especially when handling them alone, without a backup partner. His throat felt scratchy, his lungs tight from the smoke. In the zip-up, fire-resistant, pale yellow jumpsuit, he felt as if he were wearing several pairs of baggy jeans at once. But David barely noticed these discomforts, so focused was the feeling that doubt had dropped away and now there was merely effort, meeting the moment entirely, with nothing held back and nothing extra.

Eventually David put down his hose, left the buildings dripping as if from a summer shower, and returned to their communications hub in the stone office, hoping that the fire hadn't taken out the radio phone or their one remaining satellite line.

Inside the office, he needed a light to see—all of the windows and the door were now sealed with the fire-resistant wrapping. The Firezat dampened the sounds outside, but he heard rocks dislodging and crashing downslope into the creek, and he heard the sound of the fire: the whoosh of ignition, the roar when it had wind beneath it, the crackling sound when it found fuel.

David called Jamesburg to say that they'd geared up. "The fire's here! It's coming down behind the stone office, by the hill cabins, behind the zendo—," he began. Then Graham's voice came over his radio, something about lighting a backfire at the hill cabins.

"I've got to go!" said David, and hung up the phone, noting the fleeting question: Would this be the last time anyone would hear from them?

He recalled that a Big Sur resident who'd lit a backfire on his property had been arrested, so David called George Haines, the CAL FIRE unit chief who'd tried to get backup at Tassajara, to make sure they were within their legal rights to do it and to get some direction. He told Haines that the fire had surrounded Tassajara and begun its descent into the valley, slow enough that they thought they could respond. "It's near the cabins on the hill. Can we light a backfire?"

Chief Haines had the legal codes on his desk. In California, a private property owner has the right to light a backfire on his or her land if there is imminent danger to life and property. "I'll stand behind you in a court of law if need be. Be sure you ignite from a high point," Haines said, "and keep a clear path of egress."

Over the phone, he walked David through the technique. David relayed instructions by walkie-talkie to Mako and Graham up at the hill cabins, then left the office and stationed himself at the base of the stone steps to the cabins with a hose to protect their way down.

Up on the hill, Graham took an emergency flare attached to a metal pole and tipped it into the dry grass between the first hill cabin and the main fire. Ordinarily when fire crews light backfires or backburns, they use special handheld drip torches filled with a mixture of gas and diesel to deposit flames onto the ground. Lacking actual drip torches, the five at Tassajara had raided the abbot's car for flares and fashioned homemade flares on sticks with duct tape and whatever materials they could find in the shop. They'd joked about making drip torches from wine bottles left by guests and lantern wicks. But a car flare would do.

The fire sounded to Graham like a 747 coming in for a landing on the top of Hawk Mountain. Flames threatening the cabins were only fifty feet away, below the solar panels, burning downslope through the low grasses and chaparral. "We were given the impression that fire doesn't burn downhill," Graham told me later. "It drops stuff, and that stuff lights on fire and burns back up. But I was seeing fire burn downhill. It was burning up, it was burning down, it was burning horizontally."

From what he knew about backfires, which wasn't much, he had a vision of how one ought to look. "I think of a backfire as lighting a big swath of fire that burns right into the main fire," he said. But his backfire didn't look like that. It burned here and there where he'd put fire on the ground, but it didn't form a solid, moving mass of fire. Because they'd run Dharma Rain all night, everything was fairly wet up by the hill cabins. And Mako stood nearby with a hose, spraying down the eaves.

Abbot Steve watched from down below in the work circle. He saw fire sweep around the cabins and reach for the shoulders of the slope, threatening to cut off Mako and Graham from the path down. Over his walkie-talkie, he pleaded with them to come down. Mako heard but stayed put, wetting down the cabins and keeping an eye on the distance between Graham and the approaching flames. I'm not one of your daughters, she thought. If it was just Graham up here, would you be telling him to drop it?

That morning, after returning from the Overlook Trail, Mako had walked by the pool pump and called Graham on her walkie-talkie, asking if she should start it. They'd planned to start Dharma Rain around noon, and it was about that time. When Graham had answered in the affirmative, Abbot Steve had radioed that he ought to help her, not knowing that Mako had trained Graham on the pump in the first place. "The fact that I'm a woman might have made Steve feel protective," she told me later. "It's understandable. But at the time it just pissed me off."

When the wall of flame crested the Overlook ridge at twelve forty p.m., she'd started hosing down the hillside and wooden deck behind the stone office, following her first instinct to protect their safe zone directly below that ridge. "I was ready and waiting, but it just kind of trickled over. I remember feeling like, there's nothing happening over here. Things are happening over there. I need to go!" Around one p.m., she'd walked around to the front of the stone office, seen Graham up on the hill, a canopy of fire behind him, and climbed the path inlaid with stone steps to help.

"Mako, Graham!" Abbot Steve tried again. "Please come down from there! Do you see the fire moving toward the steps?"

Fear sharpened the abbot's voice, seeing that their exit from the burning hillside could be cut off. But it was more an urgent request than an order. The couple looked at each other, knowing the backfire wasn't a success but that they'd done what they could with what they had on hand. The rest of Tassajara needed tending to.

Mako set down her hose. As David wet the area around her, she descended the set of eighty stone steps back to the work circle. Graham ran straight down a firebreak built by the inmate crew.

The firebreak let Graham out on the dirt road that leads from the work circle out to the bathhouse and flats area. The road is flanked on one side by the steep lower slope of Hawk Mountain, on the other side by the creek. He walked toward the flats, where he'd watched roiling smoke less than thirty minutes before. Now, looking upstream from the bathhouse, toward the flats at the far western edge of the Tassajara valley, he saw so many spot fires that he didn't know where to begin. The bathhouse fence on the women's side was burning. Fire fringed the tree trunks and flashed on the uphill side of the dirt road. Seeing this, Graham hesitated—he didn't want to get cut off from central Tassajara. Debris clattered constantly downhill, rocks like giant, rough-hewn hockey pucks.

Because of the smoke, he couldn't see past the tent yurt. Had it all burned when the head of the fire swept through? He stopped near the large sycamore tree in front of the bathhouse. A dozen small fires encircled its trunk. Though the area had been cleared repeatedly, more leaves had fallen, and the fire had found fuel. He needed to put out the burning fence on the women's side of the bathhouse, but flames stood between him and that fire. Because the building was flanked by the creek on one side and the road on the other, the residents had chosen not to wrap it. Graham reached for his radio. "The bathhouse is on fire."

He picked his way through patches of burning grass and shrubs toward the nearest standpipe to turn it on, putting one foot carefully in front of the other. He pointed the attached hose at the closest flame, a burning bush at the base of the sycamore.

Even with his goggles on, his eyes watered. The smoke found the smallest opening. His bandanna filtered some of it, but not enough. He could taste smoke, smell it, feel it filling his nostrils, coating his throat. He felt dizzy, sick to his stomach. Then the coughing started. At first he covered his mouth with his elbow, a relic of zendo decorum, where you cough into your sleeve to preserve both the silence in the zendo and, if you are ill, the health of those near you. But soon the coughing took over. It wasn't the kind of cough you could cover. It was a sputtering, full-body spasm.

Smoke inhalation causes more deaths from fires than burns do. In the most serious cases, the fire sucks up all the available oxygen, leaving none to breathe. But the chemical by-products of fire can also do great damage, interfering with respiration at the cellular level. Too much carbon monoxide, a toxic gas released during incomplete combustion, can cause loss of consciousness and death. Hydrogen cyanide is another gas often found at poisonous levels in firefighters and civilians who have succumbed to smoke inhalation. Though typically of more concern to structural—as opposed to wildland—firefighters, hydrogen cyanide exposure can cause fatal respiratory arrest.

Still coughing, Graham peered through the smoke, trying to see if the yurt was burning. A fresh fist of nausea punched his stomach. It occurred to him that he shouldn't be alone. If he passed out, which seemed increasingly possible, he couldn't fight fire or even keep himself safe. He couldn't tell whether he'd been at the bathhouse for five minutes or five hours. Where was everyone? Hadn't he called for backup? He realized then that he'd merely announced that the bathhouse was on fire and assumed he wouldn't be the only one to respond.

He asked for help on the radio, his words broken by fits of coughing.

Mako copied immediately: "We're on our way. Over."

She and David looked for Graham on the men's side of the bathhouse, closer to central Tassajara, first. The air was soupy with smoke, bent by the heat of the fire, and they couldn't find him. Mako reached for her radio: "Graham, where are you?"

"I'm at the bathhouse." He sounded as if he were holding his breath.

"We're at the bathhouse!" she cried.

Eventually, Mako found him on the far side of the building. Through his goggles, Graham's eyes were rimmed red. He looked pale, even under a coating of fire grit.

"Are you okay?" she asked.

He handed her the hose, walked away, sat down in the middle of the road with his head in his hands, and coughed until he didn't need to cough anymore.

Forty-five minutes after speaking with David, Leslie James dialed the number again for the stone office. "Answering machine," she told the others gathered around the table in Jamesburg, and replaced the phone in its cradle, her lips tugged together.

It seemed a good sign that the machine was picking up. It meant that at least one phone line was still intact. It also meant they weren't in the office to answer. This bit of deduction reassured: They weren't hunkered down in the middle of a burnover, they were probably out fighting fire. But it also disturbed: They were out fighting fire.

Leslie had conceived her oldest daughter during the Marble Cone fire. Now sixty-one and a grandmother, she preferred her current role as Tassajara's communications point person to lugging hoses. Based on her knowledge of how the 1977 fire had unfolded and, later, the 1999 fire that almost reached Tassajara, Leslie had felt sure of the safety and defensibility of the monastery. During the three weeks since the first evacuation, she'd had a phone to each ear from six in the morning until ten at night. Over and over again, she'd reassured anxious callers: Don't worry. The fire is going to come in slowly. We have plenty of water, a safe place to retreat to. When the five had turned around at Ashes Corner the prior evening, she'd felt mostly relief.

But Mako's call later that night, describing fire like a volcano, had pierced Leslie's confidence. For the first time, she'd thought: Maybe something could go really wrong here.

First of all, the fire wasn't coming in slowly. According to David, it had swept around them like a stampede of wild horses.

"Don't fight the fire," she'd urged him. "Don't do anything stupid. Just be safe."

Leslie, *Sitting with Fire* blogger Slymon, and several evacuated residents sat around the dining table in the corner of the office, a long, narrow room just off the kitchen in Jamesburg—breathing, not saying much. Leslie found herself praying. To whom, she wasn't sure, but definitely praying. Jack Froggatt had already stopped by with mostly worrisome news: more hot weather and fire across the road in several places. They'd recited a chant for protecting life, several times. Now, there was nothing to do but wait for word in the heavy midday heat.

Zen Center president Robert Thomas sat at a nearby desk, punching numbers into a second phone. Since their last contact with Tassajara, he'd been working his way down a list, reaching out to Zen Center's political connections to plead for help. Governor Jerry Brown, then attorney general, had helped procure resources for Tassajara in the 1977 fire during his first tenure as governor, but he wasn't on Thomas's list. A friend of Zen Center who knew Brown personally from his visits to Tassajara in the 1970s with then girlfriend Linda Ronstadt had offered to make that call. Thomas had already called every number he had for the USFS and CAL FIRE. He'd spoken with Los Padres National Forest deputy supervisor Ken Heffner as the fire roared into Tassajara. Heffner complained to Thomas that the monks had put him in a bad situation by refusing to evacuate; he'd made it clear they weren't going to provide firefighting resources to protect Tassajara. Thomas could tell Heffner was under pressure, but he raised his own voice in reply: "You should do the right thing and send some help in there, whether it's water or people!"

When the phone rang in Jamesburg, Leslie leaped up. "Tassajara," she answered. She kept her voice low so as not to disturb Thomas, who was on another phone call, though a helicopter churned overhead and made it hard to hear.

"There's five still there now," she told the reporter on the other end of the line, one of many calling that morning to check on the status of the monastery and the monks. She glanced at her husband, Keith Meyerhoff, who fought the 1977 fire and who has driven the stage back and forth to Tassajara for about twenty years. His mouth was set in an uncharacteristic frown, his eyes downcast. He got up from the table then and left the kitchen. She'd find him later, lying down in bed, not sleeping.

"We don't know. We're waiting to hear," Leslie said when the reporter asked what the monks were up to in there. It was an odd sensation for someone used to being a ready source of information, adept at sorting out the daily logistical puzzles that come with running a monastery located in the wilderness, at the end of a fourteen-mile dirt road. She didn't have answers to the reporters' questions. She didn't know anything.

The bathhouse had never seemed so big before. Mako sprayed the scattered fires around the entrance and the section of engulfed fence on the women's side. If that fire spread, it could potentially demolish the whole creek-side structure, with its wooden benches, sundeck, and steamroom.

After Graham recovered, he had left to attend to the pumps. David had stayed on the men's side of the bathhouse to prevent the fire from spreading in that area and protect their only path back to the central area, but eventually he left the area, too, heading downcreek to put out spot fires at the opposite end of Tassajara, near student housing. Mako found herself alone.

Once the fence fire on the women's side of the bathhouse seemed to be out, she pulled a hose attached to the closest standpipe toward the yurt, which was smoking on its backside. The hose wouldn't reach, but just then Abbot Steve arrived carrying a shovel. He had heard the call for help on his walkie-talkie. He went around behind the yurt, an area thick with sticky burrs and poison oak, and directed Mako where to aim: "Over to the left! Now over to the right! More to the right!"

The tent yurt's days were already marked. Tassajara planned to dismantle it and build an expanded retreat center in its place. Hoping the poison oak smoke wouldn't stick to their lungs, they set out nonetheless to save it. It was there now, the next thing to demand their attention.

Abbot Steve pried a burning wooden step away from the yurt deck with the shovel and dragged it through the dirt to where Mako could hose it down. Then he headed to the bathhouse, where a burning stump near the fence threatened to ignite the structure again. He entered the women's side and emerged with a bucket of water he'd dipped into the outdoor plunge. He doused the stump, then filled his bucket again and returned to the yurt to wet the remaining steps, while Mako arced the one hose attached to the bathhouse standpipe around the yurt's backside, guessing from the smoke where she ought to aim.

The irritation she'd felt earlier with his protectiveness had evaporated. The abbot and the head cook worked together seamlessly, a sort of water-bearing tag team moving between the yurt and the nearby bathhouse and a small, freestanding bathroom, putting out the same fires again and again. The bathhouse fence and sycamore stump fires kept reigniting, like trick birthday candles.

Fire heats, wind moves, water wets, earth is solid. Abbot Steve had studied these lines from the eighth-century Harmony of Difference and Equality Sutra in a recent practice period, teaching that each of the elements has its place in the universe and in our bodies. How vibrantly alive those words were now!

Each of the myriad things has its merit, expressed according to function and place. Fire wasn't a malevolent force bent on destroying life. Fire's life was simply to burn. The flames kept coming back, but he didn't feel anger. He saw the fire as simply a coming together of various elements. Not a thing-in-itself, but a constantly-coming-into-being-with. "There actually isn't any fire," he told me later without a shred of irony.

To say there isn't any fire is to remember the importance of an open and pliant mind. Right then, Abbot Steve just knew there were places he didn't want this particular fire to go, and he was going to draw a line and try to protect those places with water, which contains and wets, and earth, which covers and supports.

After leaving the bathhouse, David patrolled between the cabins in the central area and along the creek, putting out spot fires on the other side of Tassajara Creek so that they couldn't jump to the backside of the cabins. Fiery logs and broken tree limbs tumbled down the steep hill below the Overlook Trail and continued to burn wherever they stopped, lodged against a boulder or a tree.

Eventually he walked all the way to student housing, at the far down-creek end of Tassajara. One well-placed spark and these old, ramshackle buildings, once an actual barn and stable, could go up as quickly as the zendo did in 1978. The barns were far from luxurious, but they deserved equal attention. David hosed down the surrounding area, putting out drifting embers beyond Dharma Rain's reach. He was grateful for his hard hat as rolling debris slammed into the buildings and he heard what sounded like a rock slide farther downcreek.

Once the area seemed stable, David headed back upcreek, passing Graham on his way to refuel the pool pump. Back in the central area, David stopped at the stone office to check the answering machine in case it offered good, though unlikely, news—a water drop or a fire crew on its way.

Around three p.m. in San Francisco, a crowd gathered around Abbot Haller's desk, including treasurer Greg Fain, Zen Center secretary Dana Velden, and a few others. Ironically, the landlines at City Center were down, so David had called Velden's cell phone with an update.

When he'd phoned earlier in the afternoon, they'd been sitting on the floor on meditation cushions. Velden had put her phone on speaker and placed it on a zafu in the middle of the circle, so that everyone could hear David describe the fire's three-pronged advance: "It's coming over Flag Rock. It's coming over Hawk Mountain. It's coming over the Overlook. There's fire everywhere. I've got to go!" They'd stared in silence at the phone on the cushion after David hung up, trying to take in what they'd just heard.

Now, with David on speakerphone again, Haller asked, "What's going on there?"

David struggled to describe the scene. It was like trying to describe parachuting from a plane, in the middle of the jump, to someone on the ground a hundred miles away.

"We're all fine," he said. "Dharma Rain subdued the fire when it got about seventy-five feet from the valley floor. We decided we didn't have to shelter in place. We're doing what we can."

"Where is everybody now?" asked Haller.

"Colin's at the shop. Mako and Steve are down by the yurt. Graham's at the pool pump. We've got radios. We're talking to each other."

Just then Colin's voice broke over the walkie-talkie, reporting fire tearing down the hill above the gatehouse, across from the shop.

"Call Jamesburg and update them. I've got to go. I'll call again as soon as

I can," said David. He put on his goggles, pulled his bandanna over his mouth, and went out to meet the fire.

In college, Colin had to translate part of the Aeneid *for a final* exam. He'd looked at the page of Latin his teacher placed in front of him and thought: No way in hell. But then he started. He took a blank piece of paper, covered up everything but the first line, and translated it: "I sing of arms and a man first come from Troy." Then he went on to the next. Working line by line through the poem, one small piece at a time, he completed the exam.

It was like that when the fire came in the way it did, not gradually backing but shooting down the hillsides all around as they stapled Firezat to the stone office windows. The only way Colin could keep from being completely overwhelmed was to take a single step and not worry about the one after that. Our first priority is the shop, he told himself. Okay, I'm going to the shop.

While the others moved from one edge of Tassajara to another, he stuck to the shop, patrolling the steep hills that flank the building for rolling branches and floating smoldering leaves. He wanted to protect the shop's flammable cache of lumber and fuel but also the vital buildings that stood near it: the zendo and, across dry Cabarga Creek, the abbot's cabin and founder's hall. Rocks hailed down around him, keeping him on high alert. Stuart had often told them: Watch your back. Colin looked over his shoulder constantly, as if checking the rearview mirror on his motorcycle, to make sure nothing had started behind him.

When fire flared on the slope above the gatehouse cabin around two p.m., Colin didn't want to turn his back on the shop, so he radioed for help. David showed up immediately and hosed down the hillside, Abbot Steve a few minutes later. After they managed to extinguish the flames, Colin was alone again at his shop post, with only his radio to connect him with the others.

It had been hard to stay put when the fire first entered Tassajara, listening to Steve shout to Mako and Graham to get down from the hill cabins. What if there was a medical emergency? What if someone broke an ankle, passed out, or was burned? The shop was a one-thousand-square-foot matchbox. He couldn't leave it. Yet he knew he would if one of his friends called out in distress.

After his coughing fit at the bathhouse subsided, Graham had walked to the opposite end of Tassajara to top off the pumps. He opened the tank on the permanent pool pump and peered inside. Simple enough, but quite dangerous. It's risky to fuel a running pump even when the forest all around isn't on fire. One little lapse of attention, a splash of gas on the exhaust manifold, and you could have a flash fire on your hands.

David had told Graham that things were quiet down past the pool for the moment, so when Graham finished filling the pool pump and the portable Mark 3 at the creek, he headed back upstream, toward central Tassajara. On his way to the pool, Graham had stopped to put out some burning fence posts in the garden. He wanted to make sure they were still out. But in the minutes it had taken him to tend to the pumps, the pool bathroom had burst into flames.

The bathroom structure itself wasn't a high priority. He could see that it probably wasn't possible to save it. But the building was separated from a nearby two-story wooden yurt cabin, one of Tassajara's newer structures, by just a few feet of ground and a fence. And the fence was on fire. It wasn't hard to imagine flames enveloping the yurt cabin, traveling across the path on overarching tree branches to a redwood cabin, then to an adjacent cabin in a domino effect. The bathroom fire could become the runaway flame that brought down all of Tassajara. Graham grabbed a nearby hose and opened the line, soaking the sides of the yurt and the fence, kicking down burning boards, and backing away at the first sign that the smoke was starting to get to him.

Chlorine and muriatic acid for cleaning the fifty-thousand-gallon pool—unused for weeks by now, littered with soot—were stored on shelves outside the nearby changing room, about eight feet from the bathroom. If mixed, these chemicals create something like mustard gas, the toxic brew that burned the eyes, skin, and lungs of World War I soldiers, sometimes fatally.

But Graham didn't know this. Unaware of the danger, he stayed at the pool bathroom until he was sure the fence was out and the yurt cabin safe. Then he walked past the garden again. The fire had tried to penetrate it, without much success. A few vertical posts in the deer fence were burning, but there wasn't much available fuel. Cosmos and lilies bloomed in the beds, a nodding swath of soft-petaled, unlikely pinks and reds amid Tassajara's black-and-brown palette. The grass pathways shimmered a deep green from all the extra watering. Graham watered the beds again, just to be safe. Dry mulch could still catch a spark.

Tassajara's two yurts sit on the periphery, at opposite ends of the grounds. That Mako happened to be fighting fire at one while Graham defended the other was a coincidence, but the image accurately reflects the intimate yet independent nature of their relationship. Mako wasn't worried about Graham, even though the last time she'd seen him he'd been choking on smoke, any more than she was worried about herself. There wasn't time to dwell on anything other than the task at hand. Nearly an hour after she'd first arrived at the burning tent yurt, that task was to move on. Abbot Steve had left the area. Mako didn't see smoke spirals or flames around the canvas yurt anymore. Everything was drenched, including her, and subdued. The air felt cool and damp, more like November than July. She decided to venture out to the flats, where she heard popping fire sounds.

The cabin where she and Graham ordinarily lived appeared untouched, still cloaked in Firezat wrap. Where the ground had burned around it, the earth was a dingy black, silvered with ashes. Various brush piles burned in isolated fires, as if small incendiary bombs had dropped from the air. The wood storage and compost sheds shimmered and smoked. Flames flickered from the stacks of cut wood.

Mako had to choose which fire to try to put out. But first she needed a hose. A heap of them lay scattered about, streaked with char marks. They'd been abandoned when Stuart Carlson had called off the activation the day before. The five who'd returned to Tassajara had decided to leave the hoses out, so they'd be ready for use if the fire arrived over the hogback. They hadn't thought about the possibility that no one would be present when the fire came through there or that the hoses themselves could burn.

Many of the plastic nozzles had melted. Several hose lines, heavy with water, crisscrossed. She planted her feet and summoned her strength to heave the hoses apart. She managed to free one unburned line from the heap, charged it with water from the standpipe, and opened the hose on the compost shed. Water sputtered out the nozzle's sides, wetting Mako more than the fire.

There was barely any pressure in the line. While flames licked the roof of the compost shed and darted out its open windows—the already hot pile of decomposing organic matter inside had caught fire—Mako disconnected the ruined nozzle and tried in vain to find a usable one. She grabbed an extinguisher attached to the side of the shed, pulled the pin, and sprayed it back and forth on one burning corner as she'd practiced when she first became a member of Tassajara's regular fire crew. The flames subsided under a snow of retardant, then popped right back up again. She tried a second extinguisher. The fire disappeared for a few seconds and then—*whoosh!*—picked right back up where it had left off.

The flames flickering across the roof of the shed reached farther, faster. The fire was heating up. And every nozzle she picked up seemed to have been kissed by a blowtorch.

If she'd wondered about saving the tent yurt, the same question applied to the compost shed. For as long as she could remember, people had said that it needed to be rebuilt. Should she just let it burn? But that didn't feel right. Someone would have to rebuild it, sooner rather than later, and they were all going to have enough to do after this fire.

"High things in high places, low things in low places," wrote Dōgen in *Instructions for the Zen Cook*—good, practical advice: You don't put a heavy pot on a high shelf that you can reach only on your tiptoes. But ultimately, Zen holds that there actually are no high and low places. Such hierarchies exist only in our minds, in the air of our opinions. To reinforce this teaching, the head student for a practice period at Tassajara, an honored position that marks the transition from student to teacher, is asked not only to give lectures, but also to clean toilets and turn compost.

Standing in front of the burning shed, not long before she would become head student herself, Mako recognized how generously the structure had served them, taking in heaps of discarded peach pits, eggshells, coffee grounds. She wanted to make an effort to save it. She simply needed to find a nozzle that worked, a hose that wasn't burned, and hope for decent water pressure.

She got on her walkie-talkie: "I need a nozzle out at the flats!"

David arrived several minutes later with a replacement nozzle he'd unscrewed from a hose at the bathhouse. But he couldn't solve Mako's pressure problems. The flats area is the highest ground in the Tassajara valley, requiring an uphill slog through the pipes for the water supply. They'd have to get a Mark 3 pump out there if they wanted to boost the flow. David called Graham on his walkie-talkie to see if he could fix the water pressure problem. When Graham didn't respond, David went looking for him and found him at the smoldering pool bathroom ruins.

While Abbot Steve, who'd arrived at the flats shortly after David, tried again to sort out hoses, Mako did what she could with what she had at that moment, one unburned hose and one good nozzle. She screwed on the new nozzle and leveled a few burning debris piles with the toe of her boot, then doused them with the hose. She liked the sizzling sound the embers made when the water hit them. Even when the piles burst into flame again, she found the sound distinctly satisfying.

The sound of fire meeting water.

While Mako, David, and Abbot Steve were out at the flats and Graham dealt with the burning pool bathroom, fire slipped through the temple gate, a traditional Japanese-style gate with a roof. Colin attacked it for a while with a dry chemical fire extinguisher, but moments after he thought he'd put it out, the gate blazed again. Rocks and flaming clumps of roots and branches still tumbled down the hillside above the shop. The hoses on hand wouldn't reach the gate. Still hesitant to leave the shop for long, he radioed the others, "The temple gate is on fire!"

Abbot Steve arrived first, with his shovel. He'd left Mako at the flats after the compost shed fire was under control and walked to the upper lot, where guests parked. They'd left the lumber truck there the night before. Too late. A falling rock had left a spiderweb-shaped fracture on the Ford's windshield. He'd moved the vehicle into the center of the lot, then Colin had called for help.

Abbot Steve had stood at the gate many times for the opening and closing of the monastery, first as a student and then, more recently, presiding. Now he hacked at it with his shovel. Soon, David arrived with a couple of fire extinguishers. While he smothered the fire, Abbot Steve wrangled hoses again, attaching one line to another so that the length would reach from one of the shop area's two standpipes to the gate. When pine needle duff on the gate roof ignited, he was there with the hose to stop the spread.

Once the gate fire was out, David walked downcreek again, patrolling the large area between the Cabarga Creek bridge and student housing. But Abbot Steve stayed in the shop area manning a hose, helping Colin watch for flaming debris tumbling down from Flag Rock, the kind that had probably started the pool bathroom fire. The abbot's instincts told him to stay close. The zendo, the abbot's cabin, and the founder's hall were all nearby, directly under the shower of embers from Flag Rock, and only the backsides of the abbot's cabin and founder's hall were wrapped.

The two priests listened, and when they heard the telltale sound of a chunk of burning wood careening downhill, they followed the source of the noise and hit it with water. They basically watered the entire slope, over and over and over, grateful for the endless supply the pumps drew from Tassajara

Creek. Like any vigil, it was tiring. Dangerous enough that you have to stay awake and alert, but not so dramatic that you are oblivious to the fact that you are hungry, thirsty, and impossibly tired.

Colin had long ago drained his water bottle. During a quiet stretch, when it seemed that maybe it would be safe to turn their eyes away from the burning mountain for a moment, he turned to Abbot Steve.

"I need a drink. There's got to be some Gatorade around."

"That sounds pretty good." Being abbot was a round-the-clock job. But this was the hardest work Abbot Steve had ever done. Even when he was young and working on the farm, "from can see to can't see," as they say, it was never as intense, as continuous, as this. He hadn't been off his feet, had anything to eat, or taken a drink for hours. The fire wasn't finished, but they couldn't go on like this for much longer without giving their bodies some sustenance.

Colin pressed the talk button on his radio: "This is Colin. David, we could use some Gatorade up here at the shop. Over."

After a brief silence, a voice replied: "Copy. This is Mako. The Gatorade's on fire. Over."

Colin and Abbot Steve looked at each other, unsure what to make of the response.

"Copy. Um, we need some Gatorade here. To drink. Over," Colin clarified.

"Copy. There's a case of it burning out here at the flats. Over."

Someone had carried out a case of Gatorade before the activation the prior afternoon. It had been left by the fence in front of the massage gazebo, and the plastic bottles were actually burning around the liquid inside.

Mako put out the Gatorade fire, then salvaged an undamaged bottle from the pile and drank it.

Eventually Colin and Abbot Steve got their Gatorade, too. Theirs was actually cold, as David had fetched some from the walk-in and delivered it.

Not long after their break, around four p.m., Colin saw fire on the slope above the gatehouse. At first he thought it was just a torching shrub.

Within seconds, he realized that it was in fact the birdhouse cabin, completely engulfed in flames, its silver Firezat wrap flapping in molten sheets. He announced it to the others, but just a few moments later, he radioed again: "The birdhouse is toast."

Of all the cabins that could have burned, why this one, relatively new, with its private deck and penthouse view of Tassajara?

On his way back from the garden when he heard Colin's announcement, Graham ran to the work circle, picked up a hose line, and opened it on the birdhouse.

"It's toast, Graham!" shouted Colin, not understanding why Graham was making the effort. It was already just a skeleton of blackened posts, well past saving.

"I wasn't trying to save it," Graham told me later. It was the big oak tree growing next to the cabin that he wanted to spare, with a plaque nestled in a fork at the base of its trunk:

An ancient buddha said:
The entire universe is the true human body,
The entire universe is the gate of liberation . . .

But it's not quite right to say the oak grew next to the birdhouse; the cabin practically perched in the old tree's expansive branches—thus the cabin's name. Tree and cabin seemed to be holding each other in place on the steep hillside.

Graham stood there for a while, watering the oak. They could rebuild the birdhouse in one work period. But no amount of effort or charitable labor could rebuild a tree that had been growing there for at least a hundred years.

Runaway embers rolling downhill from the blackened frame of the birdhouse cabin now threatened to ignite the gatehouse, where residents had taken a group photo the prior afternoon with the Indiana crew. Fire also continued to skid down the slope of Flag Rock. Like a marathon runner in the last leg of a race, Colin rallied energy from somewhere, because he had to. He couldn't let down his guard now and allow the fire to sneak up on the founder's hall the way it had on the birdhouse. He knew from watching the birdhouse go up in flames that it could happen instantly, while you had your head turned for a moment.

The love Suzuki Roshi's students felt for him is in each stone of the *kaisando,* built when he was still alive. In contrast with the sprawling shop, the founder's hall is an intimate space, about the size of a large bedroom. Occasionally, when yoga workshops take over the zendo during the summer guest season, afternoon service is held in the founder's hall. Chanting in there, as in the closed space of the steamroom in the baths, is a powerful, resonant experience. While nobody would cry if they lost the shop—for years people had wanted to move it out to the flats, out of sight—if the kaisando burned, hearts would ache.

Colin dragged a hose up from the Cabarga Creek standpipe on the west side of the founder's hall, across from the zendo. During the weeks they'd been clearing in preparation for fire, they'd dumped raked leaves and trimmed branches into the dry creekbed—too close to the buildings, he could see now, though there wasn't anything he could do about it.

Abbot Steve took his place on the east face of the hall, near the abbot's cabin, where a stone basin in a rock garden built by Suzuki Roshi reflects the pre-dawn stars. For an hour or so, from their respective positions, they followed the crashing course of rocks and flaming branches down the slope and poured water on anything that had burned, was burning, or just might burn.

*Throughout this time, Mako stayed at the flats, repeatedly extin*guishing fires she thought she'd taken care of. Every time she turned around, there was some new fire to tend to or an old fire that had resurrected.

Around four thirty p.m., the woodshed fire took off. The three-sided structure with corrugated metal roofing was chock-full of kindling for the wood stoves in the stone and pine rooms and a handful of other cabins—much fuller now in summer than it would be in winter. As Mako sprayed the burning piles with the meager flow from her hose, she began to worry about the volume of available fuel. If it got hot enough and all of it went up, it would be a much bigger fire than she could handle alone. Already the smoke and heat were intense, and strangely, she smelled burning rubber.

The center stack was burning the hottest, so she started toppling the pile with a McLeod, part hoe and part rake. She'd hook on to the wood with the hoe part, pull out the burning pieces, then water them down. Because the water pressure was weak, she had to get up close to the fire to work this way, within five feet. The woodpiles on either side of her were burning, too, and the smoke began to pierce her eyes and prick her throat.

When she started to feel nauseated, she set down the hose and stepped out of the woodshed to get some relief. As soon as she felt better, she picked up her hose again. She moved in and out like that for a while, in a kind of waltz with the need to take care of herself and the need to put out the fire.

Mako saw that the tires on the wood splitter, parked at the edge of the central woodpile, were on fire. That was why she'd smelled burning rubber. But as she sprayed down the machine, she instinctively took a big step back. Was there gasoline in the tank? What if it exploded? "For all I knew," she told me later, "twisted hunks of metal shrapnel were about to come flying at me."

There was a time when female Zen students deliberately disfigured themselves—often with a hot iron—in order to renounce any attachment to their beauty and to demonstrate their fierce commitment to entering a monastic practice that was once exclusively male. But San Francisco Zen Center has had female abbesses. Many American Zen teachers are women. Neither Mako nor the generation of female Zen students before her required such extreme measures to earn a teacher's respect or manifest their will. If the wood splitter exploded, much harm and no good would come of it. With her heart galloping in her chest, Mako called for help, making no attempt to disguise her fear.

"This is Mako. Graham, Colin, is there gas in the wood splitter? Over."

Graham was still salvaging the oak tree. Standing on the Cabarga Creek bridge, Colin answered first: "Copy. Colin here. Uh, yeah. . . . Why? Over." Of course there was gas in the wood splitter, but he had no idea how much.

"It's on fire! Is it going to explode?"

Colin heard the fear in Mako's voice, and it surprised him. He'd never heard her sound panicked.

"Don't worry," he told her. "Just keep it wet. Graham and I will bring out the Mark 3."

"Hurry!"

They'd moved the portable pump in from the flats earlier in the day, at Colin's suggestion, because they didn't want to get cut off from it. Now, Graham and Colin wheeled it back in a garden cart to set it up in the creek. Two-stroke Mark 3 engines are high-powered but notoriously difficult to start. This moment was no exception. Graham and Colin took turns yanking on the cord. While one of them tried, the other radioed Mako, who couldn't see them down by the creek from where she stood, to tell her they were working on it.

She had to back away. The side piles were burning intensely and it was too hot to stand in the middle of the shed, armed with the water pressure of a squirt gun. She could feel the heat searing her throat. She snugged her bandanna back up over her mouth and nose. It gave some relief, but not much. When a blast of smoke hit her in the face, she coughed so deeply she wretched.

David had also responded to Mako's distress call. He too tried to sort out the maze of hoses left over from the activation, his old rotator cuff injury acting up as he lifted the waterlogged hoses. Finally, Graham got the Mark 3 going. Colin had rolled out a new hose that hooked directly into the Mark 3. The line was too long, and it kept kinking, but once he'd smoothed it out and the pump was running, water blasted through the nozzle.

It was the first time that Colin had left the central area, the first time Mako had glimpsed him or Graham in hours, the first time they were all together since the fire arrived—except for Abbot Steve, who had stayed to keep an eye on the shop when Colin left. The four of them tried to lift the metal roof to soak the wood burning hottest directly underneath it, dodging gusts of smoke. The wind tipped the clouds rising from the woodpiles into Colin's face at one point, and he thought he might puke on his boots.

When the woodshed fire was mostly under control, Mako wandered off—she couldn't remember later where she'd gone or why she'd left; maybe she'd just needed to use the bathroom. Eventually, David and Graham left as well. Colin looked up and found himself alone. Hey, where did everyone go?

The woodshed looked like a huge, abandoned campfire. It had been transformed from neat stacks of cured firewood to ashes and cinder, a mix of scorched and unburned wood. "Firewood becomes ash, and it does not become firewood again," Eihei Dōgen wrote. "Yet, do not suppose that the ash is future and the firewood past. You should understand that firewood abides in the phenomenal expression of firewood, which fully includes past and future and is independent of past and future. Ash abides in the phenomenal expression of ash, which fully includes future and past. Just as firewood does not become firewood again after it is ash, you do not return to birth after death."

Tassajara residents knew this passage well, having chanted it many times. It awakened a changed relationship to time, to reality itself, in those able to enter its meaning. But Colin wasn't thinking about Dōgen or about returning to anything but a state of rest. He was so done in that he could barely hold the hose, too tired even to get on the radio and tease the others for abandoning him. He propped a couple of hoses on a stump, pointed them at the smoldering woodpile, and left the flats.

After leaving the woodshed, David returned to the stone office and listened to the messages on the answering machine. There were at least three from Leslie. She wasn't the type to make a fuss, but he could hear the immense relief in her voice when he finally called back, around five p.m. Relaying a message from City Center, she gave David the name and number of an information officer to call. "Something about air support. It might be a private thing, somebody with a helicopter. I don't really know."

Things were cooling and quieting down, but David radioed the others anyway to tell them about the potential water drop. "Where do you think we could we use it?"

After a long pause with no answer, Mako responded: "Ummmm, they want to drop water *now*?" It was like someone sauntering into the kitchen as dinner was coming out of the oven and asking, What can I chop?

David never reached the information officer. He left a voice mail saying that yes, they would welcome a water drop at Tassajara. The pool bathroom and birdhouse were beyond saving, but more water couldn't hurt. He didn't say, Where were you when we needed you?

When Walter and Joanne Ross checked Sitting with Fire *on the* morning of July 10, they were certain Graham had turned around during the evacuation and Mako, too, but it was just a hunch. There's a three-hour time difference between California and Ontario, so the names of those who'd gone back hadn't yet been posted. Joanne sent an e-mail inquiring about her son and received a reply that the identities of the remaining residents weren't being released until the individuals had given their consent.

The Rosses spent the next few hours wrestling with their frustrated need to know whether Graham and Mako were still in Tassajara and a stubborn intuition that they were. "I just knew that whatever fear Graham experienced, he wouldn't shy away from it," Joanne told me when I talked to her and Walter together after the fire. She'd watched her young son guard the net on the hockey rink, ready to face whatever came flying at him. She'd be gritting her teeth in the stands, but he wouldn't flinch.

Throughout the morning of July 10, she tried to busy herself with errands. Walter Ross stayed home, glued to the blog. By the time Joanne returned home around lunchtime, *Sitting with Fire* had confirmed her suspicion, listing Graham and Mako as two of the five now at Tassajara. The post noted that Jamesburg was in regular phone contact with them. Joanne resisted the urge to call and see if she could get more information, figuring it was better to keep the phone lines open. "We just had to trust and wait to hear," she told me.

If you weren't inside Tassajara, you didn't have much choice but to sit with fire—to pass the time as best you could with uncertainty, without letting worry carry you away.

The origin of the word *worry*—it comes from the Old English *wyrgan,* for "strangle"—accurately depicts the state of breathless torment that anxiety can bring. The Rosses could have picked up the phone and spread their anxiety or aired their frustration on *Sitting with Fire*. Other distressed family members did, understandably. When there's a pair of hands clutching your throat, your instinct is to pry them off.

But the Rosses, who are not Buddhists, chose to let go. They didn't know where their son was, and once they did, they couldn't be sure he was safe. "I was agitated at first," said Joanne later. Then she added, "But really, what would it have changed to know?"

Finally, after they'd knocked back the woodshed fire at the flats, there was a palpable shift, like the moment the sun dips below the horizon, an atmosphere of finality and transition.

"We knew it was over when the fire bell finally sounded," David joked when I met with the five all together for the first time after the fire. The others laughed, knowing intimately the desperation that can set in after hours of zazen, when your legs are on fire and you're perched on the edge of your cushion, waiting for the period's end, pleading silently with the person watching the clock, seated at the bells.

"It was pretty clear," said Abbot Steve, recalling what they could plainly see. "Everything on the perimeter is burned. It's not going to burn again."

Firewood becomes ash, and it does not become firewood again.

It had been nearly a month since the first threat of fire when David called Zen Center president Robert Thomas from the stone office to report, surprised and somewhat awed: "I think we saved Tassajara!"

Twelve

UNBURYING BUDDHA

Disaster could be called a crash course in Buddhist principles . . .

—REBECCA SOLNIT, *A Paradise Built in Hell*

Thursday, July 10, six p.m.

*There were cheers in San Francisco and Jamesburg. Within min*utes, the good news traveled to the dining room at City Center and caused an eruption of applause and whistles. A similar scene unfolded across the Golden Gate Bridge at Green Gulch Farm. But it wasn't all jubilation. Evacuated priest Judith Randall wept when she saw the photo of the five in their fire gear, simultaneously realizing and releasing the depth of her concern.

Once her own tears stopped, Jane Hirshfield posted an e-mail from a friend whose construction crew had built many of Tassajara's newer buildings, announcing that Steve Stücky "and the boys" had stood their ground. She didn't think to point out that there was a woman among those boys. In the moment, *who* hardly mattered.

When leaving Tassajara with most of the students at the end of June, Jane had tried to quietly convey to Mako and Graham that they were about to be blessed with the kind of experience that sears itself into one's bones, and also, that it would be fun. Months later, when I interviewed Jane, the mention of Mako's name stirred up emotion. "There's something about seeing another person do, thirty years later, what I once did," Jane said. "It made very real the cyclical nature of time. It's a nonrepeatable universe, as Baker Roshi used to say, yet every thirty years the mountains will burn."

When the 1977 fire was over, Jane told me, it was like "sitting in the middle of a dying-down bonfire. Everywhere you look there's a heart of a tree glowing red, especially at night." It was a landscape humans didn't usually get to see.

A tangle of blackened, rust-red-barked manzanitas grew out of an ash beach. An upturned, forgotten broom hung on the side of the compost shed, bristles singed off, a scorched halo on the wall behind it. Around six p.m., leaving the flats, Mako spotted a helicopter flying low over Tassajara—the first she'd seen all day. The aircraft flashed a spotlight at her. She couldn't see the faces of the pilot or passengers or read the markings, but she had the impression that whoever was up there, hovering overhead, was relieved to see her alive and walking around. She wondered if maybe it was branch director Jack Froggatt and gave a reassuring wave.

In the stone office, Mako took off her fire suit, carefully extracted her throbbing feet from her boots, and put on tennis shoes. She left on her hard hat and the bandanna around her neck. Her clothes were soaked, as if she'd been walking through a light rain for hours. Dōgen compared enlightenment to walking through fog: You could get wet without even realizing it. She'd gotten wet without realizing it under the fire gear. The dampness had kept her cool. As she set out walking downcreek, she actually felt chilled.

Outside of the intact, unlikely green of the central area, everywhere she looked was shorn down to bare skin. Brown, withered leaves clung to the surviving trees, their black bark blistered and serrated. Some wore burn skirts at the base of their trunks. Some had shed large branches or snapped and fallen over completely. Foot trails, suddenly exposed, meandered forlornly across the bare earth. Rocks lay everywhere in the road, loose dirt heaped at the base of ravines. Smoke trails emanated from smoldering piles of leaf and wood debris. Water spurted from burned pipes. Whatever didn't glow with embers was gray, brown, black, marbled with ash.

Deck chairs, dusted gray, were still arranged around the pool, a number of them twisted by flames, surrounded by a confetti of rocks. Tables had been crushed, their plastic tops misshapen by the fire's heat. The vertical posts of the pool bathroom still stood, pitted and charred, framing the air, but the birdhouse cabin on the hill had completely collapsed, a heap of still-warm rubble. The Cabarga Creek bed seemed to have widened, scraped clean of grasses and ferns. The hillsides, stripped of vegetation, seemed even more vertical. In the fire's twilight, a dusky haze hung over Tassajara.

Mako wanted to wander farther but asked everyone over the radio to meet in the central area at seven o'clock. The five gathered at the work circle below the burned husk of the birdhouse. Mako focused her camera on her firefighting companions, propped the Panasonic on the zendo steps, set the camera's timer, then jogged over to stand between Graham and David. She threw one arm around David's shoulder and tucked the other around her partner's waist.

In the photo, Graham appears to be saying something or breathing out an exhausted sigh. His jumpsuit is smeared with soot. A hose threads across the grass in front of the group and trails through Colin's boots, out of the frame. They're all wearing bandannas in the same triangular configuration around their necks. Every bandanna is a slightly different color, just as each of the five experienced the fire from a slightly different perspective. Each one of them would tell a different story.

The photo was eventually posted on Flickr with a caption: "The Five Tassajara Fire Monks." Later, the phrase would be abbreviated to the "Tassajara Five," but not by the five themselves. "We were just a group of people in a situation," Colin told me months later. Countless beings had contributed to this moment's unfolding, too many to enumerate or even to see. There are five monks in the picture, but so much that supported them is outside the frame. As with any story, there's always something cropped out of our perception, some side we can't see.

. . .

At seven thirty p.m., the five finally ate a celebratory meal of left-overs: baba ghanoush, pita bread, tabouleh, and Gatorade. They reviewed the events of the day, filling one another in and trading stories.

Later that evening, Mako went to the bathhouse and had the women's side to herself, a first. The quarter moon, normally suspended over the Overlook ridge on a lattice of stars, was rubbed out by smoke. The valley seemed uncommonly still—as if, as Jane described it, every living thing held its breath.

Graham called his parents in Toronto to report that he was fine and that they'd lost only a few structures. "Just to hear that he was there and alive, I was a babbling nutcase at that point," said Joanne later, recalling her relief. The abbot made some calls, too, then he lay down in his cabin and, within moments, fell asleep.

David and Colin had volunteered for the first patrol shift, from eight p.m. until midnight, to watch for flare-ups and refuel the pumps. "Various spot fires continue to burn or reignite throughout the night, and burning logs, branches, and pinecones tumble down the mountainsides, often casting sparks in their wake," wrote David later in his public account of the day of the fire. When we talked, he described wandering the devastated landscape at night, dousing the glowing remains of spot fires with water until he was alone again in the darkness, then stumbling upon yet another smoldering pile or tree stump, smoke rising in the beam of his headlamp. "It was nothing compared to the sight of fire rolling down the mountainsides from all directions," David told me, "but it was eerie. The night was filled with the sound of crackling, creeping, still-gasping fires and falling rocks"—and the steadfast murmur of the creek.

During that first evening patrol, a flaming tree trunk rolled down below the Overlook Trail, directly across the creek from the guest dining room. David climbed onto the dining room roof to hose it down, but the fire never completely extinguished. It smoldered quietly for days. They'd all seen how persistent fire could be, equaled only by the persistence of water.

Dharma Rain hissed steadily, reassuringly, on the rooftops. Above the tops of the mountains, the sky still glowed, reflecting fire in the distance, fire not yet burned out. But the high-vigilance atmosphere of the afternoon had waned. The worst, it seemed, was over.

They wouldn't know until the following morning, when the incident management team released its daily status report, that the Basin Complex fire had spread nine thousand acres on July 10—more than fourteen square miles—with Tassajara right in the middle. A few more days would drift by before an article ran in the *Monterey Herald* describing the fire on Tassajara Road, witnessed by a crew stationed there on July 10: "The unit was forced to pull back before noon . . . because the fire had kicked up substantially, expelling a plume so large that at one point it obscured the midday sun. As an airtanker flew toward the massive smoke, it looked as small as a sparrow flying toward Niagara Falls."

Friday, July 11, the day after the fire, felt to the five like the day after a marathon. "I was so dehydrated, I don't think I peed for a couple of days," Colin told me. The smoke gave them headaches. The by-products of exertion and adrenaline pooled in their muscles, sapping their energy. They were used to going without sleep and enduring pain during long stretches of meditation, but this was different. "It was something deeper in the bones than normal sleep deprivation that can be cured by a good night or two of rest," Mako said later. But the road was closed. The mountains around them smoldered. Despite their exhaustion, they needed to stay active and alert.

Abbot Steve's dawn patrol shift doubled as a post-fire inspection. A few buildings would need to be entirely replaced: the pool bathroom, the woodshed at the flats, and the birdhouse cabin, probably the compost shed, too. Many structures and some of Tassajara's infrastructure would need repairs: sections of fence at the bathhouse, front gate, and garden, some redwood decking at the pool, wooden steps at the yurt and the trail to the solar array, the lumber truck windshield, the radio phone, and the spring box—the source of Tassajara's drinking water.

He walked from one point to another, upcreek and then downcreek again, as if making his usual incense offerings at several altars before entering the zendo, but each place, each patch of ground, was now an altar.

The center of Tassajara was untouched. The grass glistened a deep green on the stone office lawn. The wisteria-draped trellis shaded the gravel walkway, as it has for decades. A cluster of tall sycamores fanned the bocce ball court. The creek continued to flow down the length of Tassajara, continuous, selfless, ever-present. If you blocked out the periphery and the hoses strewn about, you could imagine there hadn't been any fire. But lift your eyes a little and you saw the blackened hearth the fire had made of the mountains, the remains of the buildings the fire had consumed. Life and death, right next to each other, braided together, as they always are.

That morning while Abbot Steve was on patrol, Mako ventured out with her camera again. Near the bathhouse, she found a dead Steller's jay, eyeless, beak tucked in a wing, a shock of blue feathers against the dirt. Out past the flats, she discovered a dead buck, stiff on his side, twig-thin legs splayed, fur singed from the lower half of his belly. Its carcass lay just feet away from an old children's playground, where a metal swing stood, untouched by the fire. Many of the animals, except these unfortunate ones, had fled before the fire. Shortly after, they reappeared. Foxes and rabbits—not commonly seen in the valley or just ordinarily hidden in the brush—trotted and hopped in plain view. Squirrels scurried across rocks. Lizards sunned themselves on the fire hoses.

Abbot Steve continued his patrol past the yurt toward the Suzuki Roshi memorial, a pilgrimage he makes each time he arrives at Tassajara. How curious it was to see how the fire had touched some places and not others. They'd taken down and stored the wooden post that usually marked the place where some of Suzuki Roshi's ashes rested, beneath a large white-veined stone from the creek, but they'd left the markers for Katagiri Roshi, who had helped guide the practice of Zen in the West, and Trudi Dixon, the student who had painstakingly edited the lectures for *Zen Mind, Beginner's Mind*. In a field of ashes, the wooden markers stood upright, though Katagiri's was charred at the base.

Later that morning, Abbot Steve and the others put on their priest robes. They held a service in the zendo to express their gratitude. There were just enough of them to fill the positions—one to ring the bronze bell and one to strike the hollow wooden drum shaped like a fish, one to lead the chanting, one to be the *doshi,* or lead priest, and one to be the doshi's attendant. The Buddha was still buried in the bocce ball court. They bowed to an empty altar and dedicated their chanting to everyone and everything that had supported them and Tassajara, including fire.

Around one o'clock that afternoon, Abbot Steve was walking back to the abbot's cabin for a short nap after lunch when he heard a crackling sound coming from the shop area. A moment later, the air horn shrieked. The woodshed across from the shop had burst into flame. Colin had called it out on the radio first and reached for the air horn when he got no response. Abbot Steve ran to help on weary legs.

They'd thought the fire was over. The standpipes weren't charged. The pumps weren't on. And the woodshed fire roared across from the shop, flames flickering twenty feet high. Several overhanging trees had caught a spark. Their burning branches swayed toward the shop and its flammable contents.

They tried opening the hoses connected to the nearest standpipe, but gravity worked against them. The water pressure was half what it would be with the pumps running. Colin and Graham wrestled with the Mark 3 again so they could charge the hose lines directly from the creek, while David smothered spot fires just a few feet away from the propane tanks with fire extinguishers. But by the time Colin and Graham got the pump started, they could only soak the woodshed ruins.

The fire wasn't over, they were sharply reminded when the shop woodshed burned. It could flare up anywhere, when they least expected it, and would require a state of readiness for a while longer.

. . .

Sitting with Fire reported the shop woodshed blaze a few hours later, and an intense debate stirred up in the comments section. The debate had actually started the day before, as the fire descended into Tassajara, when a blog reader threw out this firebrand: "Attachment . . . heroism . . . lobbying for help . . . magnificent drama . . . jaded . . . blah."

To read the comments in what came to be called "the woodshed post"—all 225 of them—is to experience Tassajara, and the people who relate to it, across a range of perspectives. Kindness and empathy are on display, as are cruelty, suspicion, and condemnation. The comments provide a perfect illustration of what happens when people forget that they are connected and what can happen when they remember. An anonymous neighbor on Tassajara Road who resented having to pay for a bath in the hot springs criticized the greed of "buddha boys and girls as they weep over stone and mortar . . . and feel triumphant in their practice." An evacuated Tassajara resident responded. "Dear neighbor," she wrote, "Thank you for inviting me to study my ignorance and greed . . . Anything I can do to help you with your fire preparations?" Later, she repeated her offer to lend a hand and posted the phone number at Jamesburg. Two days later, the neighbor revealed his identity and thanked the resident and other posters for their comments, "for having started such a conversation."

When *Sitting with Fire* launched, Zen Center president Robert Thomas had mixed feelings. He recognized that opinions expressed on the blog wouldn't necessarily be shared by Zen Center leadership or be friendly to Zen Center. An organization with the size and profile of San Francisco Zen Center can't be all things to all people. But Thomas felt strongly that the blog needed to exist as a gathering place and open forum. He knew that if he could listen beneath the words for what was really being said, it just might be instructive.

Still, it pained him to read some of the comments—to hear how Tassajara's neighbors suffer from the impact of summer traffic on the road, how some people experience Zen Center as aloof, arrogant, and selfish: "i see fancy cars, i see much attachment to the possible loss of material stuff . . . i see that the boss buddhists come down when the wood and sticks are in danger . . . and i see a growing detachment from neighbors and fellow carmel valley residents . . . i would have thought i would have seen the tassajara folks going door to door with shovels . . . or working at the displaced persons center at carmel valley middle school . . . ," wrote lifetraveler, a frequent poster.

Browsing *Sitting with Fire* on the stone office computer, Mako read some bits aloud to Colin, like this post from lifetraveler: "If a cash register catches fire in the woods, can they hear it in San Francisco?" Colin left the room. "I didn't want to hear that kind of mean-spiritedness," he told me later. His choice to defend Tassajara had nothing to do with money. He lived on a stipend of a few hundred dollars a month.

Throughout the week after the fire, clashes cropped up periodically on *Sitting with Fire,* debates about selfless action versus self-interest, questions about whether the proper Buddhist response to a burning building is to save it or to accept reality and let it burn. Is it hypocritical to speak of meeting the fire and then to shoo it away?

"Turning away and touching are both wrong," Abbot Steve told a student afterward, adapting a line from a sutra chanted regularly in Zen temples: "For it is a massive fire." (Normally the line reads, "It is *like* a massive fire.") You can't turn away from fire. You can't hold it, either. You have to turn toward it, not knowing what it will bring, with your shovel or fire hose or simply with your attention.

Zen is not a passive path. It's a practice of complete engagement. A zendo is profoundly still and quiet during zazen. But then the bell rings. There's work to do, relationships to navigate, dishes to wash. And there's no dividing experience into what matters and what doesn't. It all matters. "Zen practice is very straightforward and direct," Abbot Steve told me. "You take care of what is in front of you. You do what you can, and when you can't, well, okay, then you can't."

In the end, the five at Tassajara didn't need to pull out fire shelters and jump in the creek. They had what Abbot Steve called "concerning moments." Certainly their lives were in harm's way. But they felt more focus than fear. As part of the body of Tassajara, they worked to save Tassajara. With bodies that know the element of fire from within, they tamed the element of fire from without. They concentrated on the task at hand, ready to drop what they were doing at any moment if necessary but determined to make an effort for Tassajara.

They would no more let Tassajara burn knowing they might save it than they would let their own bodies waste away without food or water.

For CAL FIRE captain Stuart Carlson, there's no question. Of course you make an effort to save a building—whether home, church, school, or doghouse—when you safely can. That's his job as a firefighter.

After the evacuation on July 9, Stuart had returned home long enough to get an eye-rolling look from his unit chief hinting that Stuart had stepped on some toes in pushing for resources for Tassajara. He was quickly assigned to another fire, but he checked in with Leslie James by phone as soon as he could, reaching her on July 10, after the fire had passed through Tassajara.

"They were lucky," Stuart said when Leslie told him that fire had descended from all sides and they'd lost only a few minor buildings. "Really lucky. I'm just so happy it all turned out okay."

He paused, then added, "I never would have left if I'd had some support."

"I know." He'd told Leslie as much, several times, before he left Jamesburg. "Well, they couldn't have done it without your help, Stuart. Thank you for everything."

Stuart batted away the compliment with a sharp exhalation. "I just wish I could have been there with them. There's no way to know, you know? You just never know how it's going to go."

Now that he knew they were okay, Stuart could move on. For a firefighter, the only fire that really matters is the one right in front of you. His job required him to make quick transitions, and he'd gotten good at it over the years.

"Did people stick around?" Stuart asked Leslie, referring to the resident evacuees who'd followed his lead up the road the prior evening.

"There's just a few of us here now," she said.

Kim Leigh, who had stood on the hogback ridge with Stuart and seen a fire he didn't want to fight, had left Jamesburg on the morning of July 10, in a car headed toward San Francisco. He lived in Sonoma, a good hour from the city. "I had no clue how I was going to get home from that point," Leigh told me later. "It was kind of like a leaf detaching itself from the tree. There was no ride headed my direction. I just started catching buses. It gave me time to reflect before I got home and realize what a wild ride it had been."

The wild ride had ended unexpectedly, with Leigh taking a bus across the Golden Gate Bridge instead of fighting fire at Tassajara. But Leigh had seen the difficulty of the conditions and Stuart's position, his legitimate concern for the safety of the community. "We were the only ones with wildfire experience," said Leigh. "I had to align myself with his decision."

Tassajara fire marshal Devin Patel had also aligned himself with Stuart, relying on the fire captain's expertise. On July 10, Devin and his girlfriend—not knowing flames were pouring into Tassajara—rode roller coasters on the boardwalk in Santa Cruz. When Devin heard about the fire's arrival later, he was surprised to find himself feeling regret that he hadn't been there. "I took on that role of fire marshal, did all the training, envisioned how we'd protect Tassajara, had drills, then didn't get to do it. That really got to me: *I missed it*." When he returned to Tassajara for the first time after the fire and saw the scorched and denuded landscape, he felt for a moment as though he'd somehow failed the mountains, failed to express his deep love for the land and the practice.

It took that practice to hold his feelings of regret yet not second-guess himself. "The decision was still so sure and clear and fresh in my mind. Both things were there: Yeah, I left, and yeah, it would have been nice to be there. I told myself, This is natural. You're going to feel this way for a while."

Interviewed eighteen months after the fire, in the dining room at Green Gulch Farm, where he now lives, Devin said he still felt solid in his decision to leave. And he still wished he'd been there.

. . .

On Saturday, July 12, the guest named the Basin Complex fire dropped in on the neighbors before leaving the area. Fire crews were working near MIRA observatory, "firing out" to burn fuels ahead of the main fire. When the wind shifted, that "contained" fire found a gap in the fireline and sprinted through it toward MIRA. Eighty-foot flames crowned through the surrounding pines, heading for two five-hundred-gallon propane tanks. Caretaker Ivan Eberle defended the tanks and the observatory structure himself, using MIRA's own pump and fire hose.

For the following two weeks, the escaped fire threatened the communities of Jamesburg, Cachagua, and Carmel Valley. A "hard" road closure went into effect on Tassajara Road on July 12—no one, not even residents, could travel on the road. Branch director Jack Froggatt stopped in at the Jamesburg house—behind the hard closure demarcation—to tell the residents there that firefighters were waiting for air attack to dampen the area first before attempting to contain the escaped fire on the ground.

Things had been relatively quiet down at Tassajara. But that Saturday morning, two days after the fire's main run through the monastery, a large plume emerged behind the Overlook ridge, possibly from fire at the confluence of Tassajara and Willow creeks to the south. From the solar panels, Colin spotted smoke and fire downcreek—the one direction fire hadn't come from on July 10. The five briefly suited up again, started Dharma Rain, and stepped up patrols. "Graham went up to the solar panels," Colin said later, "and after a while it was pretty clear that it wasn't going to move upstream and into Tassajara."

That afternoon, they unburied the Buddha. After carefully lifting the statue from the hole, they were too fatigued to carry it to the zendo. They left the Buddha sitting on the bocce ball court, still wrapped in blankets. "We were too tired," Abbot Steve told me later, "to do more than eat our MREs." Colin said they were too tired even for that: "You have to tear them open, heat them up." It was easier to grab leftovers from the walk-in and eat them cold.

They patrolled, slept, patrolled, and slept, trying to take care of basics and recover from post-fire fatigue, dehydration, and the toll of the smoke. They walked around with a tape recorder while the memories were still fresh, reviewing the events of July 10 and inventorying damage. Somehow, they found the energy to do some non-fire-related improvements. Colin and Graham repaired the spring box and installed a wooden floor in the bin where compost buckets are stored outside the kitchen, to discourage ground squirrels. Taking advantage of the fact that he could dig a huge hole and not worry about vehicles needing to drive through, Colin built a housing compartment around some buried water valves at the base of the zendo steps. Mako cleaned out rotting food from the walk-in. With input from them all, David worked on putting together a public account of the fire.

On Sunday morning, July 13, three days after the fire's run through Tassajara, a CAL FIRE crew came to do what's known as "mop up." They untangled and rolled hoses, cleared rockfall debris, and toppled dead trees, as they had on their way down on the road. "You were very brave," they said. "We were rooting for you." Also on that day, Abbot Steve's wife e-mailed a copy of Tom Meyer's *San Francisco Chronicle* "Fire Monks" cartoon, a playful rendition of the encounter between Zen mind and a wildfire. Tassajara's story meant something to people who had no knowledge of the place or particular interest in Zen. The phrase *fire monks* perfectly encapsulated the vital interplay of action and contemplation. "But we're also earth monks and water monks and air monks and wind monks," noted Abbot Steve later, "and something completely prior to that in some ways, even more elemental."

On Monday, July 14, Colin made pancakes for breakfast. The five finally returned the Gandharan Buddha to the zendo altar. First, they unwrapped the statue and set it on a bench draped with a towel. Abbot Steve steadied the Buddha while Colin brushed loose dirt from crevices. Then, with a combination of care and brawn, four of them carried the statue back across the work circle and hefted it onto the altar, facing the creek.

On Tuesday evening, they held a simple reawakening ceremony. Abbot Steve symbolically "opened" the Buddha's eyes with a small brush. The five chanted, then they sat zazen. Afterward, Mako propped her camera on the zendo steps again, and the priests posed in the work circle as they had earlier, in the same formation, this time wearing robes. Since David had sent his hand-sewn okesa to Jamesburg, he wore only a simple black robe and his *rakusu*, the small robe both priests and lay-ordained practitioners wear that hangs by straps around the neck. Had he been a little too attached to keeping his robe in good condition, he wondered? Did sending it out to Jamesburg betray a moment of doubt in those first few days of the fire, about whether they would indeed be safe in the valley?

At dawn on Wednesday, July 16, six days after the fire's arrival, Abbot Steve drove up the road unescorted, carrying a box of food to Jamesburg—a reversal of the usual flow of supplies. He'd been at Tassajara for two weeks instead of the few days he'd intended. He stopped frequently to take in the scale of the devastation. In the early morning light, the valleys would normally be green dipped in gold, with majestic, dense scrolls of living trees laid out along the sides of the mountains. Now the mountains were desiccated, brittle, the color of bone and dust. Barren, but inexplicably beautiful. What he felt, looking at the transformed landscape, was closer to immensity, to wonder, than grief.

When the abbot passed the bathtub and came to the place on the road where he'd felt a blast of heat-stoked wind on his patrol the morning the fire came in, he stopped the car again. The fire had crossed the road here. Brown-leafed sycamores and scorched bay and madrone trees on both sides formed a vanished trellis of fire. How long after I was right here, he wondered, did it cross the road? He stopped at Ashes Corner, where the five had turned around on July 9. The frenzy of heat and noise there, when they'd decided to go back to Tassajara, had smoothed into morning's peace. But clearly, the fire wasn't over. Plumes of smoke knit the sky overhead.

A few hours later, when Abbot Steve arrived at Green Gulch Farm and walked into the dining room, he was greeted with applause. That evening, he gave a talk in the zendo and answered questions, commenting that his robe smelled like smoke, a smell he now found "quite comforting." He told the assembly that Leslie had encouraged him to get clearance from Jack Froggatt before driving out of Tassajara. "I said, 'He'll forgive me if it doesn't work. Sometimes it's better to just go ahead. If you ask, then he has to say no.'"

"So, the road is still closed officially," Abbot Steve told his audience, "although the road itself is open and quite drivable." It was just like what the Korean priest had said a few days before the fire arrived, having driven past the closure signs at the forest boundary with a group of Buddhists who wanted to see Tassajara: Yes, road closed, but also open!

The remaining four at Tassajara savored their time together, alone in the still-smoking valley. It wouldn't last long, they knew. Students and volunteers would be brought back once the road opened, to help clean up and see what could be salvaged of the summer guest season. A bond that was already there before, from having lived and worked side by side for years, was now reinforced with the strongest material available: human connection through adversity.

"There was something magical in the days after the fire even though we were exhausted," David told me later. He sensed a penetrating quiet in the valley. "This traumatic thing had happened, this cleansing, tumultuous event which left the mountains ready for something else. It's like sitting in zazen with some big emotional experience. If you sit through it, there's this sense of relief, even if you still feel the pain. There's an aftereffect of settled stillness and resolution, a sense of nourishing something new to rise from the ashes."

Gradually, in the days after the fire's passage, David began to publish accounts on Zen Center's Web site and Mako uploaded her photos to Flickr, bringing the fire story to Tassajara's wider circle of friends and supporters. Lane Olson, Abbot Steve's wife, watched Mako's video of fire on Flag Rock on her office computer and felt the first rush of fear for her husband's safety. "That's when I panicked," Olson told me later—when it was already over but she saw the ferocity of the advancing fire front with her own eyes.

On Thursday, July 17, exactly a week after the fire passed through Tassajara, David posted this report on *Sitting with Fire*:

> *A haze still hovers in the valley, despite what seems like a fairly constant breeze. Without the foliage on the mountains, it seems to be windier down in Tassajara. There's a hint of fall to the trees remaining on the hillsides, as many of their leaves are turning brown since being scorched. Ash continues to accumulate on the grounds and buildings. The sound of rock slides is heard frequently throughout the day and night. Already the lesions marking the fire's entry into Tassajara are being slowly veiled by falling oak leaves, suggesting that nature's healing process has begun. Deer are continually spotted on the grounds enjoying the green vegetation, and the squirrels only seem to grow fatter on the spoils of the compost shed treasure.*
>
> *I've been able to write up an account of the events of July 9th, the day of the third evacuation and leading up to the morning of the fire. I hope it will help to clarify the many questions people have had about how it came to be that only five people remained at Tassajara. The exercise of writing this account has helped me to better understand—and to allow a newfound spaciousness for—how we all respond to the ever-changing conditions of each moment with the best effort we are able to make at the time. The decisions we make may not be the "right" ones, but they are simply the best decisions we can make in the moment before us. . . .*

For days after the fire's passage, a doe and her two fawns feasted on the garden, now open where the fence had burned away. But on the morning of July 19, Colin and Graham found the doe crumpled at the base of an intact section of fence. Colin guessed she'd broken her neck running into the fence after getting spooked by a falling rock.

Colin grew up farming and hunting. His grandparents raised cattle, goats, sheep, chickens, and a couple of peacocks. In his teens, he'd wake up early, pack breakfast, and go out to his hunting blind. "There was nothing to do but just sit and watch. Those were some of the most peaceful moments I had as a kid. The deer would come and I'd realize I was supposed to shoot." Eventually he gave away his rifle. Hunting had been an excuse to rise before dawn and just be amid the sounds and smells of the world waking up.

Graham helped Colin load the doe's body into the lumber truck. They lifted her together, Colin holding her front haunches and Graham her tail end. Then they drove her up the road to bury her in the open air. This didn't bother Colin terribly. He'd handled many dead animals before. But for Graham, it was a new experience. "I felt really bad for Graham," Colin told me later, recalling the pained expression on Graham's face. "He seemed heartbroken."

Graham, Mako, and Colin left Tassajara for the first time in a month later that day, driving to Carmel Valley Village for dinner at the Running Iron. David stayed behind to keep an eye on Tassajara along with the first evacuated resident to return after the fire, who brought Monkeybat with her.

On the drive back in to Tassajara, Graham told me, the valleys looked like little cities, lit up here and there with flame. For the next few days, the fawns returned to the garden, but after that, he didn't see them again.

With the Basin Complex fire still far from completely contained, a new incident commander rotated into position on July 19. Before flames had reached Tassajara, retired firefighter Mike Morales had blogged that he believed the cavalry would come riding in. Afterward, he'd posted a scathing indictment of the USFS response, or lack of one. Sixteen helicopters and six fixed-wing aircraft had stood by, Morales wrote, while five monks spread out around Tassajara to try to save it. Noting that the morning incident status report on July 10 listed Tassajara as a value at risk and confirmed that some residents remained at the facility, Morales concluded, "Clearly someone in the Forest Service decided to pull the plug on Tassajara. . . . Firefighters did not turn their backs on these folks, the suits comfortably situated in offices far away did."

Attempts to speak with Los Padres National Forest deputy supervisor Ken Heffner neither confirmed nor disproved Morales's claims. "If the Forest has a response," Heffner answered by e-mail, "it will be in writing." But a written response never materialized. My Freedom of Information Act (FOIA) request eventually yielded a paper trail that shed scant light on why crews were sent to Tassajara in 1977 and 1999 to fight fire, but in 2008 the monks were left to face a wildfire alone.

Nearby structures that are similarly isolated—such as the Pico Blanco Boy Scout Camp, where Stuart earned his merit badges as a boy—did receive support on the ground during the Basin Complex fire. "Why did they save the Boy Scout camp and not the Zen Center?" Morales asked me later. "Did they write it off from the beginning because who really cares about a bunch of Buddhists? If it was a Civil War memorial, they would have had that place surrounded."

Eighteen months after the fire at Tassajara, branch director Jack Froggatt told me that the choice not to keep firefighters in the Tassajara valley was collaborative, but not his call: "The decision was made at a higher level." Members of the incident management team told me that they debated the issue at length. But the incident commander ultimately in charge on July 10—the one who denied CAL FIRE unit chief George Haines's personal request for support—a fire management officer with the Stanislaus National Forest named Jerry McGowan, also declined to be interviewed. The only glimpse of his rationale comes from his Key Decision Log (KDL), obtained by FOIA request. "By wrapping the structures no firefighting resources would be required for protection," IC McGowan noted. When considering the "downstream" cost implications of this decision, McGowan wrote something he probably never expected to be read: "Politically correct thing to do."

There are many hands on the hose in the management of a fire. All it takes is one crimp to stanch the flow or start a tug-of-war over who is responsible—not just logistically and financially, but legally. Now evidently worried about the very real possibility of litigation against them, incident commanders have grown reticent. Like IC McGowan, they are reluctant to discuss their decisions after the fact, outside of the team. Froggatt consistently defended the decision not to put a crew at Tassajara, but he lamented that in general, firefighters can't learn from their mistakes if no one is willing to talk about a mistake in the first place for fear of being sued, or even to consider that a mistake may have been made.

The KDL is intended to track the complexity of decisions made on fires, but a paper trail takes you only so far. It can't capture the many split-second, gut-level calls firefighters make on a fire. It doesn't answer one critical question: Why was Tassajara abandoned? To those affected so significantly by IC McGowan's decision not to put fire crews at Tassajara during the Basin Complex fire's passage through the valley, the decision log doesn't suffice as an explanation or do much to build trust.

In Mike Morales's eyes, IC McGowan made a mistake. An overabundance of caution—or blatant bias—led to a bad call. And Morales doesn't think this sort of abandonment is rare. From his blog: "Clearly here in the U.S. we are entering a new era where federal firefighters are backing away from directly attacking wildfires. Firefighter safety is cited as the main reason, but whatever the reason, it's becoming clear homeowners will be forced to begin taking matters into their own hands."

In a Zen practitioner's mind, there's nothing necessarily wrong with that. Dōgen advised the head cook: *Do this all with your own hands.* Take care of what is yours to take care of. This is what the Tassajara monks did during a wildfire because it's what they do every day. Some help would have been nice, but when no help came, they didn't dwell on it—during or after the fire.

Whenever we talked, Abbot Steve blamed no one for how events unfolded during the fire at Tassajara. He understood that fire officials made decisions they needed to make, just as he made those he needed to make. When I asked him whether or not Tassajara would consider hiring a professional crew when the next fire comes, as more than one firefighter recommended to me, he smiled and said it wasn't likely. "I think we'll always reserve final decisions to our own leadership, not pass that on to someone else."

In the 1977 fire, then abbot Richard Baker decided early on that residents would work to save Tassajara, and the community followed his strong lead. Over the decades, Zen Center has shifted to a more democratic process of group discussion and consensus seeking. Still, many felt that an abbot's presence during the 2008 fire was essential—some even wondered why one hadn't gone to Tassajara sooner. For Jane Hirshfield, the question of authority and leadership in a crisis was one of the most interesting aspects of the fire's unfolding. Could David, as director, have made the same decision on the road to turn back, taking others with him? Jane thought it might have been more difficult—the abbot's voice is the one already entrusted to speak from a place of deep practice.

At the same time, she quickly added, "In a crisis, anybody can be abbot."

Given a sense of responsibility and appropriate authority, both by the sangha and within oneself, anyone could take the kind of decisive lead that Abbot Steve did.

Zen fosters self-reliance and trains you to be your own boss. But the practice also points to something beyond the ordinary notions of these terms. Taking responsibility includes letting go. You accept the consequences of your actions even as you realize that your actions completely depend on the totality of circumstances in any given moment.

Two weeks after the fire, residents began to return to Tassajara, though a backburn operation jumped a fireline and delayed their first attempt, sending them back to Jamesburg. On July 24, Shundo drove to Tassajara with Abbot Steve for the first time since the July 9 evacuation.

"It doesn't look so different," Shundo observed as they climbed to Chews Ridge.

"Just wait," warned the abbot.

Then they reached the ridge. The view opened onto mountains scraped clean, bare except for the wisps of leafless trees and a carpet of ash, black-and-tan slopes, a hazy sky still busy with smoke. A member of a USFS fire crew waved their vehicle down to warn them that his crew was cutting dead trees along the road ahead. He cautioned them to proceed slowly and keep their eyes open.

"Past China Camp, in the chaparral, the moonscape really started,"

Shundo wrote in his journal. "It looked like England in winter, bare trees, dark earth. A beautiful starkness to everything. Hazy and smoky below, the rocks standing proud . . . The Wind Caves were barren and brown, the Pines completely devastated, sticks standing, the trail clearly visible for once, winding up the valley."

At Tassajara, Shundo ran into Mako and David first—"big hugs, no need to say anything"—then headed for the baths to rinse off the travel dust, along the way embracing several others he hadn't seen since their evacuations. "I could already feel how different I was being here," he wrote. Reading his own words later, Shundo speculated that he'd meant he felt different at Tassajara from the way he'd felt in the city, but also that he felt different at Tassajara now compared with before the fire. Both closer to it and more distant.

At dinner the night Shundo returned to Tassajara, the residents were back to eating at individual tables. There were simply too many of them now for one big table in the center of the room—more than forty of the approximately sixty-five residents who evacuated had returned. But Shundo detected a fissure between those who'd stayed to prepare for the fire and those who'd left in the June 25 evacuation. Those who had stayed behind had never executed the tiered evacuation they'd spent so much time talking about, but here they were, organized according to how long they'd stayed or how quickly they'd gone, each drawn most easily to those in their tier, who shared their level of experience. He'd observed the same tendency in himself in the city, where he'd sought the reassuring company of others who'd been close to the fire preparations.

He'd spent the two weeks prior to returning to Tassajara after the fire "feeling like the fifth Beatle," unraveling the energy around the preparations he'd participated in only to evacuate at the last minute. He still felt a bit out of step—like Devin, he could have been there but wasn't. But as Shundo sat next to Graham that evening in zazen in the stuffy zendo they kept closed up, preferring heat to smoke, he had an insight. He could spend the rest of his life turning over all of the little moments that had led to his decision to continue driving up the road away from Tassajara on July 9, longing for an experience he had missed.

But then he thought: Or not. He could also trust that he'd done his best and let it go.

That evening after supper, Abbot Steve held the first of several community meetings in the dining room. They pushed aside the tables, sat in a circle, and shared what the fire was like for them, wherever they were, so that they might know something of one another's experience. Now the community that had been blown apart like the cottony wisps of a dandelion seedpod would try to reconstitute the whole bloom.

Some evacuees shared feelings of deep gratitude for everyone's efforts, both close to and far away from the fire, and reverence for the fire-dependent natural world they were part of and inhabited. Some shared painful feelings of displacement and disorientation and worries about plans to reopen the guest season. What's the rush? they asked. Can't we have a little more time to heal ourselves and this place before we throw open the gates?

Some evacuees were still upset, like the creator of the *Sitting with Ginger* mock blog—named for the monastery dog, evacuated with the residents on June 25. When it was his turn to speak, the former defense attorney challenged the wisdom of the breakaway decision the five had made to turn around and told Abbot Steve he believed they'd made a mistake. You may have saved Tassajara, he said, but you forsook the sangha, the community, more important than any building.

Abbot Steve took in the feeling that came with being criticized as well as his gratitude that the student felt free to express himself honestly. The abbot had opened the circle with his explanation for why they'd turned around on the road. He didn't repeat it. The group merely moved on to the next person in the circle when the angry resident finished speaking. "I realized a long time ago I can't convince anyone of anything," Abbot Steve told me later.

Tassajara's director, who'd done so much talking during the fire, didn't have much to say now. David felt protective of something he couldn't quite articulate, a simplicity, an essentialness expressed in the skeletal silhouettes of trees and the exposed slopes.

As he listened, he was surprised to find himself feeling unsympathetic. People complained about how hard it was to miss the fire, and he thought: But you also had three weeks of vacation! People spoke of painful feelings of displacement and exile, and David couldn't help but recall the years of being punted from one temporary home to another. A small voice inside him snipped: You want to know what real displacement is? "Later, I realized that some of the decisions I made during the fire contributed to people experiencing something similar to what I experienced as a child—though conditions were different and this displacement may have saved their lives," he told me. His own disregarded pain had made it difficult, he now understood, to take in theirs. "People wanted to hear from me, as director, how things came about, and they wanted to talk about the impact the decisions had on them, but I didn't want to explain or justify. What the fire taught me was: Stay with the essential. A lot of this was, 'Let me tell you my story.'"

David was grateful to Steve for leading the conversation. David knew it was important. But for him, the burned wilderness expressed all of their grief and gratitude with a dignity beyond words.

Much that the residents had done to prepare for the fire needed undoing to welcome back the guests. Tassajara needed a top-to-bottom cleaning. They drained the pool, tracking footprints in the soot as they scrubbed away the slimy layers. They pried protective boards off windows and eaves, wiped ash from every horizontal surface, rolled fire hose, sorted out undamaged wood, curtains, cushions, and linens, and redistributed lanterns. They began repairs on damaged structures. They sat zazen, chopped vegetables in the kitchen, and resumed the everyday tasks of monastic life. No more leftovers from the walk-in or MREs—the extras were stashed away—the head cook had meals to plan, mouths of monks to fill again.

The camaraderie that marked the early hours of fire preparations returned. "We weren't on crews," one evacuated student said. "I talked to people I'd never spoken to before." The resident whose San Francisco apartment had burned down washed dishes and turned compost for ten days straight without complaint, delighted just to be useful, to contribute in a tangible way to Tassajara's recovery.

For some others, the work fueled lingering resentment. First they'd worked their muscles raw doing fire prep. Then they'd been kicked out. Then they were asked, Can you come back and work again? Some residents didn't return after the fire. They'd made other plans during the long wait for the fire's arrival.

There was a calmness, a regal feel, to the landscape, a quiet and dramatic vitality. The air smelled of crushed leaves and wood smoke. By late July, tender new shoots sprouted from the bases of burned trees. Bright green ferns unfurled from ashes in the Cabarga Creek bed. As the land began to mend itself, the sangha worked together and tried to heal. "I had this dream my first night here," said one young resident-evacuee in an interview for the *Sitting with Fire* documentary. "The roots of the trees were cracking underneath the soil. Maybe that's what's actually happening." It *was* what had happened with the shop woodshed, ignited when fire had smoldered underground and traveled along a root to the structure. "But for Tassajara, the community, it's also like that," she continued. "We are trying to reestablish our sense of community."

On July 25, David, Mako, and Graham finally left Tassajara for vacation. On that day, in the Shasta-Trinity National Forest in Northern California, something horrible happened—just the kind of mishap Jack Froggatt had feared. National Park Service firefighter Andrew Palmer bled to death when an eight-foot-long, twenty-inch-wide sugar pine branch fell on his leg, shattering his femur and severing his femoral artery. It was his first day on the fireline. He was eighteen years old.

More than a dozen firefighters carried Palmer down a steep dozer line to a place sufficiently level for a Coast Guard helicopter to set down a litter. Other helicopter pilots had refused to make the pickup, citing too much smoke in the air. Ultimately, it took three and a half hours just to get Palmer to a hospital.

Before they left for some time off, Colin and Mako had talked about all the things that could have gone wrong at Tassajara that didn't. What if they'd lingered longer on the Overlook Trail? What if Graham's radio had failed and he hadn't been able to call for help from the bathhouse? What if one of those rock bombs dropping down from Flag Rock had hit someone or the shop's four hundred gallons of gasoline had caught fire? What if the pumps had failed or a major pipe had burst, taking down Dharma Rain? What if someone had been seriously burned—or suffered a heart attack? At the time of the fire, Mako was the only one with any current wilderness first-aid training. What if she'd suddenly had a real victim on her hands, someone she knew and cared for? Even if she could stabilize her patient, fire had rendered the road impassable. Would a helicopter have been willing to land in the narrow valley for a rescue? An old helipad on the hogback ridge, built in the 1970s, had never really been used. Safety officers for the Basin Complex fire had just looked at it and shook their heads.

What if someone *had* died saving Tassajara? Would that have made it a mistake to stay?

With more than forty years of practice guiding him, Abbot Steve won't weigh what didn't happen. Just as he learned a long time ago that he can't convince anyone of anything, he's rid himself of the temptation to deal in potentialities. Even as he could imagine the infinite ache of losing a son or daughter, brother, sister, or friend, he said, "It's not so helpful to judge it good or bad. Was it an appropriate response? That takes it beyond good and bad. . . . It is what it is. In any kind of action you take, you accept the karma that comes with it"—even though the effects of your actions can't be predicted. When five priests turned around on a smoky, windy hairpin turn on Tassajara Road to meet the fire alone, it was just a moment, not good or bad, an action connected to the past and future by spider's silk, its consequences yet unknown.

People may try to distinguish a meaningful death from a meaningless one—a preventable one, like young Andrew Palmer's. But Zen doesn't hold to such divisions. Death is just death, a transformation. "Death could be construed as a disaster. Birth, another kind of disaster, or anything unexpected that ruins our plans," Abbot Steve observed.

In a talk at Tassajara after the fire, his voice low with residual fatigue, Abbot Steve spoke about the particular suffering of "might have been." If you feel some regret for something, he said, it is your responsibility to engage that feeling. Only you can tend your own mind. He himself regretted that he hadn't taken the time at the turnaround point on the road on July 9 to call everyone together and announce the five's decision to return. "I could have done something there to better communicate," he said almost two years after the fire.

*On July 27, the Basin Complex fire was declared 100 percent con*tained at a total of 162,818 acres. Estimated suppression costs to date topped $78 million. Combined with the Indians fire, burned land exceeded 240,000 acres—the third-largest tally in California history.

On August 3, David read a statement at the temple gate to relaunch the guest season: "What, I ask, has the fire taught you? What, during these past weeks, have you discovered in the blaze of your own being that is beyond all displacement, beyond all destruction . . . ?" The first stage from Jamesburg in more than a month shuttled down Tassajara Road. The kitchen fired up its ovens and the cabin crew made beds for a few dozen guests—a smaller group than usual, yet still too many for some of the students. Though air quality had vastly improved, a smoky haze still settled over the valley in the mornings and evenings, and occasional winds transported smoke toward the monastery from the surrounding wilderness that still burned.

Shortly after guest season reopened, David was on the telephone behind the stone office, the same place he'd been sitting when lightning struck, starting the fires that became the Basin Complex. Looking around, he realized everything was arranged just as it had been before. The picnic tables in the student eating area, with jars of hot sauce and salt and pepper shakers; a pile of newspapers, folds worn from being opened and closed, on the round table near the phone; turn-of-the-century photos of Tassajara hanging on the walls. Physically, Tassajara looked the same. And yet, he knew, everything had changed, was constantly changing, each moment a complete transformation. Even when we don't see it. The fire had made that truth undeniably clear.

For days after the fire, a smoldering log or gently smoking pile of leaves would suddenly ignite. The birdhouse ruins had burst back into flame eleven days after first burning. In the same way, the fire's effects continued to smolder, lighting a flame of realization or recognition, revealing a teaching.

The fire was not just flame, David said in an interview a few weeks after the fire. It was "everything that came together during that time frame and that continues to come together. It was the firefighters helping us. It was the wilderness that was burning. It was every member of the community who came forth to meet the moment. It was the smoke in the area, the ash falling down, our fears and concerns for each other. It was how we supported each other, and it was everybody who really, even for a moment, thought about Tassajara" and what was happening for the affected communities and the wilderness around them.

Whenever someone approached one of the five directly to express their gratitude, as happened on many occasions after the fire, their practice became, How can I receive this? Mako often heard guests whisper, "There she is, she's one of the five." Sometimes Graham gave the gratitude back: "I'd thank them for thanking me."

When Jane returned to Tassajara the next summer and saw David as soon as she came through the gate, she bowed. "You're probably sick of talking about it, aren't you?"

He smiled. "I am."

"Thank you" was all she said. "For me it was a big moment," she told me later, "to be able at last to say thank you to each of them."

People wanted to express their gratitude. After the fire, nearly half a million dollars in donations poured in to Zen Center. People who visited Tassajara wanted to look into the eyes of those who were there through the heat of it and say, Thank you. It was challenging to be on the receiving end of the outpouring, but it was also difficult not to be. Sonja Gardenswartz, the ten-year resident who hadn't been allowed to stay, interacted often with guests in her position as guest manager. "I don't know" was all she could truly say in response to their curiosity and questions about the fire. "I wasn't there."

A few days after the fire passed through Tassajara, she had left Jamesburg to cook for several Tassajara retreats being relocated to Mayacamas Ranch, a retreat center near Napa. Gardenswartz lived at Tassajara for another year after the fire, but in 2009 she moved to Green Gulch Farm, feeling the need for a change. "Time has moved on, and renewal is always taking place," she told me. "I am a participant in that renewal."

*Long after Tassajara's residents thought they were done with evacu*ations, another advisory came. In the fall of 2008, two official reports by teams of soil scientists, hydrologists, and other post-fire assessment specialists predicted "extreme" risk of flooding and life-threatening rock and mud slides. The reports cautioned that Tassajara would be unsafe to inhabit during the upcoming winter rainy season. The fall practice period, led by Abbot Paul Haller, started nonetheless as scheduled in late September, but all participants and visitors had to sign waivers acknowledging their acceptance of the danger.

For Mako, the threat of being washed away in a flash flood was much scarier than the fire. Later, she laughed about it, recalling one official's recommendation that residents walk around with something tied to them so bodies could be found. There was a lot of gallows humor that practice period. At the work circle I attended in November, David announced that light rains were expected that week, and by the way, he still needed waivers from a few people. Someone made a joke about the killer rain in their midst.

They held it lightly, the danger they were in, but they also did something about it. Using some of the funds from the post-fire donations, Zen Center hired Tassajara's neighbor up the road, Little Bear Tom Nason (Grandpa Fred Nason's son), to fortify Tassajara for the rains that could pour down the now denuded hillsides, with little to slow or absorb them, for the next few years. While the residents went about their intensive practice—meditating in the zendo, working around the grounds, sewing robes, and studying sutras—a work crew placed sandbags and built retaining walls and trenches to divert water and mud away from structures and public areas.

The first winter rains were gentle. The hillsides sloughed rocks and soil, and the creek ran dark with silt. But then, on Christmas Eve day, a quiet time when Tassajara is between monastic training periods and former residents can return to practice, the unexpected happened. "Everyone has been looking to the skies for signs of impending danger. Rain, snow, wind," wrote Slymon on *Sitting with Fire*. "And so, on Sunday the earth moved to remind us that it too can cause problems." The quake was east of Salinas, but they felt the house shake in Jamesburg.

On a clear spring morning a year and a half after the fire, David settled onto his cushion, arranging his robes. He closed his eyes and breathed in the deep silence of the zendo, penetrated occasionally by throat clearing or a muffled cough. This wasn't his first talk as *shuso*, or head student, during the spring 2010 practice period led by Abbot Steve. David had already given two talks, and he had eighteen pages of typewritten notes for this one, which he placed on a lectern in front of him. So why did he have this tight feeling inside, this suspicion that there was something wrong with the words he'd carefully prepared?

After the opening chant, an evocation of gratitude for the Buddha's teachings and the ability to hear and "taste" them, David opened his notes and began to read. Typically, Dharma talks are not read, but he always prepared his. He didn't want to risk having all thoughts drain from his brain while a roomful of people waited for him to speak—and not just to speak, but to say something perceptive and inspiring.

He'd entitled this third shuso talk "Surrender." He started it by confessing his own "addiction to control"—citing as an example his desire to manage "the quality of care" the monastery and guests received from students. As he read on, he felt a strange disconnection with the material, a dislocation from his listeners, many of them good friends. But about ten pages in, he reached the section about his practice of "don't-know mind" during the fire. Something broke loose in him. He began to weep.

During the 2008 fire, he'd felt deeply responsible for the safety and confidence of others and acutely aware of how little he could actually control. But as he gave his shuso talk—twenty months later—he finally felt "the full weight of don't know, of truly having nothing to rely on," for assurance that Tassajara and its residents would survive the fire.

David felt the attention sharpen in the zendo as he spoke, the upright antennae of bodies tuned to his words. He sensed that people wanted him to talk to them in an unscripted way, about what was happening right now. For several minutes, he couldn't speak at all. He sat still, but inside he was falling. No wings, no parachute, no ground even to land on. Yet he felt as though he had to continue, for the sangha. He reached for his notes and resumed reading.

David felt raw for days after the talk. "At the time I didn't realize that it was the sangha's turn to carry me," he told me later, "and I wasn't ready to be that vulnerable." In the end, the experience schooled him on his own topic. You can't make surrender happen. You can only let go. In fact, "there can be no 'you' in wholehearted surrender," David said.

Nearly two years after the fire, the mountains around Tassajara were felted green. But David still remembered how they'd looked just burned, down to bare earth. It was as if he could finally really see them. "It was so beautiful, the way that a dying person can be," he told me. "The mountains in this form expressed a profound teaching for me: When everything extra is burned away, what's truly essential in our lives is exposed in all its beauty and defenselessness." What's truly essential cannot be defended. Vulnerability is the only solid ground beneath one's feet.

AFTERWORD

In May 2010, I walk up Tassajara Road with Abbot Steve and David, noting the contrast between the evidence of burn and the fierce display of new growth. Hillsides studded with blackened trunks have filled in with grasses and chaparral. Whorled lupine, morning glories, and hummingbird sage bloom profusely in the carbon-rich soil.

David takes short, quick steps on my right, while Abbot Steve strides long-legged on my left. For a while, we talk about the fire—David tells me that a new district ranger visited a few weeks back, interested in cultivating a relationship with Tassajara, that she and Mako had discovered that both of their mothers are Japanese. But then our conversation drifts, widens. I don't have a recorder, a notebook, or a list of questions. I simply enjoy their company as we move together up the road.

Telling the story of the fire, I came to know Tassajara and its residents in a way I hadn't before. Different people told me different stories. Some called into question the trustworthiness of telling stories at all. Memories shift, expand, and fade. A narrative is always in flux. Meaning exists only in relationship—to the storyteller, the listeners, the moment within which the story is told.

During the book's writing, I went through my own fire of sorts—or rather, the fire I'd waited for finally arrived. In 2006, my husband had been diagnosed with an incurable blood cancer called multiple myeloma, in an early, slow-growing, "smoldering" stage. For three years, we monitored his disease, watching for signs of progression but holding off on treatment—a passive approach typical with smoldering myeloma. When the cancer kicked into high gear in 2009, the year after the fire at Tassajara, and John started treatment, I felt relieved, even as I realized how little I could share of his experience, how much less I could control. Waiting for the moment of action, it turned out, was harder than meeting it when it arrived.

So I understood how it must have felt for the monks waiting for the fire. I knew myself the power of actually meeting something, not being before it or behind it but simply *in* it. When cancer spreads, when the fire finally arrives, there is no question where your life is at that moment. You become a fire monk.

By the start of the summer 2010 guest season, the compost shed and flats area woodshed at Tassajara had been rebuilt. Dozing one afternoon at the pool, I awoke to the sound of rocks skipping down the hillside and slamming into the wooden barrier fence built to receive them. There was a new pool bathroom and birdhouse cabin, each lovelier, in some ways, than the structures they replaced. Someone had propped the plaque that used to rest in the old oak tree's branches against the side of the new birdhouse on a ledge. "The entire universe is the true human body / the entire universe is the gate of liberation," it still proclaimed, a crack running diagonally across from one burned edge to the other.

Dharma Rain—"the thing that saved our bacon, hands down," as Colin once put it—had been dismantled, the piping and connectors stored in the shop. The fire shed had been restocked and a portable satellite phone purchased for emergencies. All new buildings had metal roofs. A weather station antenna measured temperature, wind speed, and humidity hourly from the top of the stone office. Plans for refurbishing the standpipe system and installing a permanent set of rooftop sprinklers were in the works.

David had moved back to San Francisco and taken on the position of Zen Center secretary—one of four officers of the temple, in charge of communications. Graham was halfway through a two-year tenure as head cook at Tassajara, and Mako had become the new director. She kept Monkeybat's ashes in a small ceramic bowl on her altar—the cat died in the spring of 2009 and was cremated out at the flats. Colin had returned to Texas. Abbot Steve came to Tassajara for short visits or to lead a summer workshop, always pausing at Ashes Corner on his way in and out.

That July, I watched the summer residents lay hoses in their first fire drill, slightly awkward in their gear. They took the exercise seriously—it was not the real thing, but everyone knew it *could* be.

Each time I arrive at Tassajara, I listen for the creek, for the first moment when I hear its rush through the valley. The creek is the voice under every other at Tassajara, and in this story. Purely just itself, never an idea of itself, it flowed through the whole fire event, through each of Tassajara's fires—past, present, and future. It flowed through the hoses and the Dharma Rain sprinklers. It revived tired bodies and filled every bowl of soup or cup of tea sustaining each human thought, feeling, and action. Named for a place it cannot stay, the creek is always there—the constant teacher and perfectly humble hero of *Fire Monks*.

In this book, I have tried to evoke the many lessons of the 2008 fire at Tassajara—about the basic safety of the valley and the importance of preparation; about the need to rediscover our relationship with wildfire; about recognizing impermanence, being one's own authority, and finding a way through instead of a way out; about the effort and courage it takes just to pay attention. "Don't chicken out!" Suzuki Roshi said to his students during long sesshins. This isn't the antithesis of firefighter Stuart Carlson's motto, "When in doubt, chicken out." It's more like: *Whatever comes, turn toward it.*

Fire will come, welcome or not. Illness comes, and with it, fear, pain, loss. Turning away, I realized when my strong, athletic husband suddenly became a cancer patient, is really not a workable option. When I look back on John's diagnosis, what I feel surprises me. It is something like longing—for the high relief of that time, for so much love drawn into focus. The disease seems to be controlled for now. Some days I don't think about myeloma at all. I'm lulled into a false sense of permanence, of having something that is mine to keep. Until someone sickens or dies and life reminds me, repeats the hard lesson: *Nothing is for keeps.*

I once asked Abbot Steve about the value of ruminating on the past within the context of a practice so completely committed to the present moment. Will the 2008 fire's lessons have any bearing the next time fire comes to Tassajara? It will be a different fire. A different Tassajara.

He looked at me, smiled, and said, "There is no present that does not include the past."

The present is the only actionable moment, but it is not a moment alone. The 2008 fire came into being because of previous conditions that prepared the forest to burn. The fire left its mark—on people, a place, the land—some more lasting than others. It's difficult to pinpoint when it ended or when it began. Even before the lightning strikes, the seeds of fire existed in the dry tree branches and roots. I could say there was fire, then there wasn't fire anymore, but the Buddha's words feel most true:

All is aflame.

—February 1, 2011
Colleen Morton Busch
Myoka Eido, Subtle River, Endless Path

ACKNOWLEDGMENTS

Many people contributed to this effort, in countless ways. I offer deep gratitude.

For trusting me with their stories: David Zimmerman, Steve Stücky, Mako Voelkel, Graham Ross, Colin Gipson, Shundo Haye, and Devin Patel. And thank you as well to all those not named elsewhere who allowed me to interview them: Alan Block, Alicia Baturoni, Andy Handler, Ann Voelkel, Bryan Clark, Caden Wang, Carl Coppage, Dana Velden, David Nicolson (aka "Spanky"), Edward Skinner, Eva Tuschman, Gina Horrocks, Greg Fain, Heather Iarusso, Ivan Eberle, Jon Wight, Joseph Schommer, Judith Randall, Kathy Early, Keith Meyerhoff, Kim Leigh, Lane Olson, Lauren Bouyea, Maria P. Linsao, Mark Ferriera, Michael Bodman, Michaela O'Connor Bono, Mikwa Strauss, Nancy Simmons, Paul Haller, Robert Thomas, Roger Broussal, Shoen Ferrell, Simon Moyes, Sonja Gardenswartz, Ted Marshall, Tim Kroll, Tom Johnson, and Walter and Joanne Ross.

For expert guidance in the world of wildfire and firefighting: Stuart Carlson, Jack Froggatt, Rick Hutchinson, George Haines, John Maclean, Matt Desmond, Steve Pyne, Ted Putnam, Mike Morales, Bill Stewart, Kelly Andersson. For her instructive film *Behind the Lines: Fighting a Wildland Fire,* Jennie Reinish. For assistance with my queries to the USFS: Jane Childers and Andrew Madsen. For fielding questions about fire weather: Ryan Walbrun. For help researching the history of temple fires in Japan: Hisayuki Ishimatsu, Alex Vesey, and John Stucky.

For consulting on Tassajara fire history: David Chadwick. For sharing their own recorded conversations and video footage: Ko Blix, Genine Lentine, and Susan O'Connell and Tim O' Connor Fraser, directors of the *Sitting with Fire* documentary. For creating and maintaining the *Sitting with Fire* blog: Chris Slymon, Kathleen Rose, and the rest of the Jamesburg crew. For her extensive local reporting at thefirelane.blogspot.com: Kelly O'Brien. For illuminating the relationship between fire and the Tassajara landscape: Diane Renshaw, with help from Barry Hecht, Reid Fisher, Sarah Richmond, and David Rogers. For sundry research and technical support: John Kuzel, Karen Sundheim, Nancy Suib, John Mogey, Walter Kieser, Jean Selkirk, and Christy Calame; also Alan Kelly, who transcribed some of my interviews.

For their insightful feedback on early drafts: Holly Rose, Suzanne LaFetra, and Kathy Briccetti. For asking the question this book tries to answer: Danny Parker. For writing words that inspired and supported *Fire Monks*: the authors whose works I cite, especially Eihei Dōgen. For paying attention to my words: Dan Kasper, Roman Sysyn, Elizabeth Stuckey-French, Henry Hughes, Patricia Henley, Marianne Boruch, Bruce Weigl, and Kathryn Arnold.

For their professionalism, talent, and warmth: Penguin Press associate editor Lindsay Whalen; *Fire Monks* jacket designer Tal Goretsky; and my publicist, Stephanie Gilardi. For their enthusiasm for this project and confidence in me: Leslie James, Michael Wenger, and especially Jane Hirshfield, whose words and encouragement thread through *Fire Monks*. For pushing this book to be its best: Michael Katz, my agent, and the incomparable Ann Godoff, my editor.

For their constant teaching: Edward Brown, Sojun Mel Weitsman, Alan Senauke, and the Berkeley Zen Center sangha. For their love and friendship: Nora Isaacs, Tove Jensen, Jeanne Ricci, Jen Richter, David Keplinger, and my family. For being both mountain and moon: John Busch. For taking care of Tassajara: monks, firefighters, neighbors, friends, guests—bodhisattvas all.

NOTES

vii **"Fire is more than an ecological process":** Stephen J. Pyne quote, from the *NOVA* documentary *Fire Wars*. Pyne has written numerous books on fire. Particularly instructive to me was *Fire on the Rim: A Firefighter's Season at the Grand Canyon* (Seattle and London: University of Washington Press, 1995).

PROLOGUE

4 **One of the monks who fought the fire:** Taken from the trailer for *Sitting with Fire*, a documentary film, www.sittingwithfiremovie.com.

CHAPTER 1: LIGHTNING STRIKES

6 **Fire had burned 51,125 acres:** From the six a.m. Indians fire incident status report, or ICS 209, for June 21, 2008, and from www.inciweb.org. Maps and information on the Basin Complex fire can be found at http://www.inciweb.org/incident/1367/.

9 **Chinese laborers built the road:** From "The First Passenger Wagon to Reach Tassajara," *The Double Cone Quarterly* 3, no. 2 (Winter Solstice 2000), p. 2.

12 **The basalt and granite walls of the stone rooms:** This and other architectural details are from *Zen Architecture: The Building Process as Practice*, by Paul Discoe with Alexandra Quin (Layton, UT: Gibbs Smith, 2008), and from interviews with Tassajara residents.

12 **A grand turn-of-the-century sandstone hotel:** Says David Chadwick, keeper of Tassajara history and lore, "Joan Crawford's ex-husband was the owner then. He was there. Some suspected him of arson. The remaining building stones were bulldozed into the basement. When we first made a garden there back in '67, I remember us digging up one big sandstone block after another." For more on the history of fire at Tassajara, visit www.cuke.com/tassfire.

15 **Refused to leave:** From a profile of Jane Hirshfield by the author, *Tricycle* (spring 2006), p. 73.

15 **Stopped in Jamesburg:** An unincorporated community named for the man who founded it in the 1860s, John James—of no relation to Leslie James.

18 **Suzuki Roshi had been looking for several years for the right place:** From *Crooked Cucumber: The Life and Zen Teachings of Shunryu Suzuki,* by David Chadwick (New York: Broadway Books, 1999), p. 265.

19 **The first known structures at Tassajara:** This and other Tassajara history comes from a file of historical documents and timelines that resides on the back porch behind the stone office, from *Crooked Cucumber*, and *The Double Cone Quarterly* article referenced above.

19 **Robert and Anna Beck purchased Tassajara:** Details about the Becks' ownership and sale of Tassajara and quotes from Robert Beck are taken from David Chadwick's interview with Beck at www.cuke.com.

20 **Now translated into Czech, Dutch, Finnish:** From David Chadwick's afterword in the 40th anniversary edition of *Zen Mind, Beginner's Mind* (Boston: Shambhala, 2010), p. 137.

21 ***Instructions for the Zen Cook:*** All quotes from this text, also known as the *Tenzo Kyōkun*, are taken from *From the Zen Kitchen to Enlightenment: Refining Your Life*, by Zen Master Dōgen and Kōshō Uchiyama, translated by Thomas Wright (New York: Weatherhill, 1983).

22 **She'd read about abuses of power:** The story of Suzuki Roshi Dharma heir Richard Baker's fall from grace and resignation from the abbacy of the San Francisco Zen Center in 1984 has been well documented. It does not need repeating here, except to say that the crisis raised issues of authority and decision making for the organization that emerged again during the 2008 Basin Complex fire—especially during the final evacuation, when Tassajara residents had to face the hierarchical power structure of the firefighting authorities and decide internally who would stay and who would leave, on the spot and under intense pressure.

CHAPTER 2: FIRES MERGE

30 **"The great way is not difficult":** A popular phrase from the *Hsin Hsin Ming*, attributed to Sêng-ts'an (Kanchi Sosan in Japanese), the third Chinese Zen patriarch, who lived in the sixth century.

30 **"It was as if the set for a play had suddenly been stripped from the stage":** Quote is from Eva Tuschman, a twenty-four-year-old summer guest cook.

32 **One student's apartment building in San Francisco had burned down:** Forty-eight-year-old Guatemala native Edward Skinner.

32 **Another lived in New Orleans:** Twenty-five-year-old Michaela O'Connor Bono.

35 **"Stay home and stay inside":** From a press release issued by the California Governor's Office, June 25, 2008.

36 **A carload of four senior students:** Shundo David Haye, Greg Fain, Simon Moyes, and Aliyu Turaki.

38 **Three other Tassajara senior staff members, also women:** Judith Randall (zendo manager), Kathy Early (treasurer), and Maria P. Linsao (work leader).

40 **In 2008, about half of the electricity used:** By the close of summer 2010, Tassajara had transitioned to 100 percent solar power.

42 **Find out for yourself:** From a talk given March 15, 1969. A transcript is available through the Shunryu Suzuki digital archives, http://shunryusuzuki.com/suzuki/base.htm.

CHAPTER 3: THE THREE-DAY-AWAY FIRE

43 **Genjo Koan:** These well-known lines from Dōgen's text were taken from the version used at San Francisco Zen Center, translated by Kazuaki Tanahashi and Robert Aitken. See http://www.sfzc.org/sp_download/liturgy/24_Genjo_Koan.pdf.

44 **Quick turn of events:** That day, Grace Dammann, a Green Gulch Farm resident who had been in a coma for weeks after a head-on auto collision on the Golden Gate Bridge, had woken up and mouthed her daughter's name—but the Tassajara evacuees didn't know this yet.

44 **"I'd just left my whole life":** Quote from forty-one-year-old resident Heather Iarusso.

46 **"There's no good place in the middle of the wilderness to fight the fires":** IC Dietrich's quote is from a KAZU report by Krista Almanzan, aired June 26, 2008.

46 **At 178,000 acres burned:** Both the 2007 Zaca fire (240,207 acres) and the 2003 Cedar fire (280,278 acres) surpassed the Marble Cone fire in size.

48 **The two-thousand-year-old stone Gandharan Buddha statue:** From Gandhara, an area along the Silk Road where Buddhism once thrived—"where Greek Hellenic culture met Indian culture through Alexander the Great," according to Abbot Steve. The region, in present-day Afghanistan and Pakistan, produced the earliest depictions of the Buddha in human form.

48 **Probably because of a faulty pilot light on a propane gas refrigerator:** Jane Hirshfield told me that the zendo fire may also have started in the kerosene-soaked rags used for cleaning the lamps: "As far as I know, no one's ever made a definitive call. I think we don't actually know."

53 **The unofficial state ecosystem:** Details on fire and chaparral in the Santa Lucias come from a talk by ecologist Diane Renshaw at San Francisco Zen Center on January 8, 2010, and many e-mail exchanges. Diane also provided the fascinating details on fire beetles in this section. For more, see *Introduction to California Chaparral*, by Ronald D. Quinn and Sterling C. Keeley (University of California Press, 2006), pp. 71–73, and Warren E. Leary, "On the Trail of Fire-Detecting Beetles," *New York Times*, May 11, 1999.

57 **Made cookies for the inmates:** Sixty-five-year-old Tom Johnson.

CHAPTER 4: IN THE SHADOW OF ESPERANZA

60 **He shot footage destined for YouTube:** Sixty-year-old Kokaku Brian Blix. You can watch this footage and interviews with some of the fire monks in Blix's online gallery at http://www.kofotofactory.me/.

61 **Leaving the crew nowhere to hide:** Details on the Esperanza fire are taken from the *Esperanza Fire Accident Investigation Factual Report*, October 26, 2006, and the U.S. Department of Agriculture, Office of Inspector General's *Report of Investigation* dated November 30, 2009. That an arsonist started the Esperanza fire made the deaths of the firefighters even more tragic. When the arsonist was convicted of murder and sentenced to death in March 2009, the mother of one of the deceased firefighters made this remarkable statement to her son's killer: "I harbor no anger, only hope that you understand the depth of pain you caused us and your family. More importantly, I forgive you for the act that took my son's life."

62 **Not mandated by their agency to provide structure protection:** CAL FIRE unit chief Rick Hutchinson, who worked in unified command on the Indians and Basin Complex fire, said of the USFS, "It is actually laced throughout numerous guiding documents for their agency that they can do structure protection. What they can't do is combat a structure fire. They can protect structures from the outside. They do in fact do that with a lot of their own infrastructure when fires are impacting them. There's conflicting info coming down from the upper levels, all the way from Washington, D.C."

62 **Memorial service for the Engine 57 firefighters:** http://www.wildlandfire.com/docs/2006/eng57/dietrich-walker.htm.

64 **Fire Sermon:** This translation from the Pali by Thanissaro Bhikkhu can be found at http://www.accesstoinsight.org/tipitaka/sn/sn35/sn35.028.than.html.

66 **A CAL FIRE captain had arrived:** David Nicolson, aka "Spanky," King City station captain.

66 **"There is water in the world":** From the Mountains and Rivers Sutra in *Moon in a Dewdrop*, translated by Arnold Kotler and Kazuaki Tanahashi (Berkeley: North Point Press, 1985), p. 106.

CHAPTER 5: GREAT FAITH, GREAT DOUBT, GREAT EFFORT

73 **"You should do it completely, like a good bonfire":** From *Zen Mind, Beginner's Mind,* by Shunryu Suzuki Roshi (New York and Tokyo: John Weatherhill, Inc., 1994), p. 62.

75 **Most of the residents present at the meeting were senior staff:** Fire marshal is not a senior staff position at Tassajara but was treated as one during the 2008 fire. At the time of the fire, Colin, as head of shop, was not technically on senior staff either. After the fire, he became plant manager and officially joined the senior staff.

77 **An overdose of adrenaline that stops the heart:** The fallen firefighter was Robe rt Roland of the Anderson Valley Fire Department, *Los Angeles Times*, July 6, 2008.

78 **Wag Dodge's quick, lifesaving thinking:** See "The Eureka Hunt" by Jonah Lehrer, *The New Yorker*, July 28, 2008, p. 40, and *How We Decide* (New York: Houghton Mifflin Harcourt, 2009). While *Fire Monks* illustrates the art more than the science of decision making, Lehrer's work offers a clear and fascinating peek into the neurobiology behind decisions.

80 ***Firefighter Blog:*** Mike Morales's blog can be found at http://firefighterblog.com/.

80 **Testified for a Senate oversight committee:** Casey Judd's June 18, 2008, testimony can be read on the United States Senate Committee on Energy & Natural Resources Web site at http://energy.senate.gov/public/.

82 **He'd walked into the bronze gong:** Tim Kroll, a thirty-three-year-old resident.

83 **When the habit of disconnection is broken:** For more on this subject, see *A Paradise Built in Hell: The Extraordinary Communities That Arise in Disaster*, by Rebecca Solnit (New York: Viking, 2009).

84 **"There is nothing to pin down, nothing to say":** From *You Have to Say Something: Manifesting Zen Insight,* by Dainin Katagiri (Boston: Shambhala, 1998), p. 60.

86 **Lit several backfires to save redwood structures on his family's fifty-five acres:** Forty-eight-year-old Ross Curtis, Big Sur resident arrested on July Fourth.

87 **Heffner kicked off the meeting:** Lacking an interview with Los Padres National Forest deputy supervisor Ken Heffner, I relied on the recollections of other participants to create his dialogue in this scene.

88 **In 2007, federal prosecutors charged an incident commander:** Ellreese N. Daniels on the 2001 Thirtymile fire in Washington State. For more on the fire, see *The Thirtymile Fire: A Chronicle of Bravery and Betrayal,* by John Maclean (New York: Henry Holt & Co., 2007).

89 **Rigged a temporary Internet connection:** Thirty-one-year-old Aliyu Turaki enabled Internet access in the stone office during the fire preparations.

94 **"Moment after moment, you should say, 'Yes, I will,'":** From an August 4, 1970, talk at San Francisco Zen Center, available at the Suzuki Roshi digital archives Web site, referenced above.

CHAPTER 6: FIRE IN THE CONFLUENCE

99 **"When we know something and rest in that knowing":** From a talk, "Not Knowing Is Most Intimate," May 21, 2006, www.everydayzen.org.

103 **"Simple answers to difficult questions":** From *Japan: A Short Cultural History,* by G. B. Sansom (New York: Prentice Hall, 2000), p. 372.

103 **"If the mind is clear, fire itself is cool":** Accessed at http://global.sotozen-net.or.jp/.

103 **Temple fires created opportunities:** Details and discussion of temple fires in Japan and the idea that architectural fires can function similarly to forest fires, from Professor Alexander Vesey, Meiji University, Tokyo.

106 **A reporter and photographer from the *San Francisco Chronicle*:** Matthai Kuruvila and Lance Iversen. Kuruvila's July 10, 2008, article, "Tassajara Monks Practice Zen of Firefighting," can be found at www.sfgate.com.

112 **"An icicle forming in fire":** From *You Have to Say Something: Manifesting Zen Insight,* p. 161. Interestingly, Katagiri's student and editor, Steve Hagen, uses the word "reality" instead of "Buddha" when quoting this Dōgen phrase in his own book, *Buddhism Is Not What You Think: Finding Freedom Beyond Beliefs* (New York: HarperCollins, 2003), p. 222.

CHAPTER 7: BUDDHA IN THE BOCCE BALL COURT

119 **"In nature, adaptation is important; the plan is not":** In *Deep Survival: Who Lives, Who Dies, and Why* (New York: Norton, 2003), Laurence Gonzales investigates what it takes to survive being stranded at sea or lost in the wilderness. One key, he finds, is the ability to accept reality and admit when you are in dire circumstances or lost, because only then can you begin to rescue yourself. Accepting reality requires a hard heart, writes Gonzales. "But it is a strange kind of hardness, for it has empathy at its center. . . . Gratitude, humility, wonder, imagination, and cold, logical determination: those are the survivor's tools of mind." They are the Zen student's tools of mind, too, tools for anyone who wants to live fully amid life's many upheavals.

120 **"After observation and analysis"**: Buddha quote is from the Kalama Sutta, accessed at http://www.urbandharma.org/pdf/dhammapadatxt1.pdf.

128 **"Skillful means"**: A famous parable in the Lotus Sutra illustrates the concept of skillful means—recognizable to parents the world over. A rich man's house is on fire. His young children, absorbed in play inside the house, ignore his pleas to leave it. Eventually the man entices his children out of the burning house by convincing them that better toys await them there. Is the man guilty of falsehood? Some may say yes, but as a disciple of the Buddha explains, "This rich man simply made it possible for his sons to escape the peril of fire and preserve their lives. He did not commit a falsehood. Why do I say this? Because if they were able to preserve their lives, then they had already obtained a plaything of sorts. And how much more so when, through an expedient means, they are rescued from that burning house!" The father is often understood to represent a Buddha, while the sons symbolize humans, born into "a burning house, rotten and old." Quotes from *The Lotus Sutra,* translated by Burton Watson (New York: Columbia University Press, 1993), p. 58.

129 **A summer student:** Twenty-five-year-old Joseph Schommer helped to carry the Buddha statue from the zendo and bury it in the bocce ball court.

132 **"I don't know myself":** This "don't know" had a different quality from the "don't-know mind" cultivated by Zen practitioners—a sense of openness to all the possibilities. David's father had often called anyone who didn't understand him stupid or a "dummkopf"—including his young sons—though he himself had learning disabilities and had dropped out of school in the ninth grade. David's discomfort with his father's lack of both education and self-awareness had spurred in him a desire not to be "ignorant"—literally through lack of learning, but also through blindness to his own self-delusion. "I didn't want to be ignorant at a much deeper level, to who I really was as a human being," David told me. "This was one of the pivotal factors that encouraged me to come out—to not lie to myself and fall victim to other people's ignorance by hiding who I was."

CHAPTER 8: THE LAST EVACUATION

137 **"Human life is messy":** From a talk given at Tassajara, April 28, 2009.

138 **"Form does not differ from emptiness":** From the Heart of Great Perfect Wisdom Sutra translation used at San Francisco Zen Center, accessed at http://www.sfzc.org/sp_download/liturgy/08_Heart_of_Great_Perfect_Wisdom_Sutra.pdf.

144 **Releasing the energy of an atomic bomb every fifteen minutes:** From *Fire Wars.*

145 **Didn't think he'd be able to look them in the eye again:** Colin recognized his own motivations later, after the fire, reading how the threat of shame can drive a company of soldiers into battle in a book called *On Killing,* by David A. Grossman (New York: Hachette Book Group, 2009). "There's no queen or country," Colin said. "You're fighting for each other. More than death itself, you fear letting the others down."

146 **Asked Abbot Steve if they could go back, too:** Aliyu Turaki (see note, chapter 5). Other residents who conveyed a wish to return at Ashes Corner included sixty-one-year-old Glenn Bradley and thirty-year-old Johan Östlund.

CHAPTER 9: NO LEAVING, NO GOING BACK

151 **The edge of your bodhisattva vow:** From "Taking Care of Fire," a talk given at Green Gulch Farm on August 17, 2008, mp3 available at www.sfzc.org.

158 **Sojun Mel Weitsman, then an abbot of Zen Center:** Weitsman is now abbot of the Berkeley Zen Center (BZC), originally established as an affiliate of San Francisco Zen Center. The eighty-one-year-old Weitsman—from whom I received lay ordination in 2006—founded BZC in 1967 but became abbot officially only in 1985.

159 **News of the evacuation on *Sitting with Fire*:** The *Sitting with Fire* blog served as a gathering ground for the Tassajara community at large as the fire closed in. But *Sitting with Fire* wasn't the only place where people were talking about Tassajara. On *Life in the Fire Lane* (thefirelane.blogspot.com), a report on the community meeting that locked Jamesburg residents out of their homes temporarily because of a misplaced roadblock included a perspective on the July 9 evacuation of Tassajara from a local volunteer fire department chief: "a bit of a head-scratcher from his point of view, since he believes that Tassajara is quite defensible." A fuels expert from the Los Padres National Forest had a similar reaction: "They were fine down there . . . they did a lot of good work. I heard on the radio they decided they were going to come out of there, which I was surprised at. . . . Because that's in a very defensible spot. It's usually better to stick around." Of course, five of the residents had stuck around—not everyone blogging had the latest information.

159 **An attempt to allay fears:** Tim O'Connor Fraser posted this summary of the meeting. He also provided technical assistance with the www.sfzc.org Web site and was, in Zen Center secretary Dana Velden's words, "a calm voice of reason" on the blog throughout the fire.

162 **"I felt a hot wind and thought I had better turn around":** From a talk by Abbot Steve at Green Gulch Farm, July 16, 2008.

CHAPTER 10: RING OF FLAME

163 **"A patch-robed monk is like a snowflake in a red-hot furnace":** This translation of a line from the *Blue Cliff Record* is from *You Have to Say Something*, p. 144.

167 **The red flag warning:** Ryan Walbrun, one of the incident meteorologists who spotted the June lightning strikes off the coast, told me that the warning was issued in part because of the preexisting fire threat and activity in the region. Forecasters were being extra-vigilant.

181 **"One continuous mistake":** From *Zen Mind, Beginner's Mind*, p. 39.

CHAPTER 11: MEETING FIRE

184 **The Ten Standard Orders:** In an e-mail, Putnam noted that since they can't be followed to the letter as currently worded, the orders are often used "to blame individual firefighters for whatever goes wrong on a fire." Putnam brings human factors into consideration on fatality and accident investigations—including a study of the burnover incident during the fire whirl on the 2008 Indians fire near Tassajara. In recent years, he has taught mindfulness meditation to hotshot crews. For Putnam's work in collaboration with Professor Karl Weick, an organizational expert, see "Organizing for Mindfulness," *Journal of Management Inquiry* 15,

no. 3 (September 2006), pp. 1–13, in which the authors propose "the necessity for continuous organizing to produce wise action."

184 **"'Ideally possible but practically unattainable'":** From *On the Fireline: Living and Dying with Wildland Firefighters,* by Matthew Desmond (Chicago: University of Chicago Press, 2007), p. 167.

186 **The right to light a backfire:** California Public Resources Code section 4426 states that "a person shall not set a backfire, or cause a backfire to be set, except under the direct supervision or permission of a state or federal forest officer, unless it can be established that the setting of such backfire was necessary for the purpose of saving life or valuable property." According to Kelly Andersson, who has worked in the fire world as a public information officer, writer, and editor, and who proofed my fire details in this book, *backfire* and *backburn* refer to slightly different actions. Backfiring eliminates fuels along the inner edge of the fireline and is usually done by hotshots. Backburning refers more generally to the burning of fuels ahead of a fire so the advancing fire dies down when it reaches the burned area. "Backburning is what they are doing here," Andersson told me. But "backfire" was the word used in the exchange between Chief Haines and David and is the terminology used in the California Public Resources Code that Haines consulted. For simplicity's sake, and since the term is commonly understood to mean any fire lit to create a safe, burned area, I have stuck with "backfire" here and throughout the book.

189 **Smoke inhalation causes more deaths from fires than burns do:** From www.emedicinehealth.com and www.firesmoke.org.

193 **Tassajara planned to dismantle it:** A new retreat center is under construction at the time of this book's writing. The canvas tent yurt will remain as the primary workshop space until the center is completed.

194 **Harmony of Difference and Equality Sutra:** By Sekitō Kisen (700–790). From the collaborative translation used at San Francisco Zen Center, http://www.sfzc.org/sp_download/liturgy/12_Harmony_of_Difference_and_Equality-cc.pdf

203 **"An ancient Buddha said":** These lines are from Dōgen's Yuibutsu Yobutsu, "Only a Buddha and Buddha." Former resident Meiya Wender made the plaque. Kazuaki Tanahashi's translation can be found in *Moon in a Dewdrop*, p. 161.

205 **A time when female Zen students deliberately disfigured themselves:** See *Zen Women: Beyond Tea Ladies, Iron Maidens, and Macho Masters* (Boston: Wisdom, 2009) by Grace Schireson, a Dharma-transmitted priest in the Suzuki Roshi lineage.

207 **"Firewood becomes ash":** From the Genjo Koan. See chapter 3 note on the translation.

CHAPTER 12: UNBURYING BUDDHA

219 **"It is *like* a massive fire":** From the Song of the Jewel Mirror Samadhi, or Hōkyō Zammai, by Tōzan Ryōkai (807–869). Accessible at http://www.sfzc.org/sp_download/liturgy/16_Song_of_the_Jewel_Mirror_Samadhi.pdf.

222 **Defended the tanks and the observatory structure himself:** According to MIRA caretaker Ivan Eberle, a contracted hotshot crew stood by taking souvenir photos and refused to help him during the fire's July 12 run at the observatory. "I did cajole one hotshot into helping me untangle and unkink the hose and hold the nozzle end for a moment while I sprinted 30 yards to turn the electric fire pump on," Eberle wrote in an e-mail to me. "He thrust the nozzle back into my hands after I did so and that was the sum of the help they gave me." In an April 17, 2009, article in the *Pine Cone*, a local newspaper, Eberle conceded that he may have brushed up against one of the firefighters while unrolling hose, but he was shocked when six deputies from the Monterey County Sheriff's Office showed up the following day to warn him that if he so much as spoke with another firefighter, he'd be arrested for interfering with operations. Eberle was eventually charged with two misdemeanors, battery on an individual and interfering with the duties of a firefighter. He told me that surely he'd have "gone down the hill in bracelets" on Sunday, July 13, had the charges already been "cooked up." He spent thousands on legal fees and hours assembling photos to assist in his defense and was fired from his caretaker job at MIRA, a position he had held for twelve years. The charges were dropped, but the fact that crews stood by and watched while Eberle attempted to knock down the flames alone rattles him still. "Asked to stay and help with the firefight by every division supervisor and branch director I encountered, and assured of structure protection and safe passage if I did, I nevertheless found myself with no engine crews nearby on the morning of July 12. . . . There was an imminent danger to the community of Jamesburg being rolled by fire within hours that was never publicly acknowledged."

227 **Sixteen helicopters and six fixed-wing aircraft:** Morales based his numbers mostly on the daily ICS 209 report for July 10. There were actually nineteen helicopters assigned to the incident that day, sixteen of which belonged to the USFS. Of the six aircraft, three were USFS planes. "I pointed my criticism at the USFS because they were in charge of the fire," Morales told me later.

228 **Members of the incident management team told me:** Retired IC Bill Molumby and CAL FIRE unit chief Rick Hutchinson (who replaced George Haines, also retired). Molumby and Hutchinson both worked in unified command on the Indians and Basin Complex fires.

229 **For fear of being sued:** In a November 11, 2006, article on www.dailybulletin.com, IC Dietrich pointed to Public Law 107-203 as the reason why "every Forest Service employee who's in a management position should have professional liability insurance." The 2002 legislation (sponsored by Senator Maria Cantwell, a Democrat, and Representative Doc Hastings, a Republican, both from Washington) requires an independent investigation when a USFS firefighter dies in a burnover or entrapment. Arguing that citizens have the right to protect their properties "when nobody else will" at a Big Sur community meeting in August 2008, Micah Curtis, whose brother Ross was arrested on July Fourth, protested: "Prosecuting commanders who lose people is crazy! Firefighting is dangerous. They don't tell these cops not to go into East L.A." Transcript available at http://www.kusp.org/fire/sur.html.

230 **Given a sense of responsibility:** Ted Marshall, Tassajara fire marshal in 1977, told me that the policy of having the abbot be the responsible leader "needs to be soberly addressed. We need to be able to entrust the most capable person to lead a firefighting effort to do just that." Marshall acknowledged the importance of the abbot's position but said it is "not to be confused with the right person to accomplish any and all tasks." Ted Putnam and Karl Weick would agree (see note, chapter 11, "Organizing for Mindfulness"): "expert decision making can arise spontaneously where it is needed most and is independent of rank, position, or expectations."

232 **Creator of the *Sitting with Ginger* mock blog:** Alec Henderson, http://sittingwithginger.blogspot.com/.

234 **Firefighter Andrew Palmer:** Details from *Accident Investigation: Factual Report*, July 25, 2008, at www.nps.gov.

237 **Donations poured in:** Revenue shortfalls from the guest season and expenses generated by the fire were compensated for by insurance payments and generous donations from sangha members. "We came out ahead," said Zen Center president Robert Thomas, "and we were trying to get there because we were anticipating a shortfall due to the fire for the following guest season." That expected shortfall did occur, and continuing fire-related repairs and building expenses chipped away at the surplus until the fire was "pretty much a wash"—in financial terms, at least.